THE

LIFE AND ADVENTURES

[OR SKETCHES AND

ECCENTRICITIES]

OF

Colonel David Crockett,

OF WEST TENNESSEE.

DAVID CROCKETT.

I am happy to acknowledge this to be the only correct likeness that has been taken of me.

David Crockett

THE
LIFE AND ADVENTURES
[OR SKETCHES AND ECCENTRICITIES]
OF
Colonel David Crockett,
OF WEST TENNESSEE.

EDITED WITH A CRITICAL INTRODUCTION BY
Michael A. Lofaro

The University of Tennessee Press
Knoxville

Frontispiece: "Congressman Crockett, painted by S.S. Osgood, 1834."
Courtesy Tennessee State Library and Archives.

Library of Congress Cataloging-in-Publication Data

Names: French, James Strange, 1807–1886, supposed author. | Lofaro, Michael A., 1948- editor.
Title: The life and adventures [or sketches and eccentricities] of Colonel David Crockett,
of West Tennessee / edited by Michael A. Lofaro.
Other titles: Sketches and eccentricities of Colonel David Crockett
Description: First edition. | Knoxville : The University of Tennessee Press, 2020. | Attributed to
James Strange French—ECIP PDF, page iii. | Includes bibliographical references and index. |
Summary: "Few images of Jacksonian America capture its curiosities and contradictions so
well as that of Congressman David Crockett, around 1833, fighting for control of his public
image with none other than Davy Crockett, the King of the Wild Frontier. Largely responsible
for this very nineteenth-century collision of myth and history was the present work, the *Life
and Adventures of Colonel David Crockett, of West Tennessee* (1833), which was the first in a series
of biographical and autobiographical books that thrust Crockett fully onto the national and
international scene. Quickly retitled *Sketches and Eccentricities*, it was also the most outlandish of the type. Mixing two contemporary genres of storytelling—the Humor of the Old
Southwest and the sketch—the work's rollicking story and canny, uneducated protagonist earned
Congressman Crockett's disavowal within a year of its publication, but survived to launch a cot-
tage industry of the Frontier hero after the latter's death at the Alamo"—Provided by publisher.
Identifiers: LCCN 2019054571 (print) | LCCN 2019054572 (ebook) | ISBN 9781621905615
(paperback) | ISBN 9781621905622 (pdf) | ISBN 9781621905639 (kindle edition)
Subjects: LCSH: Crockett, Davy, 1786–1836. | Pioneers—Tennessee—Biography. | Legislators—
Tennessee—Biography. | Creek War, 1813–1814. | Tennessee—History—19th century.
Classification: LCC F436.C95 F74 2020 (print) | LCC F436.C95 (ebook) |
DDC 976.8/04092 [B]—dc23
LC record available at https://lccn.loc.gov/2019054571
LC ebook record available at https://lccn.loc.gov/2019054572

Contents

Illustrations

Preface

When David Crockett publishes his autobiography, *A Narrative of the Life of David Crockett, of the State of Tennessee* (1834), he casts himself in the role of a straight-shooter, a reasonably accurate portrayal that few would dispute. He describes his work as an author in the preface as: "In the following pages I have endeavoured to give the reader a plain, honest, homespun account of my state in life, and some few of the difficulties which have attended me along its journey, down to this time."[1] "Most of authors seek fame," he says, but that is not among Crockett's motives for writing: "It is to correct all these false notions, and to do justice to myself, that I have written." What he then calls a "bundle of ridiculous stuff"—the "false notions"[2] that he mentions in the autobiography—are those published the previous year in the book that forms this edition.

The present text, *The Life and Adventures of Colonel David Crockett, of West Tennessee* (1833), is better known by its reissued title, the *Sketches and Eccentricities of Col. David Crockett of West Tennessee* (1833),[3] a far more accurate rebranding of the work and one that hints at the reason for Crockett's irritation. *Sketches* is examined in depth in the "Davy's First Book" section[4] of this edition; suffice it here to say that the work is not organized or presented in a manner that attempts more than a roughly chronological approach. It is instead often a barely connected series of tales, anecdotes, biography, politics, caricatures, and jokes that make clear to the reader that the Crockett legend has made quite the solid start.

In the far more historically correct *Narrative* Crockett cautions that "I am perfectly aware, that I have related many small and, as I fear, uninteresting circumstances." His words do not apply to *Sketches*. Much more apt a connection between the works is made in his concluding remarks to the reader in the *Narrative*'s preface:

> But just read for yourself, and my ears for a heel tap [the bit of liquor left in a glass after drinking], if before you get through you don't say, with many a good-natured smile and hearty laugh, "This is truly the very thing itself—the exact image of its Author, David Crockett."[5]

Sketches, the first book-length treatment of Crockett, certainly does provoke "many a good-natured smile and hearty laugh," but it is also a book of its time and place. The sketch is itself an earlier literary genre that is the progenitor of the short story. It parallels the relationship in art between a sketch and a painting. Traditionally the sketch is a brief form that has little plot or character development, and relies on stereotypes to aid audience identification and evoke emotions. Because of its emphasis on feelings, a sketch allows readers to shape the interpretation of the character and his or her actions in terms of their own current beliefs and experiences.[6] A collection of sketches likewise need not have a theme, continuity, or a single outcome, especially in this case when its description in its more popular title is paired with "eccentricities." Within some of the sketches themselves, no one will mistake the ideas that are expressed, especially in regard to minorities, as acceptable today other than as lessons to be learned from the past. In the same vein, however, *Sketches* does provide a fragmented but informative view into the popular culture of 1833 and its fascination with the frontier that can only aid present understanding.

Before going on to sample the amazing miscellany that *Sketches* contains, one last caution, again abstracted from the preface to Crockett's *Narrative* noted above. If that later work yields "truly the very thing itself—the exact image of its Author," *Sketches* yields an overflowing workbook of materials that undergird the legends spun about and by Crockett and foretell many of those yet to come. Over time these tall stories become as vital a part of the "exact image" of the frontiersman as fact. They are, however, unified in public as early as December 1833, on stage in Washington, DC. Congressman Crockett is sitting in a box seat for the benefit performance when James Hackett strides on stage dressed out in frontier regalia for his famous role as Nimrod Wildfire in James Kirke Paulding's play *The Lion of the West*. Wildfire, a character created to mimic Crockett, bows to David, and Crockett rises and bows back to him. Together they receive a thunderous standing ovation.[7] Crockett could not, despite his best efforts in the *Narrative*, ever separate himself from his growing legend, a fact for which readers of imaginative literature should all be grateful.

NOTES

1. *A Narrative of the Life of David Crockett, of the State of Tennessee* (Philadelphia: E. L. Carey and A. Hart, 1834), reprinted in facsimile, James A. Shackford and Stanley J. Folmsbee, eds. (Knoxville: Univ. of Tennessee Press, 1973), 6. Hereafter cited as *Narrative*.

2. *Narrative*, 3, 5.

3. *The Life and Adventures of Colonel David Crockett, of West Tennessee* (Cincinnati: Published for the Proprietor, 1833); *Sketches and Eccentricities of Col. David Crockett of West Tennessee* (New York: J. & J. Harper, 1833).

4. The bulk of the commentary in section 3 of "Davy's First Book" is taken from "Stereotype and Synthesis as National Compromise: The Evolution of the Early Frontier Hero" in Michael A. Lofaro, ed., *Boone, Black Hawk, and Crockett in 1833: Unsettling the Mythic West* (Knoxville: Univ. of Tennessee Press, 2019).

5. *Narrative*, 10–11.

6. Washington Irving was perhaps the last great American master of the sketch. His first trans-Atlantic success was *The Sketchbook of Geoffrey Crayon* (1819–1820), featuring the now classic tales of "Rip Van Winkle" and "The Legend of Sleepy Hollow." Rip, for example, is the stereotype of the man who never grows up; his only physical description in the sketch is that he has a long beard when he returns to his village, yet all readers "know" what he looks like. The plot is also very simple, if a plot at all—he falls asleep for twenty years and misses the American Revolution. Although Irving continued to write sketches, the domain of the sketch fell mainly into the hands of regional humorists. Crockett's *Sketches* is among the first popular examples of the Humor of the Old Southwest that flourishes mainly from the early 1830s to the Civil War. Present-day humor is still a place where the use of the sketch continues, but generally more in performances than in written texts.

7. Richard Boyd Hauck, *Crockett: A Bio-Bibliography* (Westport, CT: Greenwood Press, 1982), 47. It may be that Crockett saw one of Hackett's one-man shows that featured his outrageous speeches as Wildfire rather than the entire play. See also Richard Boyd Hauck, "Making it All Up: Davy Crockett in the Theater," in *Davy Crockett: The Man, The Legend, The Legacy, 1786–1986*, ed. Michael A. Lofaro (Knoxville: Univ. of Tennessee Press, 1985), 103–11; and James A. Shackford, *David Crockett: The Man and the Legend* (1965; Chapel Hill: Univ. of North Carolina Press, 1986), 253–57.

General Textual Methods

This edition relies upon and replicates as closely as possible the narrative of the first edition of this work. The intent is to present *The Life and Adventures of* (quickly reprinted as the *Sketches and Eccentricities of*) *Col. David Crockett, of West Tennessee* to readers as they would have seen it in print in 1833. No original manuscript of the text apparently survives. No priority of publication for the different 1833 Cincinnati editions of Crockett's *Life* (noted in the introduction as *Sketches*, its later and better known title) has been established. The copies of *Life* at Newberry Library and University of Tennessee Library each bear "E. Deming, Printer,/ No. 5, Johnston's Row, Upper Market Space." at the bottom of their copyright pages. Another Tennessee copy (missing the first eleven pages and hence missing the copyright page) demonstrates small differences in lineation and errors in typography, but is clearly a different typesetting. And the copy at the American Antiquarian Society bears numerous corrections to the Newberry and Tennessee texts, introduces some errors, and also carries the same information about the printer. It may be a later typesetting. This copy is available online at: http://gdc.galegroup.com/gdc/artemis. It thus seems likely that at least three printings of the *Life* were published in Cincinnati before its retitling.

Two areas of editorial information are presented separately after the text itself as "Explanatory Notes" and "Textual Notes." Explanatory Notes are indicated with superscript numbers in the texts and Textual Notes with lowercase superscript letters. The Explanatory Notes attempt to clarify or amplify the work by providing relevant information about people, events, concepts, and terms, that although perhaps present in general knowledge in 1833, might today prove unknown or vague. The Textual Notes record any changes made to the original text for this edition; such emendations strive to be conservative and consistent and are generally incorporated only to avoid misreadings or confusion. The very few necessary editorial clarifications are placed within the texts themselves and are enclosed by italicized square brackets, since non-italicized square brackets already appear in the texts. Again, the intent throughout is to immerse the present-day reader in the world of 1833. Most corrections deal with simple errors in typesetting, proofreading, and copyediting, with the italicized square brackets often containing omitted letters, words, and brief clarifications. Minor accidental errors, such as irregular or omitted punctuation, are silently corrected if confusing and then recorded in the textual notes, as are any misspellings that might lead to uncertainty of meaning, typesetter errors, and any matters requiring more extended comment. In general, however, no change is made to archaic usages, slang and dialect terms, the spelling of words, or for internal consistency in spelling and capitalization. Consistency of spelling advances as dictionary use becomes widespread, but Noah Webster's first *American Dictionary of the English Language* was published only five years earlier in 1828. End-line hyphens that are ambiguous are also noted in the Textual Notes.

Acknowledgments

I should like to express my sincere appreciation to all those who have offered assistance and encouragement in the preparation of this volume. I am grateful for grants from the Better English Fund, established by Dr. John C. Hodges for the Department of English, the College of Arts and Sciences, and the Office of Research of the University of Tennessee, and the American Antiquarian Society. All supported the research necessary to complete this book. I am indebted to the University of Tennessee Library's Special Collections for providing copies of the variant first editions of Crockett's *Life* (*Sketches*) and to its professional staff for their kindness and efforts on my behalf.

My special thanks is also due to former research assistants, Drs. Steven Harthorn, Katharine Burnett, Neil Norman, Matthew P. Smith, and Staci Poston Connor for their thorough work. My longtime colleagues, especially Drs. David Moltke-Hansen, Jerome Loving, Paul Andrew Hutton, Daniel Feller, Katy L. Chiles, Steven Lomazow, Charles Maland, Stanton Garner, Allen Dunn, the late John Seelye, and Mr. D. Strong Wyman, provided valuable assistance and support in my work. All have been long in the storm of this book, but always managed to muster an enthusiasm for it that energized my labors. Their support and interest, along with that of my adult children, Ellen and Christopher, and as always, my wife Nancy, has aided my continued investigation into the life and legend of Crockett, work that always repays determined effort. Likewise, my wife Nancy's insightful comments and keen-eyed proofreading made this a far better book. Any shortcomings or errors of any sort, however, are certainly my own.

A Selective Crockett Chronology

1786   On August 17, David is born to John and Rebecca Hawkins Crockett in Greene County, Tennessee.

1796   Tennessee joins the Union. The Crocketts open a tavern on the road from Knoxville to Abingdon, Virginia.

1798   John Crockett hires his son out to Jacob Siler to help to drive a herd of cattle to Rockbridge County, Virginia. Siler tries to detain David by force after the contract is completed, but the boy escapes and eventually arrives home in late 1798 or early 1799.

1799   David starts school, prefers playing hooky, and runs away from home to escape his father's punishment. He works as a wagoner, a day laborer, and at odd jobs for two and one-half years.

1802   David returns home and is welcomed by all his family.

1803   David willingly works and discharges his father's debts of seventy-six dollars.

1805   He takes out a license to marry Margaret Elder of Dandridge, Tennessee, on October 21, but she decides to marry another.

1806   Crockett courts and marries Mary (Polly) Finley on August 14 in Jefferson County, Tennessee.

1811   David, Polly, and their two sons, John Wesley and William, leave East Tennessee sometime after September 11 and settle on the Mulberry fork of Elk River in Lincoln County, Tennessee.

1813   Crockett leaves Lincoln County to settle on the Rattlesnake Spring Branch of Bean's Creek in Franklin County, Tennessee, near the present Alabama border. He names his homestead "Kentuck." In September, Crockett enlists in the militia in Winchester, Tennessee, to avenge the Indian attack on Fort Mims, Alabama, and serves as a scout under Major Gibson. Under Andrew Jackson, he participates in the retributive massacre of the Indian town of Tallussahatchee on November 3. David's ninety-day enlistment expires on the day before Christmas, and he returns home.

1814   Jackson defeats the Creeks at the Battle of Horseshoe Bend on March 28. Crockett reenlists on September 28 as third sergeant in Captain John Cowan's company and serves until March 27, 1815. He arrives the day after Jackson's taking of Pensacola on November 7, 1814. Crockett attempts to ferret out the British-trained and supplied Indians from the Florida swamps.

1815   Discharged as a fourth sergeant, David returns home to find himself again a father. His wife, Polly, dies the summer after Margaret's birth, although David found her in good health on his return.

1816   Crockett is elected a lieutenant in the Thirty-second Militia Regiment of Franklin County on May 22 and marries Elizabeth Patton, a widow with two children (George and Margaret Ann) before summer's end. In the fall, he explores Alabama with an eye toward settlement, catches malaria, and nearly dies. He is reported as dead and astonishes his family with his "resurrection."

1817   By about September, the Crocketts have settled in the territory soon to become Lawrence County, Tennessee, at the head of Shoal Creek. David becomes a justice of the peace on November 17.

1818   He becomes town commissioner of Lawrenceburg before April 1. Crockett is also elected colonel of the Fifty-seventh Militia Regiment in the county.

1819   Crockett resigns his position as justice of the peace.

1821   On January 1, he resigns as commissioner, having decided to run for a seat in the state legislature as the representative of Lawrence and Hickman counties. After two months of campaigning, Crockett wins the August election. From the very first of his political career, he takes an active interest in public land policy regarding the West. The House adjourns on November 17, and David, his son John Wesley, and Abram Henry explore the Obion River country.

1822   The Crocketts move west and settle near the Obion River after the second legislative session ends.

1823   Crockett defeats Dr. William E. Butler and is reelected to the state legislature. Crockett ends his state political career on October 22, when the House adjourns.

1825   In August, Crockett is defeated in his first bid for a seat in the United States House of Representatives.

1826   Nearly dying as his boats carrying barrel staves wreck in the Mississippi River, Crockett is brought to Memphis to recover and is encouraged to run for Congress again by M. B. Winchester.

1827   Crockett defeats General William Arnold and Colonel Adam Alexander for a seat in the United States House of Representatives.

1828   Andrew Jackson is elected president.

1829   Crockett is reelected. He splits with Jackson and with the Tennessee delegation on several issues during this term in office.

1830   Crockett attacks the Indian removal bill.

1831   James Kirke Paulding's play *The Lion of the West*, with James Hackett playing the leading character of Nimrod Wildfire based upon Crockett, opens in New York City at the Park Theater on April 25. In his campaign for a third congressional term, Crockett speaks openly against Jackson's policies. He is defeated by William Fitzgerald in a close election.

1833   *The Life and Adventures of Colonel David Crockett, of West Tennessee* is deposited for copyright by James Strange French on January 5. It is soon reprinted under the title *Sketches and Eccentricities of Col. David Crockett of West Tennessee.* Crockett defeats the incumbent Fitzgerald and again wins a seat in Congress.

1834   Crockett publishes his autobiography, *A Narrative of the Life of David Crockett of the State of Tennessee*, written with the help of Thomas Chilton. On April 25, he begins his three-week tour through the eastern states in an anti-Jacksonian alliance with the Whigs.

1835   Two Whig books are published under Crockett's name: *Col. Crockett's Tour to the North and Down East* in late March and *Life of Martin Van Buren* less than three months later. The earliest known copy of "The Crockett Victory March" (*"Go Ahead" a march dedicated to Colonel Crockett*) and the first Crockett almanac are published. The almanac was published in 1834 for 1835. Adam Huntsman defeats

Crockett in the election for Congress, and Crockett, together with William Patton, Abner Burgin, and Lindsey K. Tinkle, sets out for Texas on November 1.

1836   In January, Crockett and Patton sign the oath of allegiance to the "Provisional Government of Texas or any future republican Government that may be hereafter declared. . . ." In early February, Crockett arrives in San Antonio De Bexar. On March 6, he is captured and executed after Santa Anna's army captures the Alamo. Early in the summer, *Col. Crockett's Exploits and Adventures in Texas* is compiled and fabricated by Richard Penn Smith. The Crockett letters that begin the book, however, are authentic. That fall, Jackson's handpicked successor, Martin Van Buren, is elected president. A "new edition" *of Crockett's Free-and-Easy Song Book* is published.

1839   "Colonel Crockett: A Virginia Reel" is published. *Colonel Crockett's Free and Easy Recitation Book* is announced as "in press."

1846   The first known publication of "Pompey Smash: The Everlastin and Unkonkerable Skreamer" occurs in *The Negro Singer's Own Book; Containing Every Negro Song That Has Ever Been Sung or Printed.* Crockett is Pompey's supposed opponent.

1856   The last Crockett almanac is issued for this year.

1860   Reuben M. Potter's study *The Fall of the Alamo* is published.

1871   To honor the frontiersman, Crockett County, Tennessee, is created, and its county seat is named Alamo.

1872   The play *Davy Crockett; Or, Be Sure You're Right, Then Go Ahead,* by Frank Murdock and Frank Mayo, begins a twenty-four year run in this country and in England that terminates only with the death of Frank Mayo, who played Davy, in 1896.

1873   W. P. Zuber first publishes his "improved" account of the last dramatic days at the Alamo.

1889   The first major Crockett celebration is organized by Benjamin Rush Strong at Crockett's birthplace.

1909   The New York Motion Picture Company brings out a silent film entitled *Davy Crockett—in Hearts United.* Charles K. French plays the lead.

1910   The film *Davy Crockett* is released by Selig Polyscope Company.

1911   Davy is a minor character in the film *The Immortal Alamo* (Melies).

1915   Davy, played by A. D. Sears, again has a small part in *The Martyrs of the Alamo*, released by Fine Arts-Triangle, but his is the title role in *Davy Crockett Up-to-Date*, a slapstick farce released by United Film Service.

1916   The Oliver Morosco Photoplay Co. produces *Davy Crockett* starring Dustin Farnum. It is released by Pallas (Paramount).

1926   The last Crockett silent film, *Davy Crockett at the Fall of the Alamo*, is released by Sunset with Cullen Landis playing Crockett.

1934   Constance Rourke publishes *Davy Crockett*, a legendary life of the frontiersman, using tall tales from the *Almanacs*.

1937   Lane Chandler stars in the first "Crockett talkie," *Heroes of the Alamo*, which is produced by Sunset and released by Columbia.

1939   Richard Dorson extracts 108 tales from the Crockett almanacs to produce *Davy Crockett: American Comic Legend*. Robert Barrat portrays Crockett in *Man of Conquest*, a film released by Republic.

1940   Walter Blair delineates "Six Davy Crocketts," in the *Southwest Review* 25: 443–62.

1950   The film *Davy Crockett, Indian Scout* is released by Reliance. George Montgomery plays Davy Crockett, "cousin" of the hero.

1953   Trevor Bardette plays Crockett in the film *Man from the Alamo* (Universal).

1954   Walt Disney broadcasts "Davy Crockett, Indian Fighter" in his *Frontierland* television series on December 15. Fess Parker stars. "The Ballad of Davy Crockett," written by George Bruns and Tom Blackburn, also makes its debut.

1955   The year of the Crockett craze. Two more episodes, "Davy Crockett Goes to Congress" (January 26) and "Davy Crockett at the Alamo" (February 23), were shown on television and then combined with the first episode to form the Disney movie *Davy Crockett, King of the Wild Frontier*. Two more television episodes, "Davy Crockett's Keelboat Race" (November 16) and "Davy Crockett and the River Pirates" (December 14), were also shown. Franklin J. Meine's *The Crockett Almanacks: Nashville Series, 1835–1838* is published. Arthur Hunnicutt portrays Crockett in the film *The Last Command* (Republic).

1956   The last two Disney television shows are combined into a movie, *Davy Crockett and the River Pirates,* which is released in July. James A. Shackford publishes *David Crockett: The Man and the Legend,* the first definitive biography of the historical Crockett. The film *The First Texan* is released by Allied Artists with James Griffith playing Crockett.

1958   *Remember the Alamo!,* a book for young adults by Robert Penn Warren, is published.

1959   Fess Parker portrays Crockett in a walk-on part in the film *Alias Jesse James* (United Artists).

1960   John Wayne produces, directs, and stars as Crockett in *The Alamo* (United Artists).

1961   Walter Lord publishes his study of the Alamo, *A Time to Stand.*

1975   José Enrique de la Peña's *With Santa Anna in Texas: A Personal Narrative of the Revolution* is translated and edited by Carmen Perry. It gives the account of Crockett's capture and execution.

1978   *How Did Davy Die?* is published by Dan Kilgore.

1982   Richard Boyd Hauck publishes *Crockett: A Bio-Bibliography.* It is reissued in 1986 as *Davy Crockett: A Handbook.*

1984   James Wakefield Burke's *David Crockett: The Man Behind the Myth* is published.

1985   Michael A. Lofaro's *Davy Crockett: The Man, The Legend, The Legacy, 1786–1986* is published. *Alamo Images: Changing Perceptions of a Texas Experience* is published by Susan Prendergast Schoelwer with Tom W. Glaser.

1986   The bicentennial of the birth of David Crockett and the sesqui-centennial of his death, the battle of the Alamo, and the founding of the Republic of Texas are celebrated. On June 14, the exhibit "Davy Crockett: Gentleman from the Cane" opens in the Smithsonian Institution's National Portrait Gallery and is later displayed in the Tennessee State Museum. Walter Blair's 1955 work on the life and tall tales of the frontiersman is reprinted as *Davy Crockett: Legendary Frontier Hero.* Gary Foreman's pictorial compilation *Crockett: Gentleman from the Cane* is published. Mac Davis stars in "Davy Crockett," an episode of the television program *Tall Tales & Legends* that airs on December 18.

1987   *The Tall Tales of Davy Crockett: The Second Nashville Series of Crockett Almanacs, 1839–1841* is published by Michael A. Lofaro. Crockett's autobiography is reissued with a new introduction by Paul Andrew Hutton. The television film *The Alamo: 13 Days to Glory*, based upon the book of the same name by Lon Tinkle, is aired.

1988   Disney studios brings Davy back in *The New Adventures of Davy Crockett* on *The Magical World of Disney* on television. The first episode is "Rainbow in the Thunder," starring Tim Dunigan as the young Crockett and Johnny Cash as the elder Crockett reminiscing about his exploits in the Creek Wars. It airs on November 11. The subsequent four episodes are "A Natural Man" (December 12), "Guardian Spirit" (January 13, 1989), "A Letter to Polly" (June 11, 1989), and "Warrior's Farewell" (June 18, 1989). "Alamo: The Price of Freedom" is an IMAX short (37 minutes) that features Merrill Connally as Davy Crockett.

1989   *Crockett at Two Hundred: New Perspectives on the Man and the Myth* is published by Michael A. Lofaro.

1992   Euro Disney Resort, now Disneyland Paris, opens its wilderness themed Davy Crockett Ranch on April 12.

1994   "Davy Crockett: American Frontier Legend" appears as a television episode of *Biography* on August 1.

1995   Timothy Matovina's *The Alamo Remembered: Tejano Accounts and Perspectives* and Holly B. Brear's *Inherit the Alamo: Myth and Ritual at an American Shrine* are published.

1998   William C. Davis's *Three Roads to the Alamo: The Lives and Fortunes of David Crockett, James Bowie, and William Barret Travis* is published.

1999   *Encyclopedia of the Alamo and the Texas Revolution* by Thom Hatch is published.

2001   The Bob Bullock Texas State History Museum opens in Austin, featuring one of the largest exhibitions of Crockett material ever assembled. The documentary *Boone and Crockett: The Hunter Heroes* (Native Sun Productions) airs on The History Channel.

2004   The film *The Alamo* is released, with Billy Bob Thornton starring as Crockett.

2005   James E. Crisp's *Sleuthing the Alamo: Davy Crockett's Last Stand and other Mysteries of the Texas Revolution* is published.

2008 A short (26 minutes) action feature has Andrew Sensenig play the frontiersman in *Davy Crockett Battles Kung Fu Vampires.*

2009 *David Crockett in Congress: The Rise and Fall of the Poor Man's Friend. With Collected Correspondence, Selected Speeches and Circulars* is published by James R. Boylston and Allen J. Wiener.

2012 Bob Thompson publishes *Born on a Mountaintop: On the Road with Davy Crockett and the Ghosts of the Wild Frontier*, and Jim Donovan publishes *The Blood of Heroes: The 13–Day Struggle for the Alamo—and the Sacrifice that Forged a Nation.*

2015 Ron Jackson and Lee S. White publish *Joe, A Slave Who Became an Alamo Legend.* On June 7, the comedy *Too Many Crocketts* airs with Thomas Partain starring as Davy.

2016 Paul Williams publishes *Jackson, Crockett and Houston on the American Frontier: From Fort Mims to the Alamo.* The television show *Timeless* has "The Alamo" as an October 31 episode with Jeff Kober as Crockett.

2017 *Last Stands from the Alamo to Benghazi: How Hollywood Turns Military Defeats into Moral Victories* is published by Frank J. Wetta and Martin A. Novelli.

2019 *Boone, Black Hawk, and Crockett in 1833: Unsettling the Mythic West* is published by Michael A. Lofaro.

2020 *The Life and Adventures [Or Sketches and Eccentricities] of Colonel David Crockett, of West Tennessee* is published by Michael A. Lofaro.

Davy's First Book

I

"King of the Wild Frontier"? Yes and no. Whatever the answer you choose, the life of David "Davy" Crockett (1786–1836) does more to demonstrate the history and legendary spirit of the American frontier than any man of his time. His fame as a hunter, storyteller, and humorist evolves as he moves from a local to a national political career and makes him a media darling during his life on both sides of the Atlantic. And after his death at the Alamo on March 6, 1836, the fictional Crockett explodes even more into the public arena for multiple generations a century before his television and movie depictions by Fess Parker, John Wayne, and Billy Bob Thornton.

Early on, Crockett recognizes that his military success as a militiaman in the Creek Indian War of 1813–1814 and his rise to lieutenant colonel commandant on March 27, 1818,[1] would serve him in good stead in a political life. But his humor and activities as a jokester/trickster blossom well before his first race for office. Nearly dying from malaria during his exploration of the soon-to-be formed Lawrence County, Tennessee, in the fall of 1816, he returns home to find his family in mourning, for neighbors travelling the frontier report that they have met men who helped to bury him. David's reply is "I know'd this was a wapper of a lie, as soon as I heard it,"[2] an obvious backwoods predecessor to Mark Twain's "the reports of my death have been greatly exaggerated."[3]

Election stories are a great sourcebook for learning Crockett's character. The earliest is recounted in the present volume, *The Life and Adventures of Colonel David Crockett, of West Tennessee*, which is called hereinafter by the better known title of the version reprinted in New York in the same year—*Sketches and Eccentricities of Col. David Crockett of West Tennessee*, or *Sketches* for short.[4] After Crockett's election to the Tennessee House in 1821, other members of that body refer to him as "the gentleman from the *cane*" to mock his backwoods clothing and lack of refinement. His main antagonist, the man who gives him the offensive nickname that Crockett turns to his own advantage, is James C. Mitchell, a man who fancies shirts with ruffles. When a part of Mitchell's shirt is torn off in his scuffle with a senator, David recalls in *Sketches* that "'I determined to have some fun. So, I took up his fine cambric ruffle and pinned it to my coarse cotton shirt—made it as conspicuous as possible, and when the house met, strutted in. I seated myself near M——; when the members, understanding how it was, soon filled the house with a roar of laughter. M——l couldn't stand it, and walked out'" (28, 29, this edition). Mitchell hardly knew what hit him.

Crockett is no one's fool. He knows his image and continues to manipulate it to his political advantage in his campaigns. His run against Dr. William E. Butler, who is married to Andrew Jackson's niece, in the Tennessee state election of 1823 provides other great examples of Crockett's strategic humor. Playing up his homespun image, he labels Butler as an aristocrat. When he visits his opponent's house, he takes note of the expensive furnishings and refuses to walk upon a particularly beautiful rug. Crockett features the episode as the high point in one of his speeches: "fellow citizens, my aristocratic competitor has a fine carpet, and every day he *walks* on truck finer than any gowns your wife or your daughters, in all their lives, ever *wore!*" (37)[5]; he also tells Butler that he will have a buckskin hunting shirt made with two pockets large enough to hold a big twist of chewing tobacco and a bottle of whisky. According to David, after a prospective voter spits out his tobacco to take a drink from his bottle: "I would out with my twist and give him another chaw. And in that way he would not be worse off than when I found him; and I would be sure to leave him in a first-rate good humour."[6] Crockett once even memorizes Butler's campaign speech and delivers it word for word before it is Butler's turn to talk.[7] David wins the election.

On the national political scene, Crockett serves three terms in the House of Representatives from 1827–1831 and from 1833–1835. In his first campaign, he allows his opponents—General William Arnold and Colonel Adam Alexander—to work "against each, while I was going ahead for myself.... I was as cunning as a little red fox, and wouldn't risk my tail in a 'committal' trap."[8] Here getting in a dig against then-senator and Jackson's campaign manager Martin Van Buren, who is often satirized because of his small physical stature and his slippery stances on issues (Van Buren is also known as the "sly fox" and the "Little Magician"), Crockett continues to use animal metaphors and tales to talk about the electioneering season. His speeches, in contrast to his opponents' and to the norm of the day, are brief, or, as he says, "a short horse is soon curried." And when a "large flock of guinea-fowls" settles nearby, noisily interrupting Arnold's lengthy refutation of Alexander's speech until he has them shooed away, Crockett complains to him that: "he had not had the politeness to name me in his speech, and that when my little friends, the guinea-fowls, had come up and began to holler 'Crockett, Crockett, Crockett,' he had been ungenerous enough to stop, and drive *them* all away. This raised a universal shout among the people for me, and the general seemed mighty bad plagued. But he got more plagued than this at the polls in August...."⁹

Crockett's character moves rapidly into history, fiction, and combinations of the two. In *Sketches*, the historical David Crockett is shown accurately as opposing Jackson's policies on Indian removal (which culminate five years later in the Trail of Tears, a tragedy that the historical Congressman Crockett tries to prevent, as documented in his correspondence with Cherokee chief John Ross). David likewise rails actively against Jackson's policies on a National Bank, and in favor of squatters' rights versus land sales,[10] while his growing fictional personae, soon unfettered by his death, spin tall tales of fantastic adventures, as well as those that reinforce racism and expansionism.

The tallest of the tall tales that are told about and "by" Crockett occur in those Crockett Almanacs published after his death.[11] Their seedbed, however, is in oral tradition and in the newspapers of Crockett's time and are well represented in this edition. For example, when visiting a traveling menagerie in Washington, DC, a friend looks in a cage and asks Crockett "'if they were like the wild cats in the backwoods?'—and I was looking at them, when one turned over and died. The keeper ran up, and threw some water on it. Said I, 'Stranger, you are wasting time. My looks kills them things—and you had a damn sight better hire me to go out here, or I will kill every damn varmint you've got'" (87). This story is a likely precursor to those in which Crockett successfully hunts raccoons and even bears with his stupefying grin. Political antics also continue in the "menagerie" anecdote when Crockett sees a monkey riding a pony and is asked:

> "Crockett, don't that monkey favor General Jackson?" "No," said I, "but I'll tell you who it does favor. It looks like one of your boarders, Mr. ——, of Ohio." There was a loud burst of laughter at my saying so, and upon turning round, I saw Mr. ——, of Ohio, in about three feet of me. I was in a right awkward fix; but I bowed to the company, and told 'em, "I had either slandered the monkey, or Mr. ——, of Ohio, and if they would tell me which, I would beg his pardon." The thing passed off; and next morning as I was walking the pavement before my door, a member come up to me and said, "Crockett, Mr. ——, of Ohio, is going to challenge you." Said I, "Well tell him I am a fighting fowl. I 'spose if I am challenged, I have the right to choose my weapons?" "Oh yes," said he. "Then tell him," said I, "that I will fight him with bows and arrows." (87–88)

Perhaps one of the best examples of how a tall tale grows, however, is the account in *Sketches* of Davy's wringing the tail off Halley's Comet. It occurs only as a brief reference in chapter I and in a few lines as an announcement in chapter XI (11, 67).[12] Posthumously, however, in *Davy Crockett's 1837 Almanack of Wild Sports in the West, Life in the Backwoods, & Sketches of Texas*, the reader is treated to the legend full-blown as part of his preface entitled "'Go Ahead' Reader." After noting that he has left the Almanac's "'Gastronomical calculations'" to a friend, Davy explains why he wants "nothing more to do with Gastronomy, and 'see-less-tial bodies'":

> I was appointed by the President to stand on the Alleghany Mountains and wring the Comet's tail off. I did so, but got my hands most shockingly burnt, and the hair singed off my head, so that I was as bald as a trencher. I div right down into the Waybosh river, and thus save my best stone blue coat and grass green small clothes. With the help of Bear's grease, I have brought out a new crop, but the hair grows in bights and tufts, like hussuck grass in a meadow, and it keeps in such a snarl, that all the teeth will instantly snap out of an ivory comb when brought within ten feet of it.[13]

This adventure is but a mild warm-up for America's first comic superman. In later Almanacs, Crockett convinces his pet alligator to bite his tail and churn like a paddle-wheel so he can ride up Niagara Falls inside it. He also becomes a frontier Prometheus who saves the solar system by unfreezing the "airth" and the sun that have "friz fast" to their axes by pouring hot bear cub "ile" on them, and then walks "Home, introducin' the people to fresh daylight with a piece of sunrise in my pocket. . . ."[14]

A *New-York Mirror* review of his *Narrative* (Feb. 22, 1834) predicts an early sense of the dynamism of Crockett's future portrayals in the Almanacs: "His fame rolls on, increasing, like an avalanche, and burying beneath its mass the names of all the minor worthies of the west. . . ." While in an Almanac published for 1838, for example, "Davy," dead since 1836, explains how hard it was to produce his brand of literature, the same passage also reveals how far his anonymous creators will go to create tall-tale humor: "I was born in a cane brake, cradled in a sap trough, and clouted with coon skins; without being choked by the weeds of education, which do not grow *spontinaciously*—for all the time that I was troubled with *youngness*. My cornstealers were *na*'trally used for other purposes than holding a pen; and *rayly* when I try to write my elbow keeps coming round like a swingle-tree, and it is easier for me to tree a varmint, or swallow a nigger, than to write." The sometimes racist Crockett also unintentionally defeats gender stereotypes by developing lower-class backwoods "shemales" in the Crockett Almanacs whose "domesticity" was extreme: they used knitting needles, but to kill "bars," and attended church regularly, but adorned themselves with fashionable necklaces of gouged-out eyes.[15] Given the tales spectacularly audacious nature, it is no wonder that Crockett remains an integral part of peoples' views of the early westering frontier and of the "wild" in wilderness.

The legend and story of Crockett's life reaches its initial zenith in the 1833 book that forms the present volume. It is the first book about (and, in part, by) Crockett and has long been unavailable. A true hodgepodge of genres, it mirrors the many conceptions of the man and his myths. Part biography, part autobiography, part history, part fiction and tall tale, Crockett's story is formed from interviews, quotation of actual events, outright lies, and tall-tales published in newspapers. What *Sketches* does is to consolidate a good deal of previously printed and adds new material to create the United States' first great national frontier hero since Daniel Boone (1734–1820).

Crockett, like Daniel Boone before him, is one of Rousseau's "natural men," but takes on a new mantle as well. Boone, the Providentially ordained expansionist pioneer who is dedicated and noble, gives way before David Crockett as the poor man's Andrew Jackson and Davy as "half-horse, half-alligator" legendary frontiersman who is brash and cocky. The change in heroes parallels the shift in the centers of political power from drawing rooms to taverns, from the control of the upper class to within reach of the common man. The competition is as natural as the years that separate them. Boone, born in 1734, is the contemporary of Washington and is fifty-two years old when Crockett is born. Likewise, his first short "autobiography," *The Adventures of Col. Daniel Boon, One of the First Settlers, Comprehending every Important Occurrence in the Political History of that Province* . . . appears in John Filson's *The Discovery, Settlement, And present State of Kentucke: And An Essay towards the Topography, and natural History of that important Country* . . . in 1784, forty-nine years before the present volume of Crockett is printed.[16]

Crockett's life, both as historically and imaginatively rendered in *Sketches*, undercuts traditional notions of class in its stories and, in so doing, parallels similar breakdowns in the society of Jacksonian America and provides attainable models for others to follow.[17] Like Benjamin Franklin, but less "civilized," David typifies the American Dream. He rises above his initial station in life and overcomes substantial obstacles to achieve more success than most would think possible. Due to his intimate association with the frontier, Crockett arguably does not become middle class or broach an elite status as defined by the refined society of Eastern cities, nor would he wish to do so. Yet in these stories, Crockett is able to interact with those on "higher" social levels as equals, because his bravery, self-reliance, and independence provide the self-confidence necessary to follow his own judgment. This book presents many scenes that argue persuasively for

equality. Crockett is a common man of the frontier whose life traverses and sometimes breaks class and cultural boundaries. His actions are taken from their normal sphere of the wilderness, communicated to a more educated reading public,
and become staple reading for generations to come.

II

The power that *Sketches* originally exerts over the American mind benefits
greatly from a national emphasis on internal improvements that is first high-
lighted by the dedication of the Erie Canal in 1824. As distance is conquered
through canals, turnpikes, steamboat and railroad routes, and as technological
innovations in printing lessen production costs, the influence of the printed
word and popular culture upon the imagining of the West on both sides of
the Atlantic grows exponentially. *Sketches* and other popular books like it that
are "auto"biographical—such as Timothy Flint's *Biographical Memoir of Daniel
Boone, The First Settler of Kentucky. Interspersed with Incidents in the Early Annals
of the Country* and the *Life of Mà-ka-tai-me-she-kià-kiàk, or Black Hawk . . .*
both published in Cincinnati in the same year,[18]—undergird new notions of
American exceptionalism, nationalism, and expansion. They demonstrate a var-
iegated and sometimes subversive view of the frontier to the reading public
that receives far less attention at this transformative time in American history
than does literary fiction on the subject of the frontier. Works such as James
Fenimore Cooper's first three Leatherstocking Tales (1823–1827), Catharine
Maria Sedgwick's *Hope Leslie* (1827), and William Gilmore Simms's border
romances begun in 1834 provide varying fictional portrayals of frontiersmen
and Native Americans that likewise complicate then common stereotypes in
the popular mind and, like *Sketches*, create a fresh carrying image of the West
that is problematic and fraught with nuanced associations.

Crockett's *Sketches* had at least fourteen American printings in 1833 (three
of *Life* published in Cincinnati and eleven as *Sketches* reprinted in New York
and bearing the 1833 copyright) and five London editions by 1841. Its original
publication in Cincinnati, then the westernmost hub of American publishing,
also proves a small exception to the late John Seelye's astute comment that the
mythology of the West is created in the printing houses of the East. Certainly
the bulk of the editions of *Sketches* conform to his belief, as do the *Crockett
Almanacs* that are mainly created within the Boston-New York-Philadelphia
publishing axis, but whose republished imprints range as far west as New
Orleans. Clearly through their purchases readers are voting for a change in the
conception of a major American frontier hero, one that for the first time leans
upon humor and the tall tale as well as heroic deeds.

The historical Crockett addresses the mania for frontier heroes on February 1, 1834, in his *Narrative*, as he attempts to capitalize on his enhanced fame and to refute the wilder claims in *Sketches* to pave the way for a possible presidential run. The preface to his *Narrative* makes clear both the problems and the notoriety that *Sketches* produces for the congressman.

> A publication has been made to the world, which has done me much injustice; and the catchpenny errors which it contains, have been already too long sanctioned by my silence. . . . I have met with hundreds, if not with thousands of people, who have formed their opinions of my appearance, habits, language, and every thing else from that deceptive work.
>
> They have almost in every instance expressed the most profound astonishment at finding me in human shape, and with the *countenance, appearance,* and *common feelings* of a human being. . . .
>
> Go where I will, everybody seems anxious to have a peep at me; . . . . There must therefore be something in me, or about me, that attracts attention, which is even mysterious to myself.[19]

His preface is rapidly republished multiple times nationally, including in the *Cherokee Phoenix* (May 31, 1834), the first Native American language paper.

When *Sketches* appears early in 1833, it enters a world that, despite the American Dream of upward mobility through achievement, is still bound by race and class and is replete with savage descriptions of natives and of white men who immerse themselves in the frontier, who occupy bottom rungs in the overall cultural hierarchy. Historically, Crockett is a self-made man with little or no formal education who fails to succeed, if success is measured by the accumulation of wealth or power. However, Crockett's identification with the savage wilderness, which initially limits his class mobility, increases in importance with the rise of the common man in the Jacksonian era, and also readily converts to support his status as a hero who fights for equality, fairness, independence, and freedom. The result is a new kind of hero for the West who easily traverses the boundary between regionalism and nationalism, fact and fiction, instruction and humor, as well as the barriers of race and class, to complicate and even defeat previous stereotypes in important ways.

While this bridging of barriers is not new, the numerous other examples of previous linkage, such as civilized citizens dressing as Native Americans for the Boston Tea Party, rarely incorporate humor into the behavior of "playing Indian."[20] The sense of security provided by the elapsed half-century between the end of the Revolution and the publication of *Sketches* seemingly allows the removal of the "disguises" that mask the co-opting of many of the stereotypes of indigenous savage behavior and endorses them as true indicators of nationalism for white Americans, especially those who identify the frontier as a critical part of their American identity. *Sketches* succeeds where the many attempts of high-culture literary nationalism fail as they seek to create parallel versions of classic, biblical, and Miltonic epics.[21] Even the pseudo-Miltonic epic poem that Daniel Bryan bases upon the life and adventures of Daniel Boone, *The Mountain Muse* (1813),[22] falls upon deaf ears, including Boone's. The old pioneer's reaction to the flowery rhetorical treatment given his character is less than encouraging. He says that he sincerely regrets that Bryan is his wife's nephew, for he feels that he cannot "sue him for slander," and furthermore that productions such as this "ought to be left until the person was put in the ground."[23] Bryan's book never has a second printing. The American audience has to wait until the stories of and about Crockett that this volume contains erupt in a popularity that in turn legitimizes the rowdy, unrestrained, tall-talking frontiersman as a crucial part of a foundational myth that Americans could adopt as uniquely their own. The irony is, of course, that many readers, especially in the East, are more economically and culturally distant from the ways of the frontier by 1833 than ever and indulge in the myth as nostalgia for a life that they never experienced.

Sketches is thus the first narrative to capitalize radically upon this changing idea of the frontier hero. James Strange French,[24] the purported author of the work, combines satire, history, biography, legend, newspaper accounts, and tall tales into a loose narrative that is intended as comic rather than serious. His work nonetheless mirrors a good deal of the popular culture of the time and adds new elements to the debate over savagery versus civilization inherent in earlier frontier narratives. This first book-length compilation of Crockett's life provides an apt parallel to the nation's accumulating views concerning the frontier that are widely held in the 1830s.

III

The preface of *Sketches* begins with the author quickly creating an upper-crust narrator-observer who recounts his stories about Crockett in the picaresque manner that attempts to connect them to each other. The accounts are also linked in a less obvious, yet still significant way, by the prominence he places upon traditional oral storytelling, albeit in written form.

The author opens the work's preface by satirizing the need for a "fashionable" book to have a preface and, after thus announcing to the reader his knowledge of current literary trends, states with false modesty that he does not seek fame and writes in the common language that best suits his subject (3, 4). Continuing in a flippant and light-hearted tone, he rejects the use of (but in so doing

incorporates) the manufactured frontier language soon to be the hallmark of
the Almanacs—*"'bodyaciowsly,' 'tetotaciously,' 'obflisticated,' &c."*—as completely
unrealistic, preferring instead true "quaintness of expression and originality of
comparison" (4). The slang terms that he does utilize remain, however, a similar
source of obvious humor. The author next rejects the conformity that critics
inspire, such as the use of the stereotype of the native as savage. He discards as
well any serious approach to constructing his preface ("I will write as long as
my humor prompts, or until the fit under which I am now laboring, wears off")
and to his book as a whole: "in writing for my own amusement, I had a right
to select my topics; and consequently I have been grave or merry as my humor
prompted" (4). He ends by exaggerating his achievement and proclaiming his
work a book for all—wealthy, common, learned, and philosophical—and by
assuring readers of its wholesomeness, for not a word in it will offend "the
cheek of innocence, or give license to vice" (4). Perhaps the most remarkable
statement in the preface is that "though the following memoir may wear an
air of levity, it is, nevertheless, strictly true" (4). His words are best read as both
exaggeration and satire. The work does recount some of the facts of Crockett's
life, even though it is also a collection of anecdotes focusing upon the comic
and entertaining. Similarly, the author's demonstrated disdain for the trappings
of cultured literature and the outrageous vernacular coinages that are the hallmark of popular frontier tall tales makes his work a pointed, if whimsical, cri-
tique of the literature of the day. Above all, his insistence upon the truth of his
story is clearly suspect. Let the reader be warned. Oftentimes, especially in this
period of the beginning of the Humor of the Old Southwest[25] of which *Sketches*
is a significant part, the greater the insistence upon truth, the taller the tale.

It is also true that the narrator mockingly but accurately foretells the future
merger of the historical and the legendary Crockett and of the West itself:

> The term "far off West," seems from general usage, to apply only to that section of
> our country which lies between the Alleghany and Rocky mountains. In compar-
> ison with this vast region, other portions of the globe, which have delighted the
> world with the finest specimens of history, of poetry, of sculpture, and of painting,
> dwindle into insignificance with regard to magnitude. Here Fancy, in her playful
> flights, may call into being empires which have no existence; and though perhaps
> sober reason would now chide her fairy creations yet the time will come, when
> they will only be looked upon with the conviction of truth. (5)

Imagined creations such as the outlandish tales about Crockett and the West,
according to the narrator, will become reality for readers over the passage of time.

The literary banter which marks the preface does resurface in some of the
later texts of the Humor of the Old Southwest in which a more cultured

narrator introduces and at times comments on the tales, but its structure and humor find no part in the other contemporary heroic frontier narratives, such as those of Boone and Black Hawk.[26] The method emphasizes the class distinction between the author (who cites classical authors such as Horace, Apollonius, Cicero, and Juvenal) and his backwoods subject, while at the same time joining them together by the narrator's approbation of Crockett, a view that emphasizes Romanticism, as does his mentions of Sir Walter Scott, Lord Byron, and Robert Burns. After a brief nod to his "biography of a celebrated backwoodsman" to come, the author settles into a sketch of the "'far off West,'" the land between the mountains. He waxes poetical over the vastness of the glories of nature on display there, such as the Mississippi River: "There are some portions of it very shallow; but there are others, where no bottom has ever yet been found; and could its waters be drained off, there would be left chasms into which the boldest would never dare to look; and in whose depths myriads of animals crawl and flutter, which have never yet known the light of day!" (5–6). The lure of the Romantic seems a fated higher calling for all observers that defies class and, like them, this author also sees its primeval-pastoral beauty defiled; nonetheless, for whites, he states, when the frontier is tamed it is converted into the "better" beauty of civilization. Examine the debate between the Past and the Present in *Sketches'* introduction:

> "Once, only a canoe danced lightly over your waters: now, floating palaces [steamboats] adorn them, which realize all the gorgeous tales of eastern fancy, and with all their beauty blend the power of the magic carpet—
> 'Walk your waters like things of life,
> 'And seem to dare the elements to strife.'" (6)

Rather than taking a side in the debate, the author of *Sketches* sees all of Crevecoeur's stages of civilization[27]—untouched nature, the pastoral, settlement areas, and polished societies—as existing in the space of the West and serving to fire the imagination: "The whole country spreads before us a field for speculation, only bounded by the limits of the human mind" (7). He believes Buffon's theories of degeneration in the New World,[28] and also imagines a predecessor race of giants who herd and eat mammoths as easily as sheep. In his mind, the grazing mammoths eat vast woodlands and prevent regrowth with their poisonous saliva to create the Great Plains (7). Given the highly associative nature of the front matter's "organization" in *Sketches*, the story of the tree-eating mammoths not unexpectedly gives way to a very brief Crockett tale on tree-sliding: "my hero is the only person who could ever slip down a honey-locust without a scratch" (7). This, in turn, segues into a joke about a

French epicure in America who, having eaten a pig, cries out "*waitaire!* have you no more *leetle* mammoths?"' (7). The casual slippage from Romanticism to the pseudo-science of the day to a tall tale to a joke typifies the introduction and provides the reader a fine example of the supposed methodology of the preface, as well as the book itself.

No then-contemporary discussion of the West, however, is complete without a consideration of the age and purpose of Indian mounds, and they do prove a fertile topic for the author's imagination. He calls up the spirits of the chiefs of the grandfather races buried there, likens their fame to that of Hannibal, Caesar, Napoleon, or Wellington, and, perhaps most interestingly, parallels their passing and defeat to the belief in the "Vanishing Indian." For him, as for Jackson and many white Americans, "even the last remnant of this once great people is fast disappearing from the country. A few years more and not one will remain to tell what they once were" (8).[29]

It also proves difficult to deal with a white frontier hero without some mention of Daniel Boone. The author sees Boone's home as in the wilderness and Crockett's as less desirably on the frontier, oddly contradicting his previous position on the locations' relative equality. Both individuals are superb marksmen, but Boone wages "an eternal war with the Indians" while Crockett fights "an eternal war with the wild beasts of the forest, and served his country," and has the better mind (10). (Both "eternal wars" are incorrect, and Boone's long-standing service to his country goes unmentioned.)

The author's final portrait of Crockett in the introduction focuses on his residence in West Tennessee, ironically again reversing his view of the frontier as a suitable place, thinly settled, wild, but hospitable, and specifically foregrounds the start of the *Sketches* proper, by invoking a kind of geographical determinism in which a person's behavior is formed by and parallels his or her environment. In Crockett's case, "There, far retired from the bustle of the world, he lives, and chews for amusement the cud of his political life. He has settled himself over the grave of an earthquake, which often reminds him of the circumstance by moving itself as if tired of confinement" (10).[30] The humor of the "cud of his political life" and the link between Crockett's unbridled personality and the staggering New Madrid earthquakes of 1811–1812 and its subsequent violent aftershocks paves the way for the unpredictable nature of the tales to come. Although the author has promised the reader truth, the fictional Crockett is an ever-present and irrepressible performer in *Sketches*. He garners a tip of the hat in just the third sentence of the book: "No one, at this early age, could have foretold that he was ever to ride upon a streak of lightning, receive a commission to quiet the fears of the world by wringing the tail off a comet, or perform sundry other wonderful acts, for which he has received due credit, and which will serve to give him a reputation as lasting as that of the hero of Orleans [Andrew Jackson]" (11).[31]

That so much of the biographical data duplicates that which Crockett himself provides a year later in his autobiographical *Narrative* indicates that, despite later denials, David was himself a main source for the earlier *Sketches*. These events of Crockett's life are easily accessible in the present volume (also see the preceding "A Selective Crockett Chronology"); of greater interest is how the author presents Crockett as a frontier hero and how these depictions correlate with the use of humor that creates Crockett as a new type of hero outside the traditional mold. Unlike earlier frontier heroes whose destiny it is to follow fated paths, Crockett is cast as a disruptive, trickster-like figure, one who is fun-loving, a genuine American original and, at times, an uncivilized backwoods buffoon. Historically, the Tennessean is a storyteller, fiddler, and the life of the party, a good fit for the Age of Jackson. He is also intentionally the partial author of his own legend, commencing in earnest in the late 1820s, as he moves onto the national stage with his first term in the House of Representatives (1827–1829) and becomes an irresistible subject for the news media of his day. *The Constellation* (New York) prints his condensed biography on December 18, 1830, citing the *Winchester* (VA) *Republican* as its source. Crockett is already a well-known entity in print before the publication of *Sketches* in 1833.

Much more of the initial information about Crockett appears in newspapers. Although at first a staunch Jackson supporter, Crockett arrives in Washington when John Quincy Adams is still president. One of the first stories to circulate in the newspapers is about his supposedly attending a formal presidential dinner in which the boorish "Congressman from the wild woods of Tennessee" is completely at odds with the setting. He tries to keep the whole goose for himself, charges the waiter with theft when he moves the platter to serve other guests, and holds onto his plate from then on with one hand while eating, so no waiter can "steal" it. Humor trumps truth. While labeled as "facetious," the tale takes on a life of its own and is frequently reprinted, despite Crockett's printed denials and other congressmen's printed verifications of his mannerly, proper behavior. It is likewise reprinted in this edition (82–84).[32] The editors of one newspaper, *The Ariel*, seemingly discount, however, the verification of the civilized Crockett's actions to fuel the fires of the comic report: "We are told that Mr. Crocket[t] is a sensible man, but suppose it is true that he has something of the 'half horse half alligator' in his manners." Continuing further toward the tall tale, the editors state (citing the *Middlesex Gazette*) that "Davy" is stronger than two ordinary men and had assured his travelling companions on the way to Washington that "he could wade the Mississippi with a steamboat on his back, whip his weight in wildcats, and 'ride a streak of lightning barebacked.'

Davy too is the man who proposes to whip all the animals in a menagerie, consisting of a lion, a parcel of monkeys, and a zebra."[33] Adding to these accomplishments, a reprinting in the *New-Bedford Mercury* attests that Davy's stare can frighten a wildcat to death.[34] All these boasts echo the feats that the author of *Sketches* notes in his introduction and demonstrate the attractiveness and staying power of Crockett's legends.

Not all the newspaper notices of Crockett involve far-fetched portrayals; some record his congressional votes, resolutions he introduces, his speeches, and his political philosophy. The following newspaper accounts show how *Sketches* is also based upon a solid sense of Crockett the man. One example of the historical Crockett emerges in an amendment he offers to a national road bill in 1830. The road is to begin in Buffalo, and the congressman from West Tennessee wants to divert it to Memphis, instead of New Orleans, after it passes through Washington, DC, noting that taking the easily available steamboats from Memphis to New Orleans would diminish the tax burden placed upon his constituents by making the road shorter. He omits mention of the significant benefits of his proposed route for the road to his state and district. In these excerpts from his accompanying speech on March 30, 1830, the reader gets a sense of the actual Crockett's homey, straightforward personality and language, and his gift for storytelling, in which humor and controversy are never far in the shadows.

I was elected from the western district of Tennessee, after declaring myself a friend to this measure; and I came here quite hot for the road—yes, the fever was upon me; but I confess I am getting quite cool on the subject of expending money for the gratification of certain gentlemen who happen to have different views from those I entertain. Let us inquire where this money comes from. It will be found that even our poorest citizens have to contribute towards the supply. . . . I pledged myself to the good people who sent me here, that I would oppose certain tariff measures . . . /that/ are felt to be oppressive by my fellow-citizens; and, as long as I can raise my voice, I will oppose the odious system which sanctions them. . . .

I am astonished that certain of our eastern friends have become so kind to us. They are quite willing to aid in distributing a portion of the national funds among us of the west. This was not so once. And, if I am not deceived, their present kindness is merely a bait to cover the hook which is intended to haul in the western and southern people; and when we are hooked over the barb, we will have to yield. Their policy reminds me of a certain man in the State of Ohio, who, having caught a raccoon, placed it in a bag, and, as he was on his way home, he met a neighbor, who was anxious to know what he had in his bag. He was told to put his hand in and feel, and in doing so he was bit through the fingers; he then asked what it was, and was told it was only a bite. I fear that our good eastern friends have a hook and a bite for us; and, if we are once fastened, it will close the concern. We may then despair of paying the national debt; we may bid farewell to all other internal improvements; and, finally, we may bid farewell to all hopes of ever reducing duties [taxes] on any thing. This is honestly my opinion; and again I say, I cannot consent to "go the whole hog." But I will go as far as Memphis.[35]

Crockett's sarcastic comments on easterners as false friends ready to set their hooks into the West generates a partisan sectional reply and attack by the *Newburyport Herald* (Massachusetts): "This living at Washington has operated sadly upon David's moral sense." And even further, his primitive nature has no redeeming value.

His speech is rude, clumsy, and immethodical—huddled, promisc[u]ous and destitute utterly of connection—with a diction coarse and slovenly; and abounding in low vulgarisms and epithets. . . . Our opinion is that strength of passions have been mistaken for strength of intellect; and that his hand is a good deal more powerful than his head. . . . That he can ever have any clear or far insight into subjects of legislation, as they rise in Congress, it is impossible to believe; and we think it discreditable that such an individual is to be found there.[36]

Clearly Crockett inspires controversy. Whether fictional or actual, his down-home humor, wit, colorful language, and portrayal bring him fame and scorn depending upon viewpoint of his interpreters, much the same reaction that the Humor of the Old Southwest often inspires.

The newspapers also document one reason for the historical Crockett's eventual break with Jackson—overspending; his colloquial warning is typical, comical, and mixes metaphors: "The people of this country, like the humble boatmen on the Mississippi, ought to begin to look out for *breakers!* The *fox* is about: let the *roost* be guarded!"[37] Other substantial reasons for the split include Crockett's speech and vote against Jackson's Indian Removal Bill,[38] his submission of a petition of three Cherokees to reclaim 640 acres of confiscated land, and his vote in favor of the government following "the faithful observance of the treaties" with the native tribes.[39] His Indian stance is so unpopular in his district that a *"Tennessee paper"* publishes a satire in which Crockett is negotiating a treaty with the United States to have the white citizens of West Tennessee cede their land to the federal government and move west across the Mississippi.[40] Credit Crockett for holding his ground. In his published "Circular" to the voters of his district, bearing the date of February 28, 1831, he attacks Jackson's overspending, lack of reform, and particularly his Indian policy. Referencing the situation of the dispossessed Cherokees in Georgia, Crockett states:

My heart bleeds when I reflect on his [Jackson's] cruelty to poor unprotected Indians. I never expected it of him. . . . The President, relying on the strength of his
popularity and on party spirit, persists in it, and thus brings shame and reproach
on the American name; and nothing will stop this unfeeling career of treachery
and cruelty but the ballot box, and it is now to be tried whether an honest adher-
ence to treaties with defenceless tribes is to be sustained by you, against cruelty
and bad faith. I have said this much about this because I feel much about it.[41]

At the end of his "Circular," Congressman Crockett announces his bid for a
third term and says that "You know that I am a poor man; and that I am a plain
man. I have served you long enough in peace, to enable you to judge whether
I am honest or not—I never deceived—I never will deceive you. I have fought
with you and for you in war, and you know whether I love my country, and
ought to be trusted. I thank you for what you have done for me, and I hope
that you will not forsake me to gratify those who are my enemies and yours."[42]
Sincere, simple, and holding fast to his beliefs, Crockett still loses the election
to William Fitzgerald, a Jackson man; notice of his defeat and the vote count
appear in *Niles' Weekly Register*, September 3, 1831.

Before his defeat in the election of 1831, Crockett formally withdraws from
the Jackson Party; his usual wit is noted in the newspapers stating "that he was
a Jackson man still—But Gen. Jackson was not, for that the General had left
the principles which he avowed when he was elected. Now, said Mr. Crockett,
that he is off from his principles, I am off from him." And since the president
is now against internal improvements, Crockett declares he will still support
those appropriations, and "would rather be politically buried than hypocritically
immortalized."[43] He also rails in print at the party system: "'I, for one, would
not wear a collar round my neck, with "*my dog*" on it, and the name of ANDREW
JACKSON ON THE COLLAR—THEREFORE THEY WILL NOT HAVE ME FOR THEIR
PARTISAN.'"[44]

That Crockett's notoriety builds on fact only accentuates further fictional
enhancements. In James Kirke Paulding's play, *The Lion of the West*, which opens
on April 25, 1831, the main character, a backwoods roarer named Col. Nimrod
Wildfire, is purposefully based upon Crockett's personae and quickly identified
in the press.[45] Wildfire is one direct progenitor of the outlandish Crockett of
the Almanacs, a synthesis of newspaper accounts and of Paulding's experience
and imagination concerning the West. One of the character's earliest speeches
builds upon the comic brag, an integral part of the tall tale: "of all the fell-
ers on this side of the Alleghany mountains, I can jump higher, squat lower,
dive deeper, stay longer under and come out drier! There's no back out in my
breed[.] I go the whole hog. I've got the prettiest sister, fastest horse, and ugliest

dog in the deestrict. . . ."[46] Paulding presents Wildfire as the defining spirit of the American national character, a positive development distinct from any hero derived from an English heritage, one who grows sui generis out of the frontier. But the same humor is used against the historical Crockett. A local newspaper advertised a reward for him after his break from Jackson and the rest of the Tennessee delegation:

> Strayed or stolen from the Jackson ranks, a certain Member of Congress, from the Western District, named *David Crockett*. Davy is upwards of six feet high, erect in posture, and has a nose extremely red, after taking some spirits. He possesses vast bodily powers, great activity, and can lead [*sic.* leap] the Ohio, wade the Mississippi, and carry one steam and two flat boats upon his back. He can vault across a streak of lightning, ride it down a honey locust; grease his heels, skate down a rainbow and whip his weight in wild cats and panthers.[47]

Likewise, the *Memphis Advertiser* satirizes his switch to supporting Henry Clay by playing upon the dog collar statement.[48] The local abuse is noted, and Crockett, the "plain spoken, unsophisticated individual, of whom every body has heard, and whose peculiarities have been the subject of much exaggeration," is defended in other papers. He is, for example, as a congressman, "so far from having been negligent in his duty, that, we venture to say, few Members of Congress have done their duty more faithfully to their constituents, or more conscientiously. . . . The Colonel conquered the prejudices which attended his first appearance in Congress, and has been a valuable Member, whom his associates generally would be sorry to miss, when they again come together."[49]

Loss of his seat in Congress did not deter the growth and gravitational draw of his legend. It increases both in terms of true events and statements and those that are fictional. He begins to attract stories about other people simply because they are more interesting and comic if Crockett is the protagonist rather than someone less well-known. A prime example is an 1831 newspaper story with the title "David Crockett Out-Done," which is, in fact, a false tale about Governor James B. Ray of Indiana. In it, Ray is quoted as saying that:

> I have been informed that it has been asserted, that at the time I visited Jeffersonville for the purpose of receiving Gen. Lafayette, on being invited into the house of a respectable citizen, and seeing a carpet spread on the floor, I insisted on walking around it, and when the owner of the house pressed me to walk over it, I declared I would not for the world injure his quilt by treading on it—that I spit my tobacco juice on the floor outside of the carpet, and when a negro servant stared at me, and kept fixing his gaze on the spit box—that I sung out, you black rascal, take that box away, or, by the powers that be, I'll spit in it![50]

Since Lafayette's visit is on May 11, 1825, this tale has been making the rounds for six years. However, with this reprinting under the title noted above, the association links the story with Crockett. It is then woven retrospectively into and remains part of the story of his 1823 Tennessee congressional campaign against Dr. William Butler by deleting the mention of Lafayette and with Crockett simply substituting for Ray.[51] The tale likewise highlights the divisions of class in Jacksonian America.

Expectedly the publication of *Sketches* in 1833 did nothing to tamp down the enthusiasm for Crockett and the growth of his legend. When a one-hundred-foot-long sea serpent is sighted off Cape Cod, the natural response in the newspapers is "Why not send for Col. David Crocket[t] to come and catch the rascal."[52] Whether or not the publication of *Sketches* plays a significant role in Crockett's reelection to the US House of Representatives in 1833 is hard to determine, but it certainly did keep him a subject of conversation in the newspapers. In a review, the book "is said to abound in anecdotes and stories in Davy's *own* peculiar style." And it "is a rigmarole of more than 200 pages . . . made up principally of the anecdotes and tales of the redoubtable *Colonel Crockett*, that have been going the rounds of newspapers for several years past."[53] Another review, printed on both sides of the Atlantic, best catches the ring-tailed roarer caricature that soon undergirded the Almanacs, whose tales, often accompanied by woodcut illustrations, are arguably the first superhero comic books. Here is the legend unleashed:

He is a *lettle* the *savagist critter* you ever *did see*! . . . He *liquors* on a glass of "thunder and lightning" that's hotter than Tophet [hell], and bites like a rattlesnake; or for *bitters*, sucks away at a noggin of aquafortis, sweetened with brimstone, stirred with a lightning rod, and skimmed by a hurricane! He walks like an ox, runs like a horse, swims like an eel, yells like an Indian, fights like a devil, spouts like an earthquake, makes love like a mad bull, and can whip his weight in wild cats, or swallow a *nigger* without choking, if you butter his head and pin his ears back![54]

While the word "nigger" does not appear in *Sketches*, it and similar derogatory terms are a regular part of the Humor of the Old Southwest and the Crockett Almanacs, which are marked by statements that today are considered racist, sexist, imperialistic, overtly violent, promiscuous, etc. They do, however, reveal part of the culture of the time and what some people then regarded as humorous. Crockett himself had no association with, nor did he profit from, the Almanacs.

The first illustrated comic tale about Crockett before the Almanacs appears on January 25, 1834, in the *Galaxy of Comicalities*, a weekly publication in Philadelphia, and is entitled "Crockett teaching a landlord how to Grin!" The crude woodcut illustration bears no visual likeness to the actual Crockett, and the landlord's large, exaggerated, completely round head is a grotesque that harkens back to those of British comic periodicals. Here is the violent Crockett who swaps teaching the man his famous grin for a week of the best board, food, and drink that he can provide. Davy stands behind him "and placing one of his iron shod fingers in each side of the host's mouth, he soon had it stretched from ear to ear. The poor tavernkeeper bellowed at first with pain, but his voice soon failed him, for the orifice of his mouth was opened to such an extent that his tongue no longer served as a valve, and to this day, whenever he attempts to speak, a hissing sound like the noise from the spout of a boiling tea kettle is all that comes forth from his once powerful lungs."[55] Humor that exaggerates cruelty is another staple of those times.

Crockett, the man, is still applauded and lampooned. He is "'just such a one as you would desire to meet with, if any accident or misfortune had happened to you on the high way'" and "It is surely some 'error of the Moon,' when public honors are lavished upon Buffoons. . . . 'There was nothing to make amends for the coarse vulgarity of his manners. In the main, he appeared to be quite stupid, letting off occasionally, a cant phrase, which had the effect to produce something like the amusement which is created by the antic tricks of a monkey, and nothing more.'"[56] This description demonstrates that the derogatory portrayal of the frontiersman is linked inherently to the ridiculing of other minorities. The fact and the fiction of his life are frequently joined. In noting his arrival in Washington after his reelection, it is reported that Crockett "has bespoke a double-bedded room at his boarding-house, for the accommodation of himself and Major Jack Downing, with whom the Colonel has already formed a close intimacy, and whom he is desirous to keep out of bad company."[57] (Jack Downing was a creation of Seba Smith and one of the first major successes in presenting the regional "Down East" Humor of New England in stories published first in his newspaper, the *Portland* (ME) *Courier*, starting in 1830, and then collectively as a popular book, in 1833). That Crockett stories fill the newspapers of his day is a crucial ingredient to his fame. As Thomas Hamilton, an Englishman traveling in the United States during this time, says, only through "oral eloquence, and the newspaper press" can an individual have:

> any possibility of attaining political distinction. The influence and circulation of newspapers is great beyond any thing ever known in Europe. . . . Books circulate with difficulty in a thinly-peopled country. . . . But newspapers penetrate to every crevice of the Union. There is no settlement so remote as to be cut off from this channel of intercourse with their fellow men. It is thus that the clamour of the busy world is heard even in the wilderness, and the most remote invader of distant wilds is kept alive in his solitude to the common ties of brotherhood and country.[58]

Crockett is thus significantly bandied about in the public eye, and *Sketches*, in many ways, provides a summary of his sundry portrayals. The "strictly true" (4) version of Crockett's life asserted in the introduction is again emphasized later in the work, even after the reader has been introduced to the comedy and exaggeration of his political, hunting, and Dutchman tales. Why? Because the stories are about to expand further and will become "novel in the extreme." Nonetheless, the author states again that, "My narrative has, before this, placed Colonel Crockett in situations, the truth of which, perhaps, you have doubted; but nevertheless, it is all true; and the work as far as it goes, has been, and will continue to be, an unvarnished picture of his life" (52).

Likewise affirmed are the author's use of irony, of a quirky structure governed only by whim, and of his reliance upon stories and anecdotes. The ironic nature of the volume is made quite clear in both its preface and introduction, but a moment of unintended irony occurs when the author notes that his hero Crockett has had "to withstand the fury of all the presses in his district,—which sent forth sheet after sheet of violent abuse, of ludicrous caricatures, and of biting satire" (62), but uses those self same materials throughout his book (63–66; 67; 73–74; 79–80; 80–84; 84–86; 87–88). Even more noteworthy is the claim that a speech of Paulding's Nimrod Wildfire in *The Lion of the West* is stolen from Crockett (69–70). Similar capricious reinforcement of the book's original intent of having no overt plan or guiding principle continues to occur: the author harkens back to his "right to select my topics" (4) and to create humor by adding that "My object has been, merely, to amuse myself" (66). Further awareness of *Sketches* as a collection of odd bits and pieces is given added weight when he remarks, "Indeed, I should believe any man a queer fellow, who cannot in this hotchpotch, find some page to his taste" (67). This "hotchpotch," or hodgepodge, even includes non-Crockett stories designed to amuse, such as two peddler (74–78; 101–2) and four hunting tales (92–93; 93–94; 94–95; 103–6). The last of these is the "Billy Buck" story, which has nothing at all to do with Crockett and was deleted when the *Life* was reprinted and *Sketches and Eccentricities*. Other stories, including those already noted above that the popular press repurposes, fall into four categories, all of which utilize dialect for humor: black caricatures and songs (18–20; 71–72); politics (27–29; 29; 35–36; 36–37; 37; 38–39; 63–66; 79–80; 80–81; 81–84; 84–86; 87–88); hunting (26; 33; 33–35; 39–42; 44–46; 47–50; 52–55; 61; 67–68; 95–98); and Dutchman jokes (37–38; 42–44; 52). All these tales give *Sketches* a prominent place in the early Humor of the Old Southwest.

Romance also plays a significant part in the portrayals of Crockett and expectedly serves as a countervailing force to those that emphasize humor. These depictions include his youthful adventures that characterize him as an inveterate wanderer (5–10), his experiences with love (17; 17–18; 20; 24; 25–26), and—perhaps most importantly to establishing his ties with the wilderness—his delineations as a natural man from boyhood through manhood. That he is fated to become a hero is clear when chance prevents him from going to sea early in his adolescence: "Thus did fortune force David Crockett to figure in other places than the crowded streets of Liverpool. But for this slight mishap the Western District could now have boasted of no hero" (14). And his inability to explain love's effect on him also portrays him early on as a backwoods original and natural man: "I wish I may be damned if I know how I felt; but I tell you what, it made me feel quite all-overish" (26). His relationship with nature is reflected in his lack of formal education (17), his "goodness of heart," "personal popularity," generosity, lack of "vanity or refinement," all traits that mark his early life. He is also uncorrupted and unique: "his mind, untaught by rigid rules, roved free as the wild beasts he hunted, and sometimes gave vent to expressions, and to ideas, which could never have been conceived by any other individual" (27). The lack of rules and his unbridled originality feed the extreme eastern view of the West as a place of absolute freedom or chaos, depending upon the observer, and Crockett as its clear spokesman. While the author presents the romance of the "far off West" before the start of Crockett's life in the introduction (4), and sees it as ambiguous in his dialog between past and present (6), the argument over nature versus civilization continues, sometimes validating Crevecoeur's middle landscape pastoral as best and sometimes the wilderness, both through Crockett. The scene of a harvest and its festivities, for example, are such that "his heart bounded with joy" (22); the author also comments that there is "something refreshing in turning from the dissipation of a city, to look upon a rural fete" (23). Yet, like his heroic predecessor Boone, Crockett is also a lover of isolation: "although at home above all others in a crowd, he seemed equally pleased with the deepest solitude. Here he became wedded to hunting, and the great quantity of game was well calculated to have fascinated any one. Being cut off from all society, his rifle and dogs were ever his companions. Even the face of the country he had chosen to dwell in, seemed, in some measure, the counterpart of his mind. It was wild and irregular, and, like himself subject to no restraint" (31). These effects of the frontier are feared and the cause of failure for many (30–31); but Crockett, poor and uneducated (again like Boone), is "one rising superior to fortune, and possessing at the same time the ennobling virtues of our race," (80) and disrupting the barriers of class. Frontiersmen are truly remarkable for their courage; the author notes that they "have been so long companions with danger, that they become strangers to fear. They have nothing to conceal, and are consequently frank in their manners" (87). Above all, it is the sheer volume of hunting stories in *Sketches* that most associates

Crockett with the wilderness; more than other contemporary frontier icons such as Boone and Black Hawk in 1833, perhaps by design or by default through the humor residing in his narrative alone, Crockett traverses civilization and the wilderness without falling victim to either.

IV

The subversive nature of many frontier life narratives again takes a different turn with Crockett. Still the hunter, he is linked to Indian-like pursuits, but *Sketches* provides little space for the mention of native culture or its possible appreciation after the book's front matter is concluded. The preface's promise to alter the stereotypical depiction of the savage Indian is never fulfilled. The author says that "At this time, when, in every ephemeral tale, a red hunter must be treacherous, brutal, savage, and accompanied with the tomahawk and scalping knife, I should perhaps offer some apology for speaking of them in a different light, in my introduction; but my apology is—it was my pleasure to do so" (4). But this "different light" appears only in the introduction in the discussion of the native burial mounds, never in the book proper. Readers may rightly wonder why Crockett has no interactions with Native Americans in *Sketches*, when historically, as reported in the newspapers that are one main source for this volume, they and their unjust treatment by the government are of particular concern to him.[59]

It seems clear that the destabilizing lens of Crockett's *Sketches* in 1833 complicates the American frontier for readers throughout the United States and Europe. The book is in very close contact with the expanding characterization of an American hero, to the extent of blending fact, fiction, and humor into a new reality in Crockett's case, but it is also removed from certain major problems and debates of the day, especially states' rights and nullification, women's rights, and slavery. It likewise ignores Jackson's Nullification Proclamation, John C. Calhoun's opposition to Jackson's tariff acts of 1828 and 1832 protecting northern industries at the expense of the economy of the South, and Calhoun's stepping down as Jackson's vice-president in the election of 1832, as well as the growth of married women's rights, especially in newly enacted state property laws.[60] No mention likewise is made of the Nat Turner rebellion of 1831, the formation of the American Colonization Society in 1816 (a "back to Africa" movement that foreshadows Indian Removal and results in the founding of Liberia), and attacks upon that movement by William Lloyd Garrison and the New England Anti-Slavery Society (1832), the forerunner of the American Anti-Slavery Society and its segregated companion, the Female Anti-Slavery Society (1833).[61] The only marginal group in American society to receive treatment in *Sketches* is frontiersmen.

Rather than supporting foundational views of national identity in terms solely of masculinity, race, and class, Crockett's *Sketches* presents readers with a cultural outsider who, because of his link to the frontier, gains cultural capital through the power of his stories that in turn reinforce each other and seem continually to fascinate their audiences. On August 1, 1834, the *Daily Evening Transcript* (Boston), quoting the *New York Transcript*, publishes a brief article on the "Immortality of Col. Crocket [*sic.*]." It states that:

> When the name of any person is accounted of sufficient importance to be conferred on negroes, dogs, horses, steamboats, omnibuses, and locomotive engines, he may be considered as pretty certainly on the road to immortality. This is now the case with Col[.] David Crockett, whose go-a-head name, with great propriety, has been or is about to be, conferred on one of the locomotive engines on the Boston and Lowell Railroad. This will doubtless be imitated by other locomotives, by steamboats, and by race-horses, as indicative of their go-a-head qualities; and will do more to secure the immortality of the redoubtable Colonel, than forty Lives, written by himself or by any of his friends and admirers.

The naming of the locomotive is verified the next day in the *Essex Gazette* (Haverhill, MA), and on November 12, 1834, the *Southern Patriot* (Charleston, SC) notes the building of a new steamboat, the *David Crockett*. And in 1860, the clipper ship *David Crockett* (built in 1853) establishes a speed record with its ninety-three-day voyage from San Francisco to New York around Cape Horn.

The tradition continues, with readers, in addition to the 1834 *Narrative*, soon having in hand *An Account of Colonel Crockett's Tour to the North and Down East* (Philadelphia: Carey & Hart, 1835), likely written at least in part by William Clark, and the posthumously published *Col. Crockett's Exploits and Adventures in Texas . . . Written by Himself* (Philadelphia: T. K. & P. G. Collins [Carey & Hart], 1836), written by Richard Penn Smith.[62] The *Narrative, Tour*, and *Texas* are subsequently often excerpted/combined as Crockett's life story, appearing both as a stand-alone work and also in many anthologies of the lives of great frontiersmen/pioneers/heroes of America. All these works gradually decrease the popularity of *Sketches* and eventually eclipse it before the first shot of the Civil War. The next work to revive the heights of the legendary life of Crockett by incorporating his stories, as well as many of the Almanac tales, is by Constance Rourke, whose *Davy Crockett*[63] is a best seller in 1934. And there is no discounting the impact of Walt Disney's recreation of the hero both in the 1950s and to the present day through reruns on the Disney Channel, in asserting Crockett's fame. Even the military concurs in the late 1950s by naming their M-28 or M-29 tactical nuclear recoilless gun (smoothbore), that fires the M-388 nuclear projectile during the Cold War, the "Davy Crockett Nuclear Weapon System."[64] The legendary Crockett might not be pleased that it was one of the smallest, instead of the largest, nuclear weapon systems ever built. Or perhaps he might chuckle.

The lens of humor allows *Sketches* to break new ground; it presents a hero who speaks to enduring questions concerning the relationship between the wilderness/nature and civilization, and gives the reader of 1833 an updated and revised conception of Crevecoeur's "new race of men." In the volume, Crockett is public, personal, and political in his relationships; questions culture and race, standards, values, and mores; and encourages Americans who wish to, for a considerable while, to construct their personal and national identities in light of this new, more complex range of frontier heroism. However we parse the influence of Crockett on life in the United States, *Sketches* gives us perhaps the best and most intriguing funhouse mirror of American culture, thought, and nationalism during the Age of Jackson, one that helps to shift attention from the Trans-Appalachian toward the Trans-Mississippian West and that presents the nation with a frontier hero who endures to the present day.

NOTES

1. David Crockett, *A Narrative of the Life of David Crockett, of the State of Tennessee* (Philadelphia: E. L. Carey and A. Hart, 1834), reprinted in facsimile, James A. Shackford and Stanley J. Folmsbee, eds. (Knoxville: Univ. of Tennessee Press, 1973), 138n2. Hereafter cited as *Narrative*.

2. *Narrative*, 132.

3. This quotation and many variations of it are expanded and ornamented versions of what Samuel Clemens actually wrote to Frank Marshall White on May 31, 1897. His actual comment was "The report of my death was an exaggeration." See "Reports of Mark Twain's Quip about His Death Are Greatly Misquoted," This Day in Quotes website, [2019, http://www.thisdayinquotes.com/2010/06/reports-of-my-death-are-greatly.html. Albert Bigelow Paine, Twain's 1912 biographer, likely started the process by quoting the statement as "the report of my death has been grossly exaggerated." See Albert Bigelow Paine, comp., "Mark Twain. A Biography," Gutenberg Project website, [2019], http://www.gutenberg.org/files/2988/2988-h/2988-h.htm#link2H_4_0205.

4. *The Life and Adventures of Colonel David Crockett, of West Tennessee* (Cincinnati: Published for the Proprietor, 1833); *Sketches and Eccentricities of Col. David Crockett of West Tennessee* (New York: J. & J. Harper, 1833). All subsequent page references to the present edition of the *Life* (cited often as *Sketches*) will be noted parenthetically in the body of the text.

5. See also James A. Shackford, *David Crockett: The Man and the Legend*, ed. John B. Shackford (1956; repr., Chapel Hill: Univ. of North Carolina Press, 1986), 64; and *Narrative*, 166n2.

6. *Narrative*, 169.

7. Shackford, 64.

8. *Narrative*, 203.

9. *Narrative*, 204–5.

10. While historically Crockett often draws attention to his break with Jackson, the split initially began over squatters' rights in 1829 and the Indian Removal Act of 1830. The frontiersman forcefully stated his views by saying "Look at my neck, you will not find there any collar, with the engraving 'MY DOG—Andrew Jackson.'" See *Narrative*, 205; 172; 172n17. For Crockett's sentiments before his split with the president, see this volume, 116, 118. A defense of Crockett's stand on squatters' rights and of Crockett himself appears in the *National Intelligencer* (Washington, DC) on June 23, 1831.

11. *Crockett Almanacs* were published from 1835 to 1856 by different firms, and sometimes multiple different issues appear for the same year. Those published in 1834 and 1835, for 1835 and 1836 respectively, had fewer and "less tall" tall tales.

12. The abbreviated form, an announcement, is: *"Appointment by the President*—David Crockett, to stand on the Alleghany Mountain and catch the Comet, on its approach to the earth, and [w]ring off its tail, to keep it from burning up the world.—*Impartial Recorder, printed in Tennessee."* Taken from the *Vermont Gazette* (Bennington), July 24, 1832. Crockett's mighty deed also is noted in the *Independence* (Poughkeepsie, NY), September 12, 1832; the *Eastern Argus* (Portland, ME), October 22, 1832; the *Rhode Island American and Gazette*, November 20, 1832; twice in *The Pittsfield* (MA) *Sun*, March 21, 1833, and April 4, 1833; and once in the *Rhode-Island Republican* (Newport), April 24, 1833.

13. *Davy Crockett's 1837 Almanack of Wild Sports in the West, Life in the Backwoods, & Sketches of Texas* (Nashville, TN: Published by the Heirs of Col. Crockett, 1837 [*sic.* 1836]), 2. The Nashville Almanacs were actually published in Boston, and neither Crockett nor Crockett's family had any involvement in the venture. See also Michael A. Lofaro, "The Hidden 'Hero' of the Nashville Crockett Almanacs," in *Davy Crockett: The Man, The Legend, The Legacy* (Knoxville: Univ. of Tennessee Press, 1985), 51–57.

14. Richard M. Dorson, *Davy Crockett: American Comic Legend* (New York: Spiral Press for Rockland Editions, 1939), 10–12, 16–17. There is no complete edition of the Almanac stories available in print. The largest single collection of the Almanacs resides in the American Antiquarian Society. In addition to Dorson's selection, however, all seven of the "Nashville" Crockett almanacs can be found in *The Crockett Almanacs: Nashville Series, 1835–1838*, ed. Franklin J. Meine (Chicago: The Caxton Club, 1955); and in *The Tall Tales of Davy Crockett: The Second Nashville Series of Crockett Almanacs, 1839–1841, an Enlarged Facsimile Edition*, ed. Michael A. Lofaro (Knoxville: Univ. of Tennessee Press, 1987). The latter gives the best sense of how the almanacs originally appeared with normal almanac data, as well as stories, tall tales, and their accompanying woodcut illustrations. For another edition of tales and illustrations extracted from their original format that focus upon women, see Michael A. Lofaro, ed., *Davy Crockett's Riproarious Shemales and Sentimental Sisters: Women's Tall Tales from the Crockett Almanacs, 1835–1856* (Mechanicsburg, PA: Stackpole Books, 2001).

15. The Almanac tall tale is taken from *Davy Crockett's Almanack of Wild Sports in the West, Life in the Backwoods, Sketches of Texas, and Rows on the* Mississippi (Nashville, TN [*sic* Boston]: Published by the Heirs of Col. Crockett, 1838 [*sic.* 1837]), 2.

16. John Filson, *The Discovery, Settlement, And present State of Kentucke: And An Essay towards the Topography, and natural History of that important Country: To which is added, An Appendix, Containing, I. The Adventures of Col. Daniel Boon, One of the First Settlers, Comprehending every Important Occurrence in the Political History of that Province . . .* (Wilmington: James Adams, 1784). For a chronological commentary on the changes in the conception of the American frontiersman, see Michael A. Lofaro, "Stereotype and Synthesis as National Compromise: The Evolution of the Early Frontier Hero" in Lofaro, ed., *Boone, Black Hawk, and Crockett in 1833: Unsettling the Mythic West* (Knoxville: Univ. of Tennessee Press, 2019).

17. See Carroll Smith-Rosenberg, *Disorderly Conduct: Visions of Gender in Victorian America* (New York: Alfred A. Knopf, 1985), 90–108 for another view of the breakdown of class using the Crockett of the almanacs as an example. As previous noted, there was a brief newspaper version of Crockett's life of approximately five hundred words that appeared before *Sketches*. It is stated as being copied from the *Winchester* (VA) *Republican* and appears in *The Constellation* (New York), December 18, 1830; in the *Daily National Journal*, April 28, 1831; and under the heading of "Biographical Sketches" in the *Lowell* (MA) *Mercury* on May 21, 1831. It was essentially a quick overview and summary.

18. Timothy Flint, *Biographical Memoir of Daniel Boone* (Cincinnati: N. and G. Guilford, 1833); *Life of Mà-ka-tai-me-she-kià-kiàk, or Black Hawk . . .* (Cincinnati: J. B. Patterson, 1833).

19. *Narrative*, 3–5, 7. For a letter of Crockett's discussing his being asked to run for the presidency, see the *Daily Evening Transcript* (Boston), March 7, 1834. Crockett's letter is dated February 22, 1834.

20. See, for example, Carroll Smith-Rosenberg's *This Violent Empire: The Birth of an American National Identity* (Chapel Hill: Univ. of North Carolina Press, 2012), esp. "Section Two: Dangerous Doubles"; and the first three chapters of Philip J. Deloria, *Playing Indian* (New Haven, CT: Yale Univ. Press, 1998). See also chapter 2 of Lara Cohen, *The Fabrication of American Literature* (Philadelphia: Univ. of Pennsylvania Press, 2012).

21. For a broad view of epic in early America, see Christopher N. Phillips, *Epic in American Culture: Settlement to Reconstruction* (Baltimore: John Hopkins Univ. Press, 2011). For examples of specific poems, see the works of Joel Barlow, Timothy Dwight, and John Trumbull.

22. Daniel Bryan, *The Mountain Muse: Comprising the Adventures of Daniel Boone and the Powers of Virtuous and Refined Beauty* (Harrisonburg, VA: n.p., 1813).

23. Michael A. Lofaro, *Daniel Boone: An American Life* (Lexington: Univ. Press of Kentucky, 2012), 167–68.

24. James Strange French (1807–1886) is today best known for his legal defense of Nat Turner and other slaves accused of rebellion in 1831. Five years later, he published a novel, *Elkswatawa; or, The Prophet of the West. A Tale of the Frontier* (New York: Harper & Brothers, 1836), that contained a sympathetic portrayal of Native Americans and a Crockettesque character named "Earthquake." The other possibility advanced for authorship is Matthew St. Clair Clarke (1790–1852), who served seven terms as the clerk of the US House of Representatives, including times which overlapped the service of Congressman Crockett. The strongest evidence for French's authorship is the copyright data for the *Life and Adventures*, which notes that the volume is "Entered according to act of Congress, in the year 1833, by J. S. French, in the Clerk's Office of the District Court of the district of Ohio." Edgar Allen Poe names French as the author, but gives no evidence (see his "Eureka. Marginalia. A Chapter on Autography. The Literati," Hathi Trust Digital Library, [2019], https://babel.hathitrust.org/cgi/pt?id=njp.32101068601507;view=2up;seq=408). The main case for Clarke's authorship comes from Shackford, 120, 258–64.

25. The generally stipulated beginning of regional humor as a category, although much existed previously, is about 1830, and one of the more popular forms was the Humor of the Old Southwest, with the Old Southwest essentially being the South, since, except for Missouri, no states yet existed west of the Mississippi. Significantly, much of the humor is first published in newspapers and magazines (as were the early stories about Crockett) before their collection in book form. The main characteristics of this humor were incongruity, exaggeration, violence, realism, the grotesque, outlandish language (both manufactured words and use of dialect), the use of an "outside" narrator and his framing narrative to present tales within the overall story, and the use of oral tales and storytelling. For an overview and sample, see the introduction and appropriate section of Walter Blair,

Native American Humor (1937; repr., Scranton, PA: Chandler Publishing Co., 1960); and Hennig
Cohen and William B. Dillingham, eds., *Humor of the Old Southwest* (Athens: Univ. of Georgia
Press, 1994). For the continuation of violence as a theme and its ties to Crockett, see Joseph J.
Arpad, "The Fight Story: Quotation and Originality in Native American Humor," *Journal of the
Folklore Institute* 10 (1973): 141–72. Such Old Southwest combinations of the grotesque and violence
continue in southern fiction in the work of William Faulkner, Flannery O'Connor, and Cormac
McCarthy and generate some of the same sense of black/dark/bleak humor.

26. On the Humor of the Old Southwest, see the works by Blair and by Cohen and Dillingham
cited in note 25.

27. J. Hector St. John de Crevecoeur, *Letters from an American Farmer* (1782; repr., NY: Fox,
Duffield & Co., 1904). See especially Letters III and XII. See also the analysis of the introduction
and conclusion in John Filson's "autobiography" of Daniel Boone in Lofaro, ed., *Boone, Black Hawk,
and Crockett*, xxvi-xxviii.

28. Georges-Louis Leclerc, Comte de Buffon (1707–1788) is the author of *Histoire Naturelle,
Générale et Particulière*, 36 vols. (Paris: Imprimere nationale, 1749–1788), which originally stated that
nature in the New World was inferior to that in Europe and Asia, that large game was absent, and
that Native Americans were less able to procreate. He later admitted his mistake.

29. The author next mentions that "Thousands of them are at this time marching far 'over the
border,'" (8) a reference to the early effect of the 1830 Indian Removal Act. For an informative
discussion of racial theory that informed eighteenth- and nineteenth-century views, see Joyce E.
Chaplin, "Natural Philosophy and Early Racial Idiom in North America: Comparing English and
Indian Bodies," *William and Mary Quarterly* 54 (January 1997): 229–52.

30. Crockett was "at home" as *Sketches* was written, having lost his bid for reelection in 1831 after
two consecutive terms in the House. He was, however, reelected in 1833.

31. President Jackson was the obvious standard for the heroic comparison of frontier figures
in 1833 as Crockett came to prominence. Although it does not treat *Sketches*, the performativity of
Crockett's stories and their relationship to class is noted in Teresa Coronado, "The Performance
of Class in *A Narrative of the Life of David Crockett of the State of Tennessee*," *Literature in the Early
American Republic: Annual Studies on Cooper and His Contemporaries* 4 (2012): 89–111.

32. *The Ariel* (Philadelphia), January 24, 1828, 160, and February 7, 1828, 167, noting the support
and not reprinting the story; the *National Gazette and Literary Register* (Philadelphia), January 5,
1829; a mention, not an entire reprinting, in the *Baltimore Patriot and Mercantile Advertiser*, January
7, 1829; and in the *New-Bedford* (MA) *Mercury*, January 9, 1829, not including the letters of support. On January 16, the *New-Bedford* (MA) *Mercury* notes the letters of support. On January 22,
1829, *The Star* (Raleigh, NC) reprints Crockett's letter disputing his supposedly egregious behavior
and notes the letters of support. While it may not be the same "facetious narrative," Crockett is
vehement in his denunciation of the author of a letter, calling him "so *base a scoundrel*," "a *poor con-
temptible sneak*," "a *poltroon, a scoundrel, and a puppy*," and his letter "*vile calumny*" and a "WICKED
LIE." Internal evidence suggests a different story, one in which Crockett's vote is for sale (i.e., "*in
market*"). Published in the *National Gazette and Literary Register*, February 19, 1829.

33. *The Ariel*, February 7, 1828, 167. See a version of the tale on page 87.

34. *New-Bedford* (MA) *Mercury*, January 9, 1829. See also page 81.

35. *Gales & Seaton's Register of Debates in Congress* (Washington: Gales and Seaton, 1830), March
30, 1830, 6:716–17. The joke about the bite was extracted and printed in the *Alabama State Intelligencer* (Tuscaloosa), April 30, 1830. The entirety of Crockett's speech was published as a pamphlet:
*Speech of Mr. Crockett, of Tennessee, on the Bill Proposing to Construct a National Road from Buffalo
to New Orleans* (Washington: Duff Green, 1830). The bill did not pass, but on its reconsideration

Crockett said that "He would vote to go through any gentleman's State with a road or canal, that was for the good of the Union. He did not believe he should ever give up that doctrine." Crockett's statement appeared in *Gales & Seaton's Register of Debates in Congress* (Washington: Gales and Seaton, 1830) April 15, 1830, 6:804. Reconsideration failed with Crockett as one of 88 in favor against 105 opposed (*Niles Weekly Register*, April 17, 1830, 152). For more information, see Pamela L. Baker, "The Washington National Road Bill and the Struggle to Adopt a Federal System of Internal Improvement," *Journal of the Early Republic* 22 (2002): 437–64.

36. May 5, 1830.

37. *Rhode-Island American*, April 30, 1830.

38. *Niles Weekly Register*, May 22, 1830, 244, and May 29, 1830, 267. The bill passed 102 to 97. The idea of Indian removal to the land west of the Mississippi River on a massive scale was earlier proposed by President James Monroe in his eighth annual message to Congress on December 7, 1824. See James D. Richardson, ed., *A Compilation of the Messages and Papers of the Presidents* (Washington, DC: Bureau of National Literature, 1912), 2:825–26, 830. See also Monroe's follow up message to Congress on January 27, 1825 (2:849–52).

39. *Niles Weekly Register*, February 5, 1831, 407, and February 19, 1831, 446.

40. Republished in the *Newburyport* (MA) *Herald*, January 18, 1831, the same paper that had earlier labeled Crockett as unfit for his duties.

41. The "Circular" is most easily available in James R. Boylston and Allen J. Wiener, eds., *David Crockett in Congress: The Rise and Fall of the Poor Man's Friend* (Houston, TX: Bright Sky Press, 2009), 298–99. The "Circular" is a restatement of Crockett's speech opposing the Indian Removal Bill on pages 316–19.

42. Boylston and Wiener, eds., *Crockett in Congress*, 307.

43. *Rhode Island American and Gazette* (Providence), March 11, 1831, citing the *Boston Courier* as its source for the story which, in turn, internally cites the *National Journal*. The last quotation appeared in the *National Gazette* (Philadelphia), March 7, 1831. Crockett's defection from Jackson proved a significant story.

44. *Daily National Intelligencer* (Washington, DC), March 31, 1831; *Baltimore Patriot and Mercantile Advertiser*, April 4, 1831, and referenced again on April 20, 1831. The "my dog" collar image is featured again in Crockett's *Narrative*, placed prominently at the end of the volume (211). Both the "my dog" and "politically buried" comments appear in the *Daily National Intelligencer*, February 4, 1833, and in the *Rhode Island American and Gazette*, February 14, 1832, which cites the *Boston Commercial Gazette* as its source for the story.

45. *The Constellation* (New York), May 14, 1831. For more information on the genesis and evolution of the play, see Richard Boyd Hauck, "Making It All Up: Davy Crockett in the Theater," in *Davy Crockett: The Man, The Legend, The Legacy, 1786–1986*, ed. Michael A. Lofaro (Knoxville: Univ. of Tennessee Press, 1985), 102–11.

46. James Kirke Paulding, *The Lion of the West and The Bucktails*, ed. Frank Gado (New York: Roman & Littlefield, 2003), 103–4. This idea of the comic braggart has a long history in literature. See Walter Blair and Hamlin Hill, *America's Humor, From Poor Richard to Doonesbury* (New York: Oxford Univ. Press, 1978), 133–42. Crockett's notoriety also appeared in song, as well as plays for the stage. See "A Selective Crockett Chronology" in this book for examples. After his defeat for reelection, Crockett and his stand against tariffs were the subject of a "National Song" noted in the *Boston Centinel* and reprinted in the *New-Hampshire Sentinel*, September 20, 1832. In it, Crockett vehemently opposes a tax on salt because he needs it for his "pork and greens." In an odd twist, Frances Trollope, who is roundly satirized in *The Lion of the West* as Mrs. Wollope for her attacks upon the lack of civility of Americans in her *Domestic Manners of the Americans* (1832), is a fan of

Timothy Flint, Boone's 1833 biographer. She calls Flint "The most agreeable acquaintance I made in Cincinnati, and indeed one of the most talented men I ever met." Cited in Richard W. Clement, *Books on the Frontier: Print Culture in the American West, 1763–1875* (Washington, DC: Library of Congress, 2003), 43. Her stay in Cincinnati lasted from 1828 to 1830.

47. *Essex Gazette* (Haverhill, MA), May 21, 1831, citing the *Jackson* (TN) *Statesman.*

48. Noted in *The* (Little Rock, AR) *Gazette*, August 10, 1831.

49. *Daily National Intelligencer*, June 22, 1831.

50. *The Pittsfield* (MA) *Sun*, September 15, 1831.

51. For perhaps the earliest printed mention of the story, see H. S. Turner, "Andrew Jackson and David Crockett: Reminiscences of Colonel Chester," *Magazine of American History with Notes and Queries* 27 (1892): 386–87. See also J. G. Cisco, "Madison County," *American Historical Magazine and Tennessee Historical Society Quarterly* 8 (January 1903): 29–30. The story's life continues, in works such as Buddy Levy, *American Legend: The Real-Life Adventures of David Crockett* (New York: G. P. Putnam's, 2005), 114; in Michael Wallace, *David Crockett: The Lion of the West* (New York: W. W. Norton, 2011), 184; and in recent children's books, such as Gail Herman, *Who Was Davy Crockett* (New York: Grosset & Dunlap, 2013).

52. *Newburyport* (MA) *Herald*, May 3, 1833, taken from the *Po[r]tland Courier.*

53. *New-Hampshire Patriot and State Gazette* (Concord), April 8, 1833, and *Newburyport Herald*, April 26, 1833, which mainly quotes the tale from the book of Crockett grinning the bark off a large knot of a tree because in the dark he thought it was a raccoon (61).

54. *The Derby Mercury* (England), December 18, 1833, citing an *"American Paper."* A shorter version, which does not include the statement before the ellipsis, is published in the *Independent Inquirer* (Brattleboro, VT), December 28, 1833, citing the *"N.Y. Atlas."* Not all the reviews were kind. While attacking the author more than his subject Crockett, a "Literary Notice" (reviewing an early reprinting of the *Sketches*) that appeared in *The New-England Magazine* 5 (December 1833), 514, stated: "The wit, if there were any originally in his [Crockett's] sayings, evaporates in their passage through the press, and leaves little or nothing for the reader, but what reminds him of the atmosphere of a bar-room, on the morning succeeding a feast of whisky and cigars." For a brief, illustrated treatment of monographs treating Crockett, see Clement, 113–19. The unstoppable legendary Crockett also continued the motto of his historical base—"Be Always Sure You're Right, Then Go Ahead!"—and served as an echo of the times in which a very popular slang saying was indeed "Go Ahead!" (Reynolds, 3). The motto takes hold in England as well. Quoting it, the August 27, 1834, edition of the *New York Transcript* runs an article entitled *"David Crockettism in England,"* in which a prize fighter (Tom Gaynor) begins the match by head-butting his opponent's stomach and winning the match essentially before it starts, demonstrating his "go-ahead" spirit. The buried pun is likely intentional.

55. *Galaxy of Comicalities*, January 25, 1834, 132.

56. The first positive statement is from *Niles' Weekly Register*, September 7, 1833, 20, and repeated in the *Daily National Intelligencer*, September 12, 1833. The negative response is first from the *Richmond Enquirer*, December 12, 1833, and the section after the ellipsis is from the same paper quoting the *Baltimore Republican.*

57. *Daily National Intelligencer*, November 27, 1833. Before this, on July 24, 1833, in the *Political Register*, Major Jack Downing is said to have been in the Black Hawk War. Also recorded is that the fictional major accompanied Black Hawk and Jackson on their tour, commenting that "I thought the folks looked at him [Black Hawk] and the prophet [Wabokieshiek, or White Cloud] about as much as they did at me and the President. I gave the President a wink that the Indian

fellow was taking the shine off of us a little, so we concluded we would'nt have him in our company any more and shall go on without him." See "Black Hawk," Wisconsin Local History and Biography Articles, Wisconsin Historical Society website, [2019], http://www.wisconsinhistory.org /Content.aspx?dsNav=N:4294963828-4294963788&dsRecordDetails=R:BA13613, p. 6.

58. [Thomas Hamilton], *Men and Manners in America* (Philadelphia: Carey, Lea and Blanchard, 1833), 1:245. The work is published earlier the same year in London. The Philadelphia printing is available online in Google's Digital Library, https://books.google.com/books?id=JkUTAAAAYAA J&pg=PA245&lpg=PA245&dq#v=onepage&q&f=false. For background on the newspapers of that era, see William Huntzicker, *The Popular Press, 1833–1865* (Westport, CT: Greenwood Press, 1999).

59. For Crockett's role in the Creek Indian War, see his *Narrative*, 71–124.

60. Calhoun stepped down to take the Senate seat of Robert W. Hayne, who had become governor of South Carolina. Married women's property acts are enacted in different years and differ in rights conferred. An early Connecticut law of 1809 allows women to write wills. See, for example, Richard H. Chused, "Married Women's Property Law: 1800–1850," *Georgetown Law Journal* 71 (1983): 1359–1425; and Norma Beach, "Equity vs. Equality: Emerging Concepts of Women's Political Status in the Age of Jackson," *Journal of the Early Republic* 3 (1983): 297–318.

61. Among the many books that treat these issues, see Louis P. Masur, *1831: Year of Eclipse* (New York: Hill and Wang, 2001). For nullification, states' rights, and Indian policy, see 115–68; slavery, 9–62ff. Often contemporary outside observers like Frances Trollope produce astute analyses alongside their polemics. She asks pointedly if women "were made for no other purpose than to fabricate sweetmeats and gingerbread, construct shirts, darn stockings, and become mothers of possible presidents? Should the women of America ever discover what their power might be, and compare it with what it is, much improvement might be hoped." She handily reduces racial conflict as well, while fulminating against the national character of the United States: "It is impossible for any mind of common honesty not to be revolted by the contradictions in their principles and practice.... You will see them with one hand hoisting the cap of liberty, and with the other flogging their slaves. You will see them one hour lecturing their mob on the indefeasible rights of man, and the next driving from their homes the children of the soil, whom they have bound themselves to protect by the most solemn treaties." From *Domestic Manners of the Americans* (London: Whittaker, Treacher, & Co., 1832), 225, 180, available online at the Internet Archive website, [2019], https://archive.org/details /domesticmannersooootroliala (this is the fourth edition of 1832 in one volume). The quotations can also be found on pages 217 and 168 of the Penguin paperback edition (New York, 1997).

62. See the Beinecke Digital Collections record, Beinecke Rare Book and Manuscript Library website, [2019], http://brbl-dl.library.yale.edu/vufind/Record/3518932, for the lengthy full title. Excluded from these works is "Crockett's" [Augustin Smith Clayton], *The Life of Martin Van Buren, Heir-Apparent to the "Government," and Appointed Successor of General Andrew Jackson* (Philadelphia: R. Wright [Carey & Hart], 1835), since it is an anti-campaign biography and contains mainly political invective rather than tales about or biography of Crockett.

63. Constance Rourke, *Davy Crockett* (New York: Harcourt Brace and Company, 1934).

64. For more information, see Matthew Seelinger, "The M28/M29 Davy Crockett Nuclear Weapon System," Army Historical Foundation website, [2019], https://armyhistory.org/the-m28m29 -davy-crockett-nuclear-weapon-system/.

John Gadsby Chapman's portrait of David Crockett, 1834. This painting is a copy of Chapman's life-sized portrait since lost in a fire at the Texas Capitol. Courtesy Harry Ransom Humanities Research Center, The University of Texas at Austin.

BORN TO COMMAND.

OF VETO MEMORY.

HAD I BEEN CONSULTED.

KING ANDREW THE FIRST.

"King Andrew the First." Andrew Jackson is caricatured as a despotic monarch in this 1833 cartoon likely because of his order to remove federal deposits from Nicholas Biddle's Second Bank of the United States without congressional approval. The victims of his overreach of executive power lie under and at his feet: The Federal Constitution, Pennsylvania's coat of arms (the United States Bank was located in Philadelphia), a book "Judiciary of the U[nited] States," and "Internal Improvement/U. S. Bank." Around the border of the print are the words "Of Veto Memory," "Born to Command" and "Had I Been Consulted." Crockett comes to hold a negative opinion of Jackson in the present volume and more so in his 1834 autobiography. Library of Congress.

"Set To Between Old Hickory and Bully Nick." This 1834 pro-Jackson cartoon summarily satirizes his battle against Nicholas Biddle and his Second Bank of the United States. Although
the frontiersman is identified as "Joe Tammany" and supports Jackson in the fight, the language
and demeanor of the figure may be a satire of Crockett, giving him a live house cat atop his hat
instead of the stereotypical coonskin cap so often, but mistakenly, a part of his depictions. Crockett
opposed Jackson while Tammany Hall and the state of New York did side with the president in
the conflict. An obese woman, Mother Bank, holding a bottle of port stands beside Biddle (arms
raised, at left). Behind her are Biddle supporters Daniel Webster and Henry Clay. Mother Bank
says: "Darken his day lights Nick[.] Put the Screws to him my tulip!" Webster: "Blow me tight if
Nick ain't been crammed too much. You see as how he's losing his wind!" And Henry Clay says:
"Hurrah Nick my Kiddy! Hit him a pelt in the Smellers!" On the right are Jackson's supporters
Martin Van Buren, Major Jack Downing, and Joe Tammany, in buckskins. On the ground next
to Tammany is a bottle of "Old Monongohala Whiskey." Van Buren says: "Go it Hickory, my old
buffer! give it to him in the bread basket, it will make him throw up his deposits!" Downing: "I
swan if the Ginral hain't been taken lessons from Fuller! [perhaps William Fuller, a bare-knuckle
'scientific' boxer who came to the U. S. in 1824]" Tammany: "Hurrah my old yellow flower of the
forrest, walk into him like a streak of Greased lightning through a gooseberry bush!" Below the
fight scene, a mock account of the event, as reported in the Washington "Globe," is given: "This
celebrated fight took place at Washington in 1834, Hickory was seconded by Little Van and Major
Jack Downing, with Joe Tammany for the bottle holder; Long Harry and Black Dan were Nick's
seconds, and Old Mother Bank bottle holder. Several long and severe rounds were fought, and
from the immense sums bet, many of the fancy were losers to a large amount[.] Old Mother B. is
said to have backed her champion to the tune of more than $150,000. Nick's weight of metal was
superior as well as his science, but neither were sufficient for the pluck and wind of Hickory, who
shewed his thorough training and sound condition so effectually that in the last round Nick was
unable to come to time and gave in." Library of Congress.

"View of Col. Crockett's Residence in West Tennessee" (*Davy Crockett's Almanack of Wild Sports in the West. And Life in the Backwoods. 1835.* (Nashville, Tenn.: Published by Snag & Sawyer, [1834]), 24-25. Courtesy of the University of Tennessee's Special Collections.

"Col. Crockett's Desperate Fight with the Great Bear" *(Davy Crockett's Almanack of Wild Sports in the West. And Life in the Backwoods. 1835.* (Nashville, Tenn.: Published by Snag & Sawyer, [1834]), 48. Note that Crockett's features are nearly all different in the almanacs. Courtesy of the University of Tennessee's Special Collections.

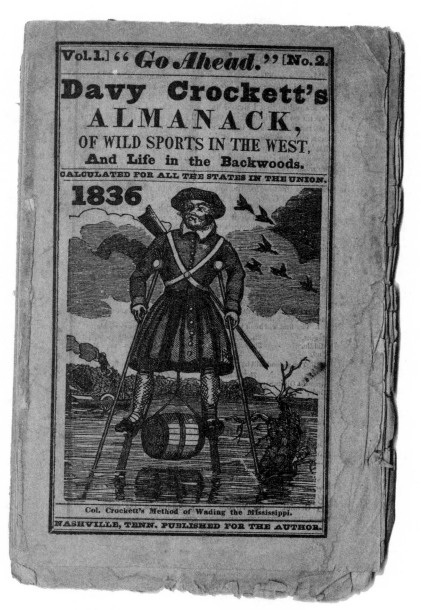

"Col. Crockett's Method of Wading the Mississippi" *(Davy Crockett's Almanack, of Wild Sports in the West. And Life in the Backwoods. 1836.* (Nashville, Tenn.: Published for the Author [1835]), cover. A close examination of the original woodcut reveals the word "Whiskey" on the barrel he carries. Courtesy of the University of Tennessee's Special Collections.

"Col. Crockett's Trip to Texas and Fight with the Mexicans" *Davy Crockett's Almanac. 1845* (Boston: James Fisher, [1844]), [29]. Often a super-nationalist in the almanacs, Crockett races into the Mexican War on his pet bear. Courtesy of the University of Tennessee's Special Collections.

"Crockett's wonderful escape up the Niagara Falls, on his Pet Alligator" *(Crockett's Almanac. Scenes in River Life, Feats on the Lakes, Manners in the Back Woods, Adventures in Texas, &c. &c. 1846* (Boston: James Fisher, [1845]), cover. In the accompanying tale, anti-British sentiment abounds because of their violation of the northern border of the United States. The woodcut shows Crockett "cocking his snoot" (thumb on his nose, holding the palm open and perpendicular to the face, and fingers extended) to deride the British soldiers as he escapes. Courtesy of the University of Tennessee's Special Collections.

CROCKETT BLOWING UP A MAN OF WAR, BY A FLASH OF LIGHTNING FROM HIS EYE.

"Crockett Blowing Up a Man of War, by a Flash of Lightning from his Eye" *(Davy Crockett's Almanac, 1847* (Boston: James Fisher, [1846]), [16]. The story notes that the vessel that Crockett destroys is a pirate ship. Note the change in the portrayal of his face. Courtesy of the University of Tennessee's Special Collections.

"Crockett's Celebrated War Speech" *(Davy Crockett's Almanac, 1847* (Boston: James Fisher, [1846]), [19]. Here Crockett is now shown as an inhuman machine of war and destruction. There is no linear progression in Crockett's depictions in the almanacs, but the general trend is toward the savage, grotesque, and outlandish. Courtesy of the University of Tennessee's Special Collections.

"Coleman's California Line for San Francisco [(] 'Be sure you'r [sic] right then go ahead.'[)] Sailing regularly on advertised days, The Celebrated A1 Extreme Clipper Ship DAVID CROCKETT. . . . This well-known and favorite vessel has made the passage to San Francisco in 115 days (and admitted by all to be one of the fastest ships afloat.). . . ." Crockett's "Go Ahead!" spirit lived on well after his death and his fame made a picture of the ship unnecessary. This advertisement for the speedy clipper ship bearing his name was built in 1853 by Greenman & Co., in Mystic, CT. It made seven successive passages from New York to San Francisco in 110 to 131 days when the previous average was 150 to 180 days." Courtesy of the University of Tennessee's Special Collections.

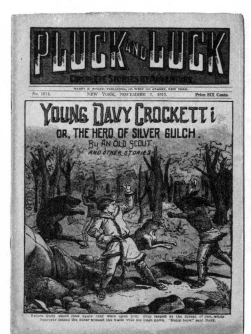

"Young Davy Crockett; Or, The Hero of Silver Gulch. By an Old Scout" (*Pluck and Luck*, November 7, 1917). This is one of the many fictional dime novels about Crockett and his prowess as a hunter and Indian fighter from the 1860s through the 1920s. Its bottom caption reads: "Before Davy could load again they were upon him. Grip leaped at the throat of the one, while Squeezer seized the other around the waist with his huge paws. 'Bully boys!' said Davy." Courtesy of the University of Tennessee's Special Collections.

Colonel Crockett, engraved by C. Stuart (ca. 1839) from the original portrait
by J. G. Chapman, (1834), Library of Congress.

THE

LIFE AND ADVENTURES

OF

COLONEL DAVID CROCKETT,

OF WEST TENNESSEE.

"Ridentem dicere verum, quid vetat?"—Hor.[1]

CINCINNATI:

PUBLISHED FOR THE PROPRIETOR.

1833.

PREFACE.

So fashionable has it become to write a preface, that, like an epitaph, it now records of its subject, not what it is, but what it ought to be. The mania for book-making has really assumed an epidemic character; for, like the late pestilence,[2] uninfluenced by all changes of weather—save that a murky evening generally aggravates its symptoms—it makes its attacks from quarters the least expected; and emanating from beneath the dim light of some rusty old lamp, sheds abroad its sleepy, yawning influence. But so fashionable has this practice become, that I should be as much surprised to meet a book without a preface, as I should be, were I, in one of midnight rambles, to meet a preface, stealing clandestinely along, unaccompanied by a book. Yet some men have been lost to all the fashions of the day, as to send forth the treasurers of genius, to enlighten and astonish the world, without this expected formality. But, as I do not aspire to that elevated niche in the temple of Fame, which such men have been allowed to occupy by common consent, I must permit my better feelings to predominate, and clothe my first born babe in all suitable garments, before I turn her loose upon a heartless world. Were I to set her adrift without this necessary appendage, my heart would smite me; and I should never meet a poor beggar, thinly clad, breasting the storms of winter, but with sorrow, I should think of the destitute condition of my pretty bantling.

Having thus resolved upon a preface, I will write as long as my humor prompts, or until the fit under which I am now laboring, wears off.

It is perfectly ridiculous, in my opinion, for a man to write a book, which he believes calculated to interest, instruct, or amuse, and then sit down and write an elaborate apology for doing so: Nor is it less absurd, to ask favor from the hands of would-be critics—self-constituted judges of modern days—whose mere dictum creates a literary vassalage—beneath whose blighting influence, the finest specimens of genius, when linked with poverty, wither and die—and whose sole duty is to blazon forth the fame of some one, whom public opinion has placed above them; or, to puff into notice another, who has money—not mind—enough to carry him along.—But as regardless of this class of gentry as I am careful of my own comfort and convenience, I have really labored under the impression, that, in writing for my own amusement, I had a right to select my topics; and consequently I have been grave or merry as my humor prompted.[3]

At this time, when, in every ephemeral tale, a red hunter[4] must be treacherous, brutal, savage, and accompanied with the tomahawk and scalping knife, I should perhaps offer some apology for speaking of them in a different light, in my introduction; but my apology is—it was my pleasure to do so.

Gentle reader, I can promise you, in no part of this volume, the wild rhodomontades of Bushfield[5]—nor can I regale you with the still more delicate repast of a constant repetition of the terms *"bodyaciowsly," "tetotaciously," "obflisticated,"* &c. Though my intercourse with the West has been considerable, I have never met with a man who used such terms, unless they were alluded to, as merely occupying space in some printed work. They have, however, been made to enter, as a component part, into the character of every backwoodsman; and, perhaps, I hazard something in leaving the common path; but my duty commands it—and though the following memoir may wear an air of levity, it is, nevertheless, strictly true.[6]

In describing backwoodsmen, it has become customary to clothe their most common ideas in high sounding, unintelligible coinage—while my observation induces me to believe that their most striking feature is the fact that they clothe the most extravagant ideas in the simplest language; and amuse us by the[i]r[a] quaintness of expression, and originality of comparison. With these remarks I submit to you the LIFE AND ADVENTURES OF COLONEL DAVID CROCKETT.[b]

I know there are those who dwell in the splendid mansions of the East, and whose good fortune enables them to tread a Turkey carpet, or loll upon a sofa, to whom a faithful representation of the manners and customs of the "far off West," will afford a rich repast; and there is another class for whom this volume will possess many charms, when I remark that it entertains for the *"blue devils"*[7] the most deep and deadly enmity. And, still farther, the learned, though they may see little to admire in the composition of this work, may yet find amusement in the peculiar eccentricities of an original mind: and to the grave philosopher, also, I here present a subject of deep and lasting meditation.

Finally, most gentle reader, I hereby guaranty, that there shall not be found, in the volume before you, a single sentence, or a single word, calculated to crimson the cheek of innocence, or give a license to vice.

INTRODUCTION.

In giving to the public the biography of a celebrated backwoodsman, a brief sketch of the country in which he resides will not be deemed irrelevant. I am aware that much has been written upon this subject; but it is a theme so fruitful in variety, that I hope, if I shall not be able to instruct, I shall at least entertain. The term "far off West," seems from general usage, to apply only to that section of our country which lies between the Alleghany and Rocky mountains. In comparison with this vast region, other portions of the globe, which have delighted the world with the finest specimens of history, of poetry, of sculpture, and of painting, dwindle into insignificance with regard to magnitude. Here Fancy, in her playful flights, may call into being empires which have no existence; and though perhaps sober reason would now chide her fairy creations yet the time will come, when they will only be looked upon with the conviction of truth.

Oft, while seated upon the margin of the Mississippi river—the greatest curiosity on our globe—have I thought, until my brain reeled with the multitude of images which crowded upon it. When I reflected on the vast region compromised in the phrase "far off West"—when I recollect that all the water which fell, and accumulated, between the Alleghany on the east, and the Rocky mountains on the west, (a section of country thousands of miles in extent,) sought, by the same outlet, its passage to the ocean—and when I beheld at my feet, that passage, in a narrow muddy stream, winding smoothly along, I was struck with astonishment. I thought it ought to boil, and dash, and foam, and fret its way, in hurried search of the ocean. Although the Mississippi receives tributaries which are navigable for several thousand miles, yet its size is not at all apparently increased. Irregular, though smooth, it forces its circuitous way along—yet restless, and ever changing its bed, as if to relieve itself from the accumulating weight of waters. Frequently does it narrow itself to within less than a quarter of a mile, Then [*sic*] how incalculable must be its depth! There are some portions of it very shallow; but there are others, where no bottom has ever yet been found; and could its waters be drained off, there would be left chasms into which the boldest would never dare to look; and in whose depths myriads of animals crawl and flutter, which have never yet known the light of day!

The "far off West" spreads before us every variety of climate—every species of soil. One would be more disposed to look upon it as a creation of fancy, than as possessing an actual existence. Here, roam and play their sportive tricks, over verdant fields, innumerable animals, whose feet are crimsoned with fruit, which the gods themselves would eat. Here, roving over our prairies, the weary hunter may repose on the beds of flowers which give the blush to all the enchantments of city gardens. Here, while I am now writing, apart from the busy hum of men, how the events of a few years rise up before me. The Past and Present both present themselves, and seek to gain my preference. The Past tells me, here, but a few years since, nature slept in primeval loveliness: her forests had never echoed to the sound of an axe: her rivers had never been disturbed by the noise of a steam boat: there was nothing to break in upon the stillness of evening, save the loud whoop of her children, the long howl of some hungry wolf, the wild scream of a famished panther, or the plaintive notes of some gentle turtle[dove], weeping for one that's far away. "Yes," cried she, "here roamed my red men of the forest, free as the breezes which fanned their raven locks. Here, no bickering disturbed their social intercourse—no right of property shed its baleful influence over their wild society—no white man was here to practice them in all the wiles of deception:—No—there was none. Here, my young daughters of the forest have led on the mazy dance[8]—here, have luxuriated in all the delightful emotions of innocent love. Here, some Indian warrior may have wooed his dusky bride. My heart grows sick, when I think of all that was lovely which has left me."

"But," cries the Present, "the scene that I could sketch is still more beautiful. Though no long howl of the wolf now announces evening; though no famished panther wakes you at midnight—yet the repose of nature is now broken by music far more delightful. The noise of children just bursting out from school—the cheerful song of the milk maid, as she performs her evening duties—or the loud crack of some driver, as he forces his weary oxen to their stalls, now tell us of the close of day. Once, only a canoe danced lightly over your waters: now, floating palaces adorn them, which realize all the gorgeous tales of eastern fancy, and with all their beauty blend the power of the magic carpet—

"Walk your waters like things of life,
"And seem to dare the elements to strife."

The West presents much variety. Some of our cities, in beauty and in all the fascinations of a polished society, vie with those of the East; while there are many portions where the wildness of nature and the first rudiments of society are struggling for the ascendency; and there are still many more, where nature yet reposes in her loveliest form. The whole country spreads before us a field for speculation, only bounded by the limits of the human mind.

Every spot shows that it was once the abode of human beings, who are now lounging idly about in the vale of eternity—not so small as the degenerate race of modern days,[9] but majestic in size, and capable, according to scripture command, of managing the various species of the mammoth tribe—even those that were *ligniverous*, whose ravenous appetite has clearly accounted for the want of timber on our great western prairies, and whose saliva, according to the MS. of a celebrated travelling antiquarian and great linguist, (which subsequent annotators seem to have overlooked)[10] was of so subtle yet deadly a nature, that when applied to a tree, it immediately diffused itself throughout its roots, and killed, for all future ages, the power to germinate.

We must ever regret that the same ingenious traveller did not inform us of their mode of eating this timber; as henceforward it must be a matter of doubt. Was it corded up like steamboat wood, and in that manner devoured? Or did this animal, after the manner of the anaconda, render its food slippery by means of saliva, and swallow it whole? If this latter be the case, I am struck with the analogy which this animal bears to the subject of my biography—for as my hero is the only person who could ever slip down a honey-locust without a scratch, so I presume that this is the only animal which has ever swallowed a tree of the same species, and received no inconvenience from its thorns. But, believing, as I do implicitly, that man was placed at the head of affairs in this lower world, I have no doubt that the time has been, when men were so much larger than they now are, that a mammoth was swung up and butchered with the same ease that we would now butcher a sheep; and it requires no great stretch of imagination to conceive a gentleman of that day, after the manner of the French epicure in America, (who, having dispatched a pig, asked the waiter if there were no more *leetle* hogs,) crying out "*waitaire!* have you no more *leetle* mammoths?"

The multitude of tumuli, or Indian mounds, which every where present themselves, alone form a subject for deep meditation. The idea that they were used solely for burying places, seems to me absurd, and were it now proper, I could adduce many arguments to the contrary. These tumuli, however, are found in all situations, of various heights, and different sizes; sometimes insulated, at others linked together for an indefinite distance. In Arkansas and Missouri, you frequently meet with chains of these mounds: east of the Mississippi they are generally insulated, and now remain but as a memento of what once was. Sometimes they are surrounded by a ditch, now almost effaced, from the decay of vegetable matter, which gives them the appearance of works thrown up for defence. But, for what they were intended—when they were built—what was their height—are all questions which cannot be answered. Tradition has never dared to affix a date to any of them; nor can any Indian tribe now in existence give any clue which will enable us to solve the mystery. Large trees growing on their tops have been felled, and their ages counted; and though some of them would reckon years enough to be looked upon as the patriarchs of the forest, yet that gives no direct clue—for, how long the mounds were in existence before the trees grew up, we cannot tell.

Bones of the aborigines, in many places yet whiten the soil: sometimes you meet with them so deposited as to leave little doubt that the last honors of war were once performed over them. How often, while travelling alone through our western forests, have I turned my horse loose to graze, and lolling upon one of these mounds indulged in meditation. Fancying it a depository for the dead, I have called before me all its inmates; and they rose up of every grade from hoary age to infancy. There stood the chief of his tribe, with wisdom painted in his furrowed cheeks; near him a warrior, in all the bloom of youth. There stood one, who, with all the burning fervor of eloquence, had incited his tribe to warlike deeds; near him a blushing daughter of the forest, cut off while her beauties were just opening into day. And, to extend the picture, and view the wide expanse of the mighty West, methinks there rose up before me warriors of the forest, whose fame was once as fair as is now that of Hannibal or Caesar, Napoleon or Wellington. Yes, methinks, they each had a Cannae or a Pharsalia, an Austerlitz or a Waterloo.[11] Yes, how often here, have I wandered over fields which, perhaps, were once hallowed by the sacred blood of freedom, or which have been consecrated by deeds of high and lofty daring. Could the "far off West" give up its history, the chivalry of darker ages would have no votaries. But even the last remnant of this once great people is fast disappearing from the country. A few years more and not one will remain to tell what they once were. Thousands of them are at this time marching far "over the border."[12] To see such a multitude of all ages, forced from a country which they have been taught to love as their "own native land"—to hear their wild lamentations at leaving the bones of all who were dear to them, to wander over a region which has for them no tender recollections, touches all the finest chords of the human heart. Feelings of sympathy will ever kindle at the recollection of the fate of the

Indians, whose history, at some future day, may be read in the following brief epitaph:

"Alas! Poor Yorick!"

Throughout the west innumerable prairies abound, covered with every flower which can delight the senses, either rolling like the gentle heavings of the ocean, or level as the surface of an unruffled lake. These form another subject of fruitful meditation; at least with those (if any should be found) who doubt the existence of the Tree-eater. What has caused them? Why do you meet with them of all sizes, (the richest land we have,) without a shrub, surrounded by dense forests? Why, as soon as the whites begin to graze them, do they spring up in a thick undergrowth, when if they do not graze them, they retain their former appearance? Have they not been cultivated? Were they not plantations? And were not the inhabitants who then resided here, entirely destroyed by Indian tribes who took possession? Is not their present appearance owing to the fact that the Indians have burned them regularly since they were cultivated, in order to preserve them as pastures for their game? I am aware that some of the prairies, from their great size, would seem at once to put an end to these speculations. But, on the other hand, there are many proofs of the great antiquity of our country, and many convincing arguments that its former proprietors were much farther advanced in civilization than the present natives. In support of this position I will simply refer to a circumstance generally known, that in digging a well near Cincinnati, two stumps were found some sixty or seventy feet below the surface, which had been cut off by an axe, and upon one of which the remains of an axe was found. Further, to prove that its former proprietors were somewhat enlightened, I would remark that in digging a salt well at one of the licks near Shawneetown, Illinois, an octangular post was discovered some twenty feet below the surface, bored through precisely similar to that now used for a pump. Also, in the same state, a large rectangular smooth stone was found, covered with regular hieroglyphical characters. Coins, brick, and forts, the result of a certain degree of civilization, have been everywhere found.[13]

That there were many prairies once in cultivation, many ingenious arguments may be brought to prove. These views are given, merely with a hope that they may induce an examination into this subject. I have already entered farther into speculation than the nature of this work demands, and shall be gratified if my suggestions call into action talents more suited to the task.

The country which I have but slightly sketched, in its wildest state was the home of BOONE, the great pioneer of the west, who now lives in sculpture in the rotunda of your capital.[14] In a frontier, and consequently less attractive state, it is now the home of DAVID CROCKETT, whose humors have been spoken of in every portion of our country, and about whom there is less known than of any other individual who ever attained so much notoriety. I intend no regular comparison between these two personages, for each will live while the "far off West" has a votary; but I must run a parallel only for an instant. Each lived under the same circumstances: the one waged an eternal war with the Indians, and hunted game for recreation: the other waged an eternal war with the beasts of the forest, and served his country when his aid was wanted. Each could send the whizzing ball almost where he wished it. Mr. Knapp, in a beautiful sketch which he has given the world of Boone, mentions that frequently to try his skill, "he shot with a single ball the humming bird, as he sucked the opening flower, and spread his tiny wings and presented his exquisite colors to the sun; and brought down the soaring eagle as he poised in majesty over his head, disdaining the power of this nether world."[15] I cannot say that Col. Crockett has ever performed either of the above feats, but often have I seen him seated on the margin of a river, shooting with a single ball its scaly inmates, when only for an instant in wanton sport they glittered in the sun: the rifle cracked, and ever was there some little monster struggling on the top. The task of William Tell would give no pain, for in idle sport does he sometimes shoot a dollar from between the finger and thumb of a brother, or he will plant his balls between his fingers as pleasure suits. In point of mind, Col. Crockett is decidedly Boone's superior. I do not found this remark on the authority of the common sketches of the day, which are little better than mere vagaries of the imagination, but gather my information from a gentleman[16] who now knows Col. Crockett, and who, with Boone for a companion, has often hunted the buffalo on the plains of Kentucky.

The country which it falls to my lot most particularly to describe, is the western district of Tennessee; and of that, to me the most interesting spot was Col. Crockett's residence. There, far retired from the bustle of the world, he lives, and chews for amusement the cud of his political life. He has settled himself over the grave of an earthquake, which often reminds him of the circumstance by moving itself as if tired of confinement. The wild face of the country—the wide chasms—the new formed lakes, together with its great loneliness, render it interesting in the extreme to the traveller.[17] But above all, the simplicity and great hospitality of its thinly scattered inhabitants makes one turn to it with pleasure who has ever visited it. The many stories in circulation of deadly struggles with wild animals, and the great distance sometimes found between settlements, create in this country much interest for the traveller; but for a more particular history of these things I refer you, gentle reader, to the following pages.

LIFE AND ADVENTURES
OF
COLONEL DAVID CROCKETT.

CHAPTER I.

DAVID CROCKETT, the subject of the following memoir, was born in Greene county, East Tennessee,[18] of poor and respectable parentage. He was the ninth child, and the extreme indigence of his father rendered him unable to educate all his children: so that when David became old enough to go to school, his father's situation made it necessary that he should go to work. No one, at this early age, could have foretold that he was ever to ride upon a streak of lightning, receive a commission to quiet the fears of the world by wringing off the tail of a comet, or perform sundry other wonderful acts, for which he has received due credit, and which will serve to give him a reputation[19] as lasting as that of the hero of Orleans.[20] But David was always a quirky boy, and many and sage were the prophecies made of his future greatness. Every species of fortune-telling was exhausted to find out in what particular department he was to figure; but this was for ever[c] shrouded in mystery. No seer could say more than that David was to be great. In the slang of the backwoods, one swore that he would never be *"one-eyed"*—that is dishonest: another, that he would never be *"a case"*—that is flat, without a dollar. But let us pursue an even narrative of his life, and see how far those various prophecies proved to be correct.

While David was yet young, his father removed from Greene to Sullivan county,[21] and settled upon a public road for the purpose of keeping tavern. David's duty here was to wait about the house and stable, and the labor devolving on him was already too great for a boy of his years. Spending his time in this way, he remained at home until he reached his twelfth year, when he became acquainted with a Dutchman[22] who resided about four hundred miles distant, and who was in the habit of regularly driving cattle to the western part of Virginia. To this man was David hired by his father, and at the early age of twelve years, entirely uneducated, was forced to bid adieu to home, and thus commence his entrance into life. But a few days elapsed after the contract was made, before the old Dutchman, having bought up his cattle, was ready for the journey. After an agreeable though laborious trip they arrived at their place of destination. David was treated with much kindness, and many efforts were made to wean him from a too great fondness for his parents. His activity and general acquaintance with business for a boy of his years, made him a valuable assistant to the old Dutchman, who was anxious to retain him. But the menial offices which it soon fell to his lot to discharge, rendered him unhappy and dissatisfied; and after remaining five or six months, he asked permission to return home, which was denied him. He immediately formed a resolution to do so at all hazards.

While playing in the road one Sunday evening after his resolution was formed, he met with an opportunity of carrying it into effect. Many wagons passed, and with them he recognized a wagoner whom he had frequently seen, and who was then on a journey to his father's. David soon told him of his situation, and his desire to get home, and received from his new friend a promise of protection, provided he would go along with him. This David readily agreed to; and not being able to leave at that time, he found out where the wagons would encamp that night, and promised, after getting his clothes, to overtake them.

He then returned to the house, succeeded in bundling up his little all, and having conveyed it to the stable unsuspected, went about his regular business. At supper he was even treated with more than usual kindness, which caused him to regret the step he was about to take; but his resolution was fixed. David with the rest of the family retired to bed as usual. He soon fell into a light sleep, from which he awoke about two o'clock, arose, dressed, and gently opening the door, left the house. After getting out he found it extremely cold and snowing, with several inches of snow already upon the ground. His resolution for a moment faltered; but he resolved to go on. Groping his way to the stable, he obtained his bundle, and soon was in the public road on his way to the camp of the wagoners. The place appointed for their meeting was distant about seven miles. The snow was now falling fast, and driving in his face; the excessive darkness of the night much impeded his progress, and he was only enabled to get along by avoiding the woods on either side, and pursuing, by feeling with his feet, the smooth track of the road before him. The desire of reaching home, or rather the fear of being overtaken by his master, produced the excitement which alone enabled him to accomplish his purpose.

The shades of night were giving place to the dark gray light of morning when David came in sight of the wagons. His friend was already stirring, and believed rather that an apparition had presented itself than that his young acquaintance was before him. However, he received him with much kindness, and paid him that attention which his situation deserved—making him drink whiskey freely and by degrees thawing his frozen limbs. He also quieted his fears about being overtaken by his master, promised him protection, and convinced him from the fact that the snow was still falling, that no trace could be left of his escape, the prints of his feet being filled up almost as fast as created. This adventure was quite an undertaking for a boy so young; and one would be disposed to look upon it merely as a premonitory symptom of similar adventures in after life. He soon became a favorite with the wagoners, spent his time pleasantly, and arrived in safety at his father's, whom he satisfied for having left his first master.

Here for a year or two he remained, performing the drudgery in and about his father's premises—a situation ill calculated to improve his mind or inculcate correct morals. His ideas seem to have run far ahead of his years, and he appeared as if out of the sphere for which he was intended. With an ardent desire to be sent to school, he was admonished by his father's poverty that it was entirely impracticable. So becoming dissatisfied with the tedious monotony of his life, he neglected his business, and his father resolved again to hire him out, and accordingly did so, to a cattle merchant who was about to set out for western Virginia.

During this trip he suffered much, was very badly treated, and having arrived at the end of his journey, was dismissed, though several hundred miles from home, by his employer, who gave him only the sum of three dollars to pay expenses. David insisted it was not enough; but he could get no more; and meeting with a young acquaintance who had been engaged in the same employment, with one horse between them they set out upon their return. This trip served to convince him that cattle driving was not exactly "*the thing;*" and if his earlier associations could have had any influence upon his after life, he would certainly either have become a grazier, or have labored forever under an insuperable antipathy to beef.

It will be seen from a perusal of the following pages, that David was ever mere sport for fortune. She was not always unkind to him, but tricky; rather sportive than otherwise: so that his starting to a place was no proof that he would ever reach it. He was almost sure to diverge, and in his wanderings appears to have been governed by the principle, that there was more beauty in a curve than in a straight line.[23]

David, with his companion, trudged along several days, when the latter, being the larger, insisted upon his privilege to ride exclusively, which so much offended David, that, meeting with a wagon going in a counter direction to his home, he bade adieu to his late comrade and took a passage. Upon enquiry he found out that the wagon was bound for Alexandria, D.C. So, not caring where he went, he entered into a contract to accompany it as a wagon boy. He visited Alexandria, and then determined to return with the wagon home. After having travelled for several days, his friend, the wagoner, entered into an engagement to do some hauling in the neighborhood, and David, in the interim, hired himself to a farmer as a ploughboy. In this situation he remained until he had accumulated the sum of eleven dollars; when meeting with a wagon bound for Baltimore, he resolved to go along with it. With the driver he deposited his money for safe keeping, and entered into an agreement upon small wages. Arriving in the suburbs of the city, some accident happened which delayed the farther progress of the wagon. The time necessary for repairing gave David some leisure. High with hope, the whole world as he imagined spread before him, and down the streets of Baltimore he strolled until his faculties became confused with the "*sights*" he saw, and he stood gazing for the first time at a ship lying alongside of the wharf, with a part of her canvass floating loosely in the breeze. The sight was novel, her appearance inviting, and on board stepped David. Some of the crew observing the admiration with which he gazed on the rigging and on every part of the ship, asked him, familiarly, if he would not take a passage in her for Liverpool, the port for which she was bound. But a few moments elapsed before he was employed as a common sailor, to set out on a voyage of three thousand miles, who perhaps an hour before was not aware that there was such a thing as a sea or a ship in existence. The ship was to sail that evening, and with a promise that he would return so soon as he could gather his clothes, David sought his wagon. With ideas of the world much enlarged from having seen Baltimore, and the fact that this ship was to take so long a voyage, and with a boundless prospect for adventure before him, light hearted and happy he danced his way back. Occasionally his golden visions were clouded by the probability that the wagoner would not permit him to go; but this was not calculated to have much effect upon a mind sanguine in its own resources. Presenting himself before the wagoner, he asked him for the money he had deposited with him for safe keeping, and also told him of his intention to go to Liverpool. The wagoner positively refused, and threatened him severely should he dare to leave. However, David taking advantage of his momentary absence, bundled up his clothes and started for the ship. But as fate would have it, in strolling along a crowded street, whom should he run full tilt against but his friend the wagoner.

Thus did fortune force David Crockett to figure in other places than the crowded streets of Liverpool. But for this slight mishap the Western District could now have boasted of no hero. In a common scrape no one would have said, "Now the way he fights is a sin to Crockett"—and when any thing wonderful happened, "Now I tell you what, it is nothing to Crockett." However, the day after this adventure, David was on the public road, bound for home; but dissatisfied and blubbering along after the wagon demanding his money. A stranger met them and finding out from David the cause of his distress, threatened the wagoner with an immediate whipping unless he would refund the money. This he was unable to do, having previously spent it; so that David, collecting his clothes, bade adieu to the wagon without a cent, and was again thrown upon a heartless world. He stopped at the first house he reached, where he was employed as a common laborer. Here he remained until he had accumulated a small sum. He then again started for home; but getting out of money in the western part of Virginia, he was forced to work. His necessities induced him to hire himself out merely for his clothes; which after having obtained, being still without money, he bound himself as an apprentice boy to a hatter for four years. Here he remained several months, when the hatter failed and he was again thrown out of business. He then hired himself as a laborer, acquired a small sum of money, and set out for East Tennessee, where, after many adventures for one so young, he arrived and stopped with some relations, distant from his father's about one hundred miles. Here he sojourned until he either was or fancied himself an unwelcome guest. He then set out determined to reach his father's, having been absent about two years, and never having communicated a syllable to his relations during his wanderings.

The shades of a winter evening were setting in, when David, neatly though plainly dressed, came in sight of the house of his father. Walking in with his bundle, he complained of fatigue and asked permission to remain. His father, rather infirm, was discharging the duties of his house; his mother was preparing supper; and a sister was engaged in some other household occupation. These, with a traveller or two, formed the little circle collected within. Withdrawing himself into a corner of the room, David remained a silent spectator of the scene before him—feeding his imagination upon the anticipated pleasure which was to burst forth upon his being recognized. Perhaps an hour elapsed, when the little party were summoned to supper. David's features, from the extreme silence he had preserved, were anxiously scanned by all present so soon as he came to the light. His sister recognized him, and a happy meeting, with a gentle chiding for the strange manner in which he had introduced himself, closed the evening.

CHAPTER II.

DAVID's wanderings had caused his parents much uneasiness, and they had long since given him up for lost. A prosecution had been commenced against the cattle driver who had carried him off, which was compromised; and for a time a ray of sunshine seemed to play over the family, while David amused them with his adventures, or called into action all their tender sympathies by a recital of his sufferings. Occasionally would he gather a crowd of his associates around him and create as much astonishment by a narrative of what he had actually seen, as he could have done had he just dropped from the clouds. But these halcyon days were of short duration. David had now arrived at an age when he began to feel his ability to support himself, and was anxious to engage in some laudable pursuit. He had, as yet, not received the first rudiments of the most common education. He felt a great desire to learn to read and write; but his father so far from being able to afford him an opportunity actually required his services. Being indebted to a merchant in a little village not many miles distant, he resolved to hire his son out to him, until his labor should discharge the debt. The village had a bad character, and David protested against going; but upon the entreaty of his father, and a promise that if he would discharge the debt he should thenceforth be his own man, David went to work. About six months of the closest labor (a fact stated by himself) enabled him to release his father. He then quit the village, and hearing that the Quakers, many of whom resided in the village neighborhood, were remarkable for their kindness, he resolved to seek employment among them. The first to whom he applied offered to employ him and give him liberal wages, provided he would take in payment a note which he held, executed by his father for the sum of thirty dollars. These were hard terms to a boy just entering into life, dependent entirely upon his own exertions for support. But reflecting upon the situation of his father, his extreme poverty and great age, his goodness of heart prevailed, and he resolved to cancel the demand. He applied himself diligently to work, and in a little less than six months, the Quaker gave him his father's note. In this part of life, he has a perfect recollection of never having failed to work a single day while in the employment of his friend the Quaker. It however served to give him a good character, and he never wanted for employment afterwards.

Although within twenty miles of his father's, he had not visited there for about twelve months: so, taking his note along with him, he went home, and after knocking about awhile he presented it to his father, who told him he was entirely unable to pay it. David remarked it was not presented for payment, but intended as a gift, and stated how he became possessed of it. His father was much affected and even mortified—perhaps for having forced his son to work at a place counter to his wishes. Being much in want of clothes, and hearing that the Quakers were famous for their workmanship, David went to work among them until he was genteelly dressed. His desire of learning to read again returning, he went to see a Quaker who kept a school in the neighborhood, and with him made the following bargain: That he, David, would labor in the field two days for being allowed to go to school three. He soon became a favorite, progressed rapidly, and remained here some five or six months, strictly complying with his bargain. This was the only schooling he ever received.

After being at school some four or five months, his tutor was visited by a female relation. She was pretty and fascinating, and David began to feel a little unhappy whenever she was absent. She did not long remain ignorant of the impression she had made, nor could she recollect that a handsome stripling was interested in her welfare without feeling her spirits flutter with delight. They for some time conversed with their eyes, a language least liable to be misunderstood; and David found out that she was not altogether indifferent to him. While things were in this situation she had an offer of marriage from a wealthy neighbor, which was exceedingly gratifying to her relation. David saw that with him all was over—that it would be idle to press his claims while a wealthy suitor was soliciting her hand. He subdued his passion. She was courted, and but a short time elapsed before it was necessary to make a parcel of pens. Pigs, turkeys, geese, chickens, &c. were restricted from taking exercise, and forced to sit and eat, preparatory to their being sacrificed on a day appointed, when Miss ———— was to become a wealthy bride. An unusual bustle, with the arrival of all the neighbors, announced the evening. "About this time," says David, "I began to feel unhappy, but did not know why. I thought the devil and all was in women—that there was nothing on earth like them."

Among the crowd that assembled on that evening was a pretty little girl whom David had often seen; and he, with her for a partner, waited on the bridal couple. The touch of her hand conveyed a thrilling sensation, and he found out that he was doomed to fall in love—so to work he went. He was modest and retiring and at first made but slow progress; but several old fashioned plays were introduced, which served to help him along amazingly. Being a handsome fellow and a favorite where he lived, his attentions were kindly received, and ere they parted next morning not only had the stolen glances of her eyes indicated an interest in his welfare, but her hand had been solicited, and that with her heart pledged irrecoverably to David.[24] With regret the crowd parted, and not one experienced more heartfelt sorrow than our loving couple. A day not far distant was appointed when David was to pay a visit and ask for his bride. Time rolled heavily along. David could neither work nor go to school, but lounged idly about, thinking of her who was dearest to him.

At length the day arrived, and borrowing a horse he set out in high hopes, filled with those natural yet exciting fears which render love so delightful. Upon getting within a few miles of the home of his intended, he heard of a great dance, and met a party going on for fun and frolic. He stopped. That evening was the time appointed by him to ask for his bride—that evening a frolic was to take place, and he was now in reach of it. His resolution faltered— to-morrow would do to ask for his wife. So wheeling his horse about, uninvited, he determined to enjoy the frolic. Arriving at the house full of fun and life, he soon became a welcome guest, and met with a very jolly set. It was composed of the less refined portion of society, and appearances promised much sport. The house was tolerably large, with a dirt floor, which had been swept, ready for a dance. Most of the persons present had "taken a little," and were conse- quently in a good humor. Both girls and boys had on their best bib and tucker.[25] The dresses of the ladies, however, were chosen counter to Apollonius' advice,[26] being gaudy, not rich; and, expressed in fancy, they looked "very killing." There was only one pair of shoes present, and they were not allowed to be worn unless by those persons who had danced their nails off.

Had every thing been dull, the appearance of old Ben the banjo player, would have filled them with fun. He was seated in a corner upon a stool, holding his instrument, which he called SAL, and the perspiration exuded so freely that he looked very much as if he had been greased. His hair was roached,[27] and he wore an air of much dignity. His forehead was low and narrow; his eyes red and sunken; his nose not so flat, but protuberant at the sides; his lips curling, as if in scorn at each other. His teeth were not placed perpendicular, but set in at an obtuse angle, which caused them to jut out; and his lower jaw seemed to have a great antipathy to the upper, and when idle always kept as far off as possible. His apparel was in unison with his face. He had on no jump-jacket,[28] and his bosom was a little exposed. His coat hung down nearly to his heels, and was at the same time nearly large enough for a cloak; while his pantaloons (light drab) were a close fit all the way, and so short that they only came where the calves of his legs ought to have been. The contrast between his black legs and drab breeches might have made one fancy he had on boots, but that the shape of the lower extremity denied it. His leg was placed so nearly in the middle of his foot, that, with toes at each end, no one could have tracked him; and the hollow of his feet projected so far outward that it gave them somewhat the appearance of rockers to a chair. Ben also had much vanity, and thought he was looking remarkably well that evening; but with all this, his willingness to oblige, and a certain portion of good humor which played over his countenance, rendered him pleasant to look upon.

Girls and boys were all ready for fun, and never was there a more enliven- ing scene than when Sal jumped up, spun round, and swore she could "go her death" upon a jig, and cried out, "Uncle Ben, strike up!" Jinny got up, spun round, and faced Sal; and both began to shuffle. Soon the whole house was up, knocking it off—while old Ben thrummed his banjo, beat time with this feet, and sung in haste the following lines, occasionally calling for particular steps.

> "I started off from Tennessee,
> My old horse wouldn't pull for me.
> (*Ben cries out—"Now, back step an' heel an' toe."*)
> He begin to fret an' slip,
> An' I begin to cus an' whip;
> Walk jawbone from Tennessee;
> Walk jawbone from Tennessee.
> (*"Now, weed corn, kiver taters,*[29] *an' double shuffle."*)
> I fed my horse in de poplar trof,
> It made him cotch de hoopin' cof;
> My old horse died in Tennessee,
> And will'd his jawbone here to me.
> Walk jawbone, &c.

The dance was all life. They spin round—they set to—they heel and toe—they double shuffle—they weed corn—they kiver taters. They whoop and stop.

"Now, Dick," says Sal, "didn't I go my death?"

"Yes, you did, Sal. But didn't I go the whole animal."

"Yes, you did, Dick. You are the yallerest flower[30] of the forest."

They take a little, treat the fiddler, and are again ready. No—Ben has to mend his suspender, and pull up his breeches. Now they are. Out goes Tom, and calls for her favorite tune of jay-bird, but she was admonished that she had once been before the church for that same profanity, and was ordered to be seated. Names here, at that time, were no true indication of the sex, and are not entirely so to this day; for I now know a girl named Tom and a boy named Mary. However, Tom having seated herself, out walked Sal again, and called for Jim Crow.[31] Says old Ben "Miss Sal, I lub to see yur—yur so limber on de floor." But Sal had on the shoes—a proof that she had worn her nails off. So soon as Ben struck up, many joined in, and when he stopped every woman in the house was on the floor, being afraid of the consequence of the last line. This was danced in a different style from the other, and while Ben with his banjo and feet kept time, he sung the following lines:

> "My old misses she don't like me,
> Bekase I don't eat de black eye pea;
> My old misses she dont like me,
> Bekase I don't eat de black eye pea.

My old misses long time ago,
She took me down de hill side to jump Jim Crow.
Fus 'pon de heel tap, den 'pon de toe,
Eb'ry Monday morning I jump Jim Crow.

Oh Lord, ladies, don't you know
You nebber git to Heben till you jump Jim Crow.
(Repeat—"My old misses," &c.)

But even the world must have an end—so the dance closed; but not until the shoes had been worn by nearly all present.

Not one of that crowd danced more, got in a love scrape sooner, drank more whiskey, saw more fun, or sat up later than David Crockett; for next morning beheld him an early riser, not having retired during the evening, suffering the after-claps[32] always attendant upon a night of dissipation. It being the first excess he was ever known to be guilty of, nothing else was talked about. With him the only care, save for the sickness under which he was then laboring, was the fear that his intended might find it out. However, after the whiskey which he drank had evaporated, from being spread over the ground, and he had somewhat recovered, conscience stricken he mounted his horse, and unwillingly urged him on to visit his mistress. The distance diminished even faster than he wished it, and he rode up to a house, distant about a mile from the place of his destination, to enquire the news, or rather to saunter his time away. Dismounting and going in, he there met with a sister of his intended bride. After the usual common place salutations, he made some enquiry after her who was dearest to him, and ascertained that she was to be married on that very evening to another man. His riding whip slipped from between his fingers; his lower jaw involuntarily fell. With mouth open, and eyes staring wildly, he gazed upon the messenger of this unwelcome news. The remainder of the company, not knowing the cause of his surprise, gazed as wildly at him. However, the tidings being too true, and corroborated beyond all doubt, he remounted, and again sought the scene of frolicking, there to forget, amid the gay and light-hearted, his own deep suffering and mortification. He was the last to leave the place, and then went home to the Quaker's, whose sympathies were much enlisted in his favor, upon a recital of his sufferings.

CHAPTER III.

PECUNIARY misfortunes we submit to: the loss of our dearest friends we become reconciled to: but a rejection, where the feelings are much interested, creates sensations which belong exclusively to that situation. There are no terms which can define them, nor are they ever felt under other circumstances. In other misfortunes, their certainty enables us to bear them. But in a rejection, there is always a species of suspense, or hope, which will exist in the face of a thousand denials. What! Hope not exist, because a lovely woman has said *no*—because *she* has said *no*, whose only method consists in going counter to all method—because she has said *no*, whose determination, when once made, is so fixed that it has given rise to the following lines:

> "Stamp it on the running stream,
> Print it on the moon's pale beam,
> And each evanescent letter
> Shall be firmer, fairer, better,
> And more permanent, I ween,
> Than the thing those letters mean."[33]

Yet there is something very sickening in a rejection. It unhinges one—relaxes all his muscles, and produces a state of feeling very nearly allied to that which a man feels who is to be hung, from the time the scaffold is knocked loose until the rope catches him. During that single moment of descent, liver, lights, *etc.* endeavor to go out through the mouth. But I hate to think of a rejection; for I always recollect the general consolation attending it. A woman most generally tenders her friendship in lieu of her love which is asked—a sufficient requital, heaven knows! But the other sex will tell you to stand it like a man! Yes, stand it like a man, when you can't stand it! I have seen many a poor fellow, worse off than I could describe him, puffed up for an instant with this consolation. I should, myself, rather undertake to prevent the appearance of a comet, than stand it like a man. But lovely woman! all thy foibles are but graces, when understood—and though I agree with David, that "the devil and all is in woman," yet I will love thee, if my only requital be occasionally the hanging scene.

Thinking of the ladies, I have forgotten David, and I hope my reader will not require me to tell what he has been at since I left him; for, of all things, I hate to dwell upon time subsequent to a rejection. It is a horrible portion of a man's life. Besides, I don't think a man has a right to mope, and pretend to pine away, and look mad, and be disagreeable to every body he meets with, because a lady cannot love him. By doing so, he pays but a poor compliment to the remainder, and shows great ignorance of the sex:

"What careth she for hearts, when once possessed."[34]

Rather stand it like a man, and be consoled, not by the trite adage that "there are as good fish in the sea as ever were caught out of it"—for I do not mean to make so *scaly* a comparison—but, reflect that where pearls are found, more may be. There is no philosophy in one's making a blockhead of himself. If a woman don't love you, you would not marry her: then cease teasing, and *drop* it. This was the philosophy which then governed David; and so far from having to part from him on account of one small mishap, I hope to be able to place him in a situation where he may have another chance of experiencing that delightful sensation, felt only between the scaffold and the end of the rope.

Some short time after David's first misfortune, he happened to meet with a female cousin, who told him there was to be a great reaping and flax-pulling[35] in the neighborhood, at which there were to be many girls; and that she had no doubt that the woman he was destined to marry, would be among the number. This was enough. It set his imagination at work, and he returned home, once more indulging in happy anticipations. He then went over to a neighboring Quaker's, where lived an apprentice boy, his associate, and to him communicated the prospect for fun. He caught like tinder the contagion, and both resolved to go, at all hazards. The apprentice was to ask his master's permission, and David was to labor with him, when the frolic was over, to make up for lost time. However, the master would not hear of the proposition, and reminded David of the reputation he had already obtained by a frolic. But go they would, even counter to orders. So much fun could not be lost. The agreement settled upon was, that David should go over to the frolic, in the morning, and his friend would get a couple of the old Quaker's horses, and come in the evening, though about six miles, in time for the dance. The appointed day came, and away to the reaping and flax-pulling went David.

It was a lovely morning, and the scene one of life and happiness. There was only air enough to stir the dark ringlets of the girls, or impart to fields of yellow grain the gentle undulations of the ocean.

When David arrived there, he found many assembled, and already engaged in their labors. In one field, were to be seen the girls playful and happy—performing their tasks, and striving to excel. In another was to be heard the joyous song of the reapers, while their voices kept tune to the sweep of the sickle. His heart bounded with joy, and he was soon in the midst of them. The beauty of a harvest field, the universal cheerfulness which prevails over it, and the reflection that the husbandman is reaping the reward of his labor, render it one of the most interesting scenes in nature, and has served to identify it with festivity and rejoicing.

Having finished their labors, the reapers sung with full chorus the harvest home, while they bent their way to the field where the girls were engaged in pulling flax, vieing who should finish soonest. When they arrived there all was silence—nothing could be heard save the pulling of the flax. To the girls it was a moment of great interest. The young men were about to select their partners. The formality of introductions had not at that time crept into the backwoods, and David sauntered among the gathering of girls, in order to find out who was most beautiful, or who would suit his fancy best.[36] He was soon observed to pace backwards and forwards a small spot of ground, as if for the purpose of examining the features of a little girl engaged in her task, not far distant. A moment more, he was at her side, pulling flax, and endeavoring to make her excel her companions. This was the benefit of a partner; and it frequently happened that the lady who accomplished her task first, was more indebted to her beauty for doing so, than to her industry. Whether David's partner was pretty or not, I never knew. I have no doubt he thought so.

The day passed off pleasantly, and happily came on the evening dance. There was no fashion—no finery—no short frocks—no corsetts. They did not encircle each other through the many windings of a waltz; nor were they skilled in the less fashionable cotillion. But with neat plain garments of their own manufacture, and with figures such as nature made them, they met, after the toils of the day were over, to give loose to the feelings of their innocent hearts. Nor must I forget him, not who is master of ceremonies, for there was none, but he who presides over the scene.[37] His full heart overflows with joy, and brimful of hospitality, he sets before them all his little farm affords. Is it necessary that fashion should preside, or glittering show lend its ornaments, that the heart may be feasted? Is it requisite that pride or wealth should lend its influence? No—

> "For a' that, and a' that,
> Their tinsel show, and a' that;
> The honest man, tho' e'er sae poor,
> Is king o' men, for a' that."[38]

I fear, that for my city readers this simple narrative will have no charms. But to my mind there is something refreshing in turning from the dissipation of a city, to look upon a rural fete—from etiquette and rigid forms to nature as it is. It reminds one of the days which in some measure, once characterized our country, and which now characterize Scotland and part of England. It reminds one of all that is happy. It seems peculiarly the home of love.

When they met that evening, all were gladsome. Awhile they trip the country dance—then exchange it only for some amusement less fatiguing, or for one which promises more pleasure. Even conundrums (I hate them, for they always remind me of rail-road stockings,[39] which I abominate) were unknown. But, by the by, why is the loveliest and best woman we ever meet with, like the Prince of Darkness? Do you give it up? No. Well, then, I can't tell you.

The pastimes of our infancy ever interest us; chiefly from their simplicity, or else from the fact that we wonder how things so silly could have delighted us then. Plays which had been fashionable when their grandmother's [*sic*] were girls, such as Sell the Thimble, Grind the Bottle, &c.[40] were called up and wearied out. Nothing seemed to give more enjoyment than a play termed, "We are on our way to Baltimore."[41] This, from its title was probably picked up by David, during his wanderings; and derived its chief charm from the circumstance, that every couple who composed it, had to kiss each other at stated pauses. It consisted of a wild and irregular dance, during which, with measured steps, the following lines were sweetly chanted:

"We are on our way to Baltimore,
With two behind, and two before;
Around, around, around we go,
Where oats, peas, beans, and barley grow,
In waiting for somebody.
                (A kiss.)

'Tis thus the farmer sows his seed,
Folds his arms, and takes his ease,
Stamps his feet, and claps his hands,
Wheels around, and thus he stands,
In waiting for somebody.
            (Another kiss.)

David's partner was a bewitching creature, and ere they had finished dancing "We are on our way to Baltimore," she had initiated him into all the delightful mysteries of love. From the rapid progress which he generally made in the affections of his mistress, it must be conceded that he could love more in a given time than any other man. For we will here find him, though introduced as a stranger, engaged to be married, before the evening is over.[42]

About eleven o'clock, who should step in but the apprentice boy, ripe for fun—having, after his master had retired to rest, taken out of the stable, according to agreement, a couple of horses. Upon going out to put them up, there they stood, covered with perspiration; and in lieu of saddles there were two bundles of hay, upon one of which the apprentice had rode, and brought the other for his friend David.

They drank on that night their fill of amusement, and just before the break of day, David, having arranged matters with his love, and fixed upon a time for a visit, when he was to ask her mother's consent, set off with his friend for home.

They had to ride a rapid race. The first light of morning was coming forth, when, in passing a neighboring Quaker's, who happened to be out, they were discovered. A halt was called: the affair must be concealed. So David, returning, rode up to the Quaker's, made a full confession, and implored his secrecy. It was the first time he had offended; would never do so again; would be marked in his future conduct; that a discovery would forever ruin the apprentice boy. These, with sundry other arguments, finally prevailed; and on they rode. The horses were rubbed, and put away; and the friends by means of a pole, climbed in at one of the upper windows.

Scarcely were they quiet, when the apprentice boy was called by his master, to get up and be stirring. David's Sunday clothes for a moment plagued him. They went down together.

Quaker.—Why, David, how came thee here?

David.—I went over to the frolic, sir; got tired, quit, and came over here; and my friend got up and let me in.

Quaker.—Thee had better have taken my advice.

David.—Yes, sir, I wish I had; it would have saved me a long walk.

So the affair was entirely concealed, and the whole matter passed off smoothly. David's time hung heavily on his hands, until the day appointed for his visit arrived. Rigging himself in his best clothes, he borrowed a horse, and set out to see his intended. Upon arriving at the house, he was told that she was visiting a neighbor's; and over he went to see her.

Riding up to the house where she was, many people had collected; and to tell his business, or not attempt to conceal it, was more than his modesty could bear. So, feigning an excuse, he asked if they had seen any thing of a bay filley, belonging to his friend the Quaker, which had strayed off—he himself having left her in the stable at home.[43] He observed that many smiled, and looked quite knowing, as in truth they were—the mother of the girl having told the object of his visit before his arrival; not being able, in common with her sex, to keep a secret. However, David soon managed to get an interview, and persuaded his intended to take a seat behind him, and return to her mother's. As he rode off with his tender charge, some wag among the crowd cried out "I expect you have found your bay filly now!" Reader, if you were ever in love, you can imagine the feelings of David, at this specimen of backwoods humor; if not, I can give you no better idea of them, than by using his own language: "I wish I may be damned if I know how I felt; but I tell you what, it made me feel quite all-overish." Nevertheless, he spent his time very pleasantly, and had a day appointed for his wedding.

Not long after this visit, a wolf hunt was agreed on; and accordingly on a fixed day the neighbors all set out. David being unacquainted with the woods, got lost, and wandered about, not being able to ascertain where he was. Most gentle reader, methinks you seem thunderstruck at the annunciation that David Crockett was lost in the woods! But I beg you to bear in mind that he received his knowledge not by intuition, but by experience; and at this time he had not commenced his favorite pursuit of hunting.

As the day was drawing to a close, and David was expecting to spend the night alone in the woods, what should he see but a female figure wandering about, apparently lost. Upon making towards it, he beheld before him the woman who had pledged herself to be his, and his only. An explanation took place, which accounted for her situation. She had left home in the morning, in order to drive up the horses to go to meeting, and wandering off was unable to get back. David gave a narration of himself, and together did they thank kind fortune for having, in a sportive humor, brought about so remarkable a meeting.

A godsend of this sort, one never forgets: not even in the dull afternoon of life; but it is ever looked upon as a little green isle in the waste of early years, which the fancy still delights to visit and linger on as at home. They luckily, in a short time, came in sight of a hospitable roof, where they were entertained with much kindness. On the next day David attended her home; and the time fixed for his wedding being close at hand, he there remained until he was married.[44]

CHAPTER IV.

DAVID CROCKETT being married, we have now to look upon him in a new light, but in one not less amusing. We will find him in no disposition to forego pleasure or avoid a frolic; and will contemplate the outbreaking of that peculiarity of talent which has served to identify him with the country in which he lives.

I fear we shall not be able to relieve him from the poverty which was ever his attendant; for we find him for two years after his marriage living with his wife's mother, and making barely enough for a support. From this situation he removed and settled upon Elk river;[45] when, the late war[46] breaking out, he left home, and served as a volunteer in defence of his country. After serving several months, he obtained permission to return home; but having tasted the excitement of battle, the pleasure of company, etc. he became unhappy, and again sought the army.

He was in many skirmishes, and always bore among his comrades the reputation of a brave man. He was at Tallisahatchee, Talladago, Pensacola, and would have been at New Orleans,[47] but for an accident. Serving under General Jackson, he became personally acquainted with him, and was sincerely and devotedly his friend, until circumstances connected with his political life, brought about a separation.[48]

During his stay in the army, he found a field for the exercise of that talent which nature had so eminently endowed him. Without education, without the refinement of good society, perfectly a child of nature, and thrown by accident among men raised like himself, on the frontiers, and consequently uneducated, he was perfectly at home. Naturally of a fine person, with a goodness of heart rarely equaled, and a talent for humor never excelled, he soon found his way to the hearts of his messmates. No man ever enjoyed a greater degree of personal popularity, than did David Crockett, while with the army; and his success in political life is mainly attributable to that fact. I have met with many of his messmates, who spoke of him with the affection of a brother, and from them have heard many anecdotes, which convince me how much goodness of heart he really possesses. He not unfrequently would lay out his own money to buy a blanket for a suffering soldier; and never did he own a dollar which was not at the service of the first friend who called for it. Blessed with a memory which never forgot any thing, he seemed merely a depository of anecdote: while at the same time, to invent, when at a loss, was as easy as to narrate those which he had already heard. These qualities made him the rallying point for fun, with all his messmates, and served to give him that notoriety which he now possesses. Vanity or refinement were terms that he hardly knew the meaning of, and his mind, untaught by rigid rules, roved free as the wild beasts he hunted, and sometimes gave vent to expressions, and to ideas, which could never have been conceived by any other individual. This slight sketch will perhaps be doubted. But to those who doubt, I would say—go and hunt with Colonel Crockett for a week, and you will then believe, and never regret the time spent.

While Mr. Crockett was absent, fighting in defence of his country, he met with a severe misfortune in the death of his wife, which rendered it necessary for him to return, and take care of his children. This event served to wean him from all thoughts of the army, kept him closely at home, and for some time changed the general tenor of his life.

Duty to his children required that he should seek a helpmate; and accordingly he selected for his companion the widow of a deceased friend.[49] He then removed to Laurens county,[50] where circumstances forced him to figure in a different sphere. Here his popularity secured him the office of justice of the peace. Soon after this he was elected colonel; and finally a representative in the state legislature. To fill these various offices,[51] he was invited by the partiality of his friends; but his success is mainly attributable to energy of character, and to the possession of that talent, in an eminent degree, which enables a man to recognise every person he meets, whether he knows him or not; and to enquire, without being discomposed, after wives and children, who have long since been swept from existence.

Colonel Crockett was flattered by being elected to the legislature; but, satisfied that he was called upon to discharge a duty for which his early life had rendered him unqualified, he felt awkward. However, he took his seat, and the preliminary business of electing door keepers, clerks, etc. having been gone through, he discovered many persons presenting what they termed "bills," and being fresh from the backwoods, and unacquainted with the rules of a deliberative body, took up an idea, that, as many others were presenting bills, he must do so too. So he got a friend to draft a bill, rose in his seat, and with much confidence presented it. The object of it, I have now forgotten, though I was satisfied at the time of his narration to me, of its propriety. The bill was opposed by Mr. M——l,[52] who, during the discussion, thought proper to travel out of his way, to allude to Colonel Crockett, as the gentleman from the *cane*, in rather disparaging terms.[53]

The Colonel's mettle began to rise: so that, when Mr. M——l seated himself, upon many persons crying out, "Crockett, answer him—Crockett, answer him," he determined to do so. His diffidence for a time prevented him from rising—but his embarrassed situation is more happily described in his own language. "Well, I had never made a speech in my life. I didn't know whether I would speak or not; and they kept crying out to me, 'Crockett, answer him—Crockett, answer him:—why the hell don't you answer him?' So up I popped. I was as mad as hell: and there I stood, and damn the word could I get out. Well, I bothered, and stammered and look[ed] foolish, and still there I stood; but after a while I began to talk. I don't know what I said about my *bill*, but I jerked it into *him*. I told him that he had got hold of the wrong man; that he didn't know who he was fooling with; that he reminded me of the meanest thing on God's earth, a damned old coon dog, barking up the wrong tree."

But the Colonel was not satisfied; for, says he, "After the house adjourned, seeing Mr. M———l walking off alone, I followed him, and proposed a walk. He consented, and we went something like a mile, when I called a halt. Said I, 'M———l, do you know what I brought you here for?' 'No.' 'Well, I brought you here for the express purpose of whipping you, and I'll be damned if I don't mean to do it.' But the fellow said he didn't mean any thing, and kept apologising, till I got into a good humor. We then went back together; and I don't believe any body ever knew any thing about it."

"I'll tell you another story of this same man: 'twan't long after my difficulty with M———l, before he got into a fight with a member of the senate, in which he was worsted—for he had his ruffle torn off, and by accident it remained on the battle ground. I happened to go there next morning, and having heard of the circumstance, knew how the ruffle came there. I didn't like M———l much, and I determined to have some fun. So, I took up his fine cambric ruffle and pinned it to my coarse cotton shirt—made it as conspicuous as possible, and when the house met, strutted in. I seated myself near M———l; when the members, understanding how it was, soon filled the house with a roar of laughter. M———l couldn't stand it, and walked out. I, thinking he might want a fight, though I had tried him, followed after; but it didn't take place; and after a while he came up to me, and asked if that wasn't his ruffle. I told him yes, and presenting it, observed that I looked upon it as the flag of the lower house, which, in battle, had been borne off by the senate; and, that being a member of the lower house, I felt it my duty to retake it."

The "gentleman from the *cane*" was soon known to every member of both houses, and never was there a species of fun going on, but Colonel Crockett must have a hand in it. Thus did he become exceedingly popular, and his annunciation, declining to serve for another term, caused much regret.

Colonel Crockett had vested the scrapings of his industry in a mill, which was scarcely completed before a freshet[54] swept it off, and left no trace of its existence. Retiring to bed, comfortably situated, he awoke next morning flat without a dollar. So that, ever was he mere sport for fortune. But he had been schooled too deeply in *misfortune* to murmer at his luck, or spend his time in idle regret. He saw that, without capital, where he was, he could scarcely support himself. So, winding up his business, a short time found a little family, with a couple of pack horses, heavily laden, travelling on, deeper into the "far off West." In advance of this party, humming a song, walked a cheerful, light-hearted backwoodsman, with a child on one arm and a rifle on the other, followed by half a dozen dogs.

This incident in the life of Colonel Crockett, simple as it is, is fraught with philosophy; and if attended to, may compensate some reader for the perusal of this volume. How many of us, when we meet with misfortunes, are rather disposed to give way than to bear up against them. How many of us curse what we call our luck, and some even indulge in farther profanity. Yet how idle! Will our cursing or fretting restore our losses? Or will our sinking beneath the weight of misfortune, call forth tears of sympathy from a cold, calculating, interested[55] world? He is little versed in the ways of the world, who thinks so. Mankind are ever disposed to press down him who is sinking. It is human nature. We are all struggling to accomplish some object, and the more we keep beneath us the better our prospect. One is rarely assisted, unless his energy of character is forcing him ahead against accumulating circumstances: or unless he is so situated as not to require it. In either case, then, self-interest prompts assistance, and in the latter you will have it forced upon you. This idea I have often seen illustrated, when seated on the margin of a little stream, watching the fish endeavoring to get up its rapids: the larger ones ever chase away the smaller, to make room for themselves.

We curse our luck, and even call down the vengeance of heaven upon us. Yes! When—rarely is there an exception—if we analyze our loss, it may be traced to some imprudence of our own. Action is the soul of every thing. If we meet with a loss, regret is idle, and the sooner we get to work, the sooner it is repaired.

I do not mean to inculcate the idea that it is necessary to move whenever one meets with a misfortune. Nothing is more absurd: and no country can give a more forcible illustration of my remark than the "far off West." Thousands of young men, of worth, of character, and of family, have flooded the west, to better their fortunes. They come here with anticipations of immediate success; and there are so many engaged in the same enterprise, that disappointment must be the inevitable consequence. And they spend their time, either brooding over past days, which then seem happy, or fall into the too prevalent customs of our country, drinking and gaming; then sicken and die away, under the withering influence of blighted hopes. The learned professions in this country are crowded beyond any thing I have ever seen; consequently the wreck of talent is great. Often have I met with examples which chilled me to the heart. Often have I seen one, who may, by the coruscations of his genius,[56] have shone conspicuous in the circle from which he came, in some far land, and whose parents are yet shaping out "Oh! such bright hopes of future greatness," sinking into nothingness, from cold neglect. Often do they sink into despondency, lamenting the loss of that society to which they have been accustomed, and of which, here, they cannot taste the sweets.

These remarks are intended only to apply to the more unsettled portions of the "far off West," where, from the transitory nature of its inhabitants, and from the fact that they are made up of representatives from every region between the two circles, it is impossible that talent can be as much respected, or as highly appreciated as it is in a more settled society. A frontier country is no place for a man of modesty, of refinement, or of delicacy; and it must ever be, that in a society so constituted, success is as often the result of accident as the consequence of merit.[57]

But to our narrative. When Colonel Crockett was next heard from, he had settled himself about one hundred and fifty miles from his former residence, in Gibson county, Western District;[58] and was hard at work, putting up log cabins. His children were all too young to be any service to him, so that all the labor requisite for forming a new settlement was performed by himself. His cabins were built; a well was dug; a little patch was cleared for corn; and the Colonel found himself in the bosom of our western forest, forty miles from any settlement.

Colonel Crockett was never avaricious; and a change in his circumstances, from bad to worse, had no effect upon his spirits. They were too buoyant, too playful, ever to yield to any misfortune: so that, although at home above all others in a crowd, he seemed equally pleased with the deepest solitude. Here he became wedded to hunting, and the great quantity of game was well calculated to have fascinated any one. Being cut off from all society, his rifle and dogs were ever his companions. Even the face of the country he had chosen to dwell in, seemed, in some measure, the counterpart of his mind. It was wild and irregular, and, like himself subject to no restraint. Here, one moment, all nature was hushed into silence; the next, the earth seemed rocking to its centre. He had chosen to settle in that section of the country where the earthquake of 1812 was most sensibly felt, east of the Mississippi river. That country has been subject to slight shocks ever since, and the Colonel remarked to me, that frequently while at work, he has had his clothes or hat shaken down, but would merely hang them up, and continue his labor.

CHAPTER V.

THE[d] earthquake of 1812[59] has often been described; but I must mention a few incidents connected with it, as the scene of many hunting stories, as well as the residence of Colonel Crockett, lies in that section of the country where its effects were most felt east of the Mississippi river. This section of country is termed the *Shakes*,[60] and is never alluded to, in common conversation, by any other title.

The Obion river,[61] a deep and navigable stream which empties into the Mississippi nearly opposite to New Madrid, was dammed up, and two considerable lakes,[62] one nearly twenty miles long and varying in its breadth, the other not quite so large, have been formed of unknown depth. The bed of the river has been changed; and fissures, or openings made in the earth by the concussion still remain—running parallel to each other, of various lengths, from three to thirty feet wide, and from ten to forty feet deep. One, to visit these *Shakes*, would see striking marks of the gigantic power of an earthquake. He would find the largest forest trees split from their roots to their tops, and lying half on each side of a fissure. He would find them split in every direction and lying in all shapes. At the time of this earthquake, no persons were living where those lakes have been formed. Colonel Crockett was among the nearest settlers; and to this day, there is much of that country entirely uninhabited, and even unknown. Several severe hurricanes have passed along, blowing down all the trees in one direction, and an undergrowth[63] has sprung up, making these places almost impenetrable to man.

This section of country which has been visited by the shakes, forms the best hunting grounds in the west. There are bears, wolves, panthers, deer, elk, wild cats, etc. in abundance; and this is the only place within my knowledge east of the Mississippi, where elk are yet to be found.

These lakes are famed above all places for their great quantity of honey—I presume from the fact that the immense number of trees which were killed by the formation of the lakes have afforded excellent hives. A bee-hunter told me he had remained in one spot, and counted in sight eighty bee trees. They have been much hunted, and are now becoming more scarce. A few settlements for the purpose of hunting, have lately been formed on the margin of these lakes, which besides the game enumerated, are filled with wild geese, ducks, and swans. It was to this section of country, as I before remarked, that Colonel Crockett removed, after his pecuniary misfortunes.

Innumerable are the anecdotes that daily occurred, while with no companion save his favorite *Betsey*, (his rifle,) or with his son and dogs sometimes added, he roved the forest.

Still hunting is with all hunters a favorite amusement. It requires more talent, and gives a wider field for the formation of stratagems and the exercise of ingenuity than any other species of the same occupation. There are many modes practised by a wary hunter of approaching game, even in an open field, which are attended with success. One will steal up while it is feeding—remaining perfectly still, and personating a stump, when it becomes the least alarmed. His progress is gradual and at stolen intervals. The object which he wishes to shoot becomes familiarized to the stump, as it supposes, and the hunter approaches as near as he wishes. Another personating a hog, will, upon his hands and knees, root himself along, until within shooting distance. Either of these modes, when practised with skill, often proves successful. But there are a thousand plans, the best of which the hunter must select, and will be governed in his choice entirely by circumstances.

His favorite *Betsey*, as he termed her, I had the pleasure of shooting. She is a large, coarse, common rifle, with a flint lock, and from appearance has been much used. In her breech there is a wire hole or two with feathers in them, and several parts of her may be found wrapped with a wax thread, for the purpose of healing up wounds which she has received in her passage through life.

To bear hunting Colonel Crockett has ever been most wedded; first, because it is profitable; secondly, because there is danger in it, and consequently great excitement. It requires a *man* to be a bear hunter; for he is frequently thrown into situations which require as much coolness and determined purpose of mind as though he were in a regular battle. All hunters agree in saying that its meat is superior to that of any other wild game. You may drink, from its peculiar sweetness, (and it will never be attended with the slightest inconvenience,) a pint of pure bear oil at a draught.

Occasionally settlers began to locate near him, and Colonel Crockett was called on for meat. If he had it, it was theirs—if not, he would take his dogs, go over, and kill them as much as they wanted. This trait in his character, always gained for him the good will of those who settled near him.

I was amused at the simplicity with which he told me the following story. "I had'nt [*sic*] been a hunter long in these backwoods, when I had an occasion to send my little son a short distance from home; he soon came galloping back, and told me he saw two large elk cross the road just before him. I gathered up my rifle and accoutrements—jumped upon the horse—took up my son behind me, to show where they were, and rode off. I did not think it advisable to carry my dogs; for they would at once have run them out of my hearing. The sun was something like two hours high, and the evening was calm and still. I had never at this time killed an elk, and was very anxious. I found where they had crossed the road—left my little boy the horse, to go home, and followed after them. The ground was rather hard, and their tracks almost imperceptible; but I noticed where the grass was bruised by their treading, and sometimes I could see where they had bit a bush; in this way I followed after them. I went, I s'pose, about a mile, when I see'd *my* elk feeding in a little prairie: there were no trees near me; so I got down and tried to root my way to 'em, but they had got a notion of me, for they would feed a while, and then turn their heads back and look for me, and then run off a little. We soon got into the woods agin, and I begun to work 'em right badly. When they were feeding, I'd git a tree 'tween me and them, and run as hard as I could, then peep round to see 'em, and get down, root myself behind another tree, and then run agin. The woods were mighty open and I could see 'em a long way, and I'd have got a shot, but as I was creeping 'long after 'em, I see'd five deer coming towards me. I stopped right still, and they come feeding 'long close to me: when they got in about twenty yards of me, I raised old Betsy,ᵉ levelled her, and down dropped the largest; the others raised their heads and looked astonished; went up to the one which was down, and smelt him, but didn't seem afraid of me. I spoke not, and the report of the rifle was the only noise. Having loaded, I raised old Bet agin, and down come another; the others only looked more astonished. I shot down a third, and the remainder still kept looking on. Coming off in a hurry, I brought but few balls, and my fourth load contained the last. I thought I must have *my elk*; so I wouldn't shoot another deer. I have never seen any thing like that since, in all my hunting. I don't believe they had ever seen a man before; for they wasn't the least afraid of me. Well, as I was saying, I thought I must have my elk—so I just left the deer lying there, and I was sorry I'd killed them, and off I started. I found their tracks, and followed on 'till I agin see'd 'em; 'twas getting late in the evening when I come in sight of 'em; they had somewhat forgotten me, tho' they were still a little shy—so, pursuing my former plan, I gained on 'em, but they still had a notion of me, and I could'nt git a close shoot. The sun was down, and it was growing a little dim, and I found I must either shoot or lose 'em; so I resolved to take the first chance. Again getting a tree 'tween me and them, I run as hard as I could up to it; and upon peeping round, there stood my elk about one hundred and forty yards distant, in a tolerably clear place, with their heads turned back, looking for me. This was my only chance; so, raising up old Betsy, I fired at the one which was nearest to me: at the report of the gun, it run off, passing the one which was before it, about twenty yards, and then tumbled over. The other run on and stopped with it. The ball, as I found afterward, had entered just behind the shoulder, and ranged forward. I felt a little afraid, because they were so large; but I went up: when I got in about twenty yards of 'em, the one which was standing up began to paw the ground very violently, and shake his head at me; his horns were about six feet long, and he looked very formidable. I had nothing to shoot him with, and he seemed from his actions, determined for battle. I tried to frighten him, but I was not able to do so till I gave a shrill call, when off he run; so great is the effect of the human voice upon all animals. I then went rather nearer to the one which was lying down, walked round him several times, and kept throwing chunks, to find whether he was alive or not; but he did not move, so I went up to him, and sure enough he was as dead as could be. By this time 'twas dark—I'd wandered off about four miles, and had nothing with me but my knife: however, I set to work and butchered him on the ground, and then set off for home. I felt mighty proud of this act, because the elk was the first I had ever killed, and he was so large. Next morning, with the aid of pack horses, I got him home."

The chief thing which struck me in the above anecdote, was, that the Colonel should term them *his elk*, while they were running in the woods: it shows the great confidence he has in his gun; and I believe, from what I have seen, that Colonel Crockett feels as certain of a deer or elk which he may find in the woods, if he can get within one hundred and fifty yards of it, as if he had it in his chimney smoking, and would be as much offended were any one to frighten it, as he would be were the same individual to take one of his hogs.

Colonel Crockett, having hunted for some time, collected all his skins, loaded a horse, and set out for a store in order to barter them for groceries. This simple incident exerted a great influence on his after life. At the store, he met several acquaintances with whom he had served in the legislature, and together they spent a happy evening. Upon parting, they solicited Colonel Crockett again to become a candidate for the legislature; this he declined, telling them that there were several candidates already in the field, and that he could not hope for success. Moreover, he was an entire stranger; the election came on in a few weeks; and that he lived down in the cane, forty miles from any settlement. Believing the matter at rest, they parted. Colonel Crockett returned home, and devoted his time chiefly to hunting. Accident, however, soon afterwards threw in his way a newspaper, in which he saw himself announced as a candidate for the legislature, at the ensuing election. He viewed the matter as a quiz;[64] but after thinking of the subject, resolved to make a trial; and lent all his energy to the accomplishment of that object, with a hope of quizzing those who had attempted to quiz him.

He gave up for a time his favorite amusement, and began to mix among the people. He could occasionally hear of persons who intended to vote for the great bear hunter. He was becoming somewhat formidable, and the three other candidates agreed among themselves that two should withdraw in favor of the third. This was to be determined at some place where there was to be a very considerable gathering; and to that place, an entire stranger, went Colonel Crockett. He beat about among the crowd the greater part of the day, entirely unknown. When it was determined that B.[65] should run, the Colonel went up to a small crowd, and called for a quart of whiskey, for which he had to pay fifty cents. While it was passing about, the Colonel, still unknown, B. happened to pass along, Crockett hailed him,

"Hallo! B. you don't know me," (B. called his name and passed into the crowd,) "but I'll make you know me mighty well before August; I see they have weighed you out to me, but I'll beat you mighty badly." (Crockett not knowing a man.)

B.—"Where did you spring from Colonel?"

C.—"O! I've just crept out from the cane, to see what discoveries I could make among the whites—you think you have greatly the advantage of me B. 'tis true I live forty miles from any settlement; I am very poor, and you are very rich; you see it takes two 'coon skins here to buy a quart, but I've good dogs, and my little boys at home will go their death to support my election; they are mighty industrious; they hunt every night till twelve o'clock; but it keeps the little fellows mighty busy to keep me in whiskey. When they gets tired, I takes my rifle and goes out and kills a wolf, for which the state pays me three dollars; so one way or another I keeps knocking along."[66]

B.—"Well Colonel, I see you can beat me electioneering."

C.—"My dear fellow, you dont call this electioneering, do you? When you see me electioneering, I goes fixed for the purpose. I've got a suit of deer leather clothes, with two big pockets; so I puts a bottle of whiskey in one, and a twist of tobacco[67] in t'other, and starts out: then if I meets a friend, why I pulls out my bottle and gives him a drink—he'll be mighty apt, before he drinks to throw away his tobacco; so when he's done I pulls my twist out of t'other pocket and gives him a *chaw*: I never likes to leave a man worse off than when I found him. If I had given him a drink, and he had lost his tobacco, he would not have made much; but give him tobacco, and a drink too, and you are mighty apt to get his vote." Though profuse in his liberality, the Colonel boasted of his economy, saying, when alone he never spent a 'coon skin, but always carried hare skins, to buy half pints. Conversing in this way, he soon became well known; and ere he left the ground, no person was more talked of than the great bear hunter.

His fondness for fun gave rise to many anecdotes: among others I have heard this, which I do not altogether believe. Colonel Crockett, while on an electioneering trip, fell in at a gathering, and it became necessary for him to treat the company. His finances were rather low, having but one 'coon skin about him; however, he pulled it out, slapped it down on the counter, and called for its value in whiskey. The merchant measured out the whiskey and threw the skin into the loft. The Colonel, observing the logs very open, took out his ramrod, and upon the merchant turning his back, twisted his 'coon skin out, and pocketed it: when more whiskey was wanted, the same skin was pulled out, slapped upon the counter, and its value called for. This trick was played until they were all tired drinking.[68]

About this time an incident also occurred, somewhat amusing, and which will serve to give a further illustration of the backwoods. The Colonel's opponent was an honorable man, but proud and haughty in his bearing. This, of course, was laid aside as much as practicable, while he was electioneering. Standing one day at his window, he observed several of his friends passing along the road, and familiarly hailed them to call by and take a drink. They called, and upon going into the house, there was a handsome table with choice liquors, set out on the middle of the carpet, which was not large enough to cover the floor, but left on each side a vacant space around the room. On this vacant space walked B's friends, without ever daring to approach the table. After many and frequent solicitations, and seeing B. upon the carpet, they went up and drank; but left him manifestly with displeasure. Calling at the next house to which they came, where happened to live one of Crockett's friends, they asked what kind of a man was the great bear hunter; and received for answer, that he was a good fellow, but very poor, and lived in a small log cabin, with a dirt floor. They all cried out he was the man for them, and swore they would be damned sooner than support any man as proud as B. They never having seen a carpet before, swore that B. had invited them to his house to take a drink, and had spread down one of his best bed quilts for them to walk upon, and that it was nothing but a piece of pride.[69]

CHAPTER VI.

WHILE electioneering, the Colonel always conciliates every crowd into which he may be thrown, by the narration of some anecdote. It is his manner, more than the anecdote, which delights you. Having been a great deal with the Dutch, he draws very liberally on them whenever he wants to make sport.[70] I once had the pleasure of seeing Colonel Crockett the centre of some dozen persons, to whom he was telling the following story of a Dutchman, whose hen house had met with some mishap, and who, afterwards meeting with Colonel Crockett thus went on: "Well, cot tam it, what you tink, a cot tam harricoon come to my hinkle stall" (hen house) "an picked out ebery hair out de backs of all my young hinkles; so I goes ober to brudder Richards, an gets his fox-trap; an as I comes back, I says to myself, I'll catch de cot tam harricoon. So I takes de fox trap an goes to my hinkle stall, an I didn't set it outside, an I didn't set it inside, but I puts it down jist dere. So next morning I goes to my hinkle stall, an sure enough, I had de cot tam harricoon fast; an he wasn't white, an he wasn't black, an ebery hair was off he tail," (opossum) "an soon as he see me, he look so shame—ah! you cot tam harricoon, you kill my hinkles, heh! an I hit him a lick, an he lay down, an he look so sorry, he make me tink he repent; so I turn him loose. Well, now what do you tink; I goes to my hinkle stall next morning, an dere lay my old speckled hinkle, an ebery hair was out her back; so I goes ober to brudder Richards gin, an gits his fox trap, to catch de tam harricoon; an I carried it to de hinkle stall, an I didn't set it outside, an I didn't set it inside; but I puts it down jist dere; an sure enough, next morning I had de old harricoon gin; an he wasn't white, an he wasn't black, but he was white, an he was black, spotted all ober," (pole cat)[71] "an I goes up to him, ah! you's de cot tam harricoon dat catch my old speckled hinkle, heh! you de tam rascal! an I hits him a lick, an he lif he tail up, an ebery deble in hell might smell him, for I smell him de whole time."

Pursuing this course, he laughs away any prejudice which may exist against him; and having created a favorable impression, enforces his claims by local arguments, showing the bearing which great national questions have upon the interests of the persons whom he wishes to represent. This mode, together with the facility of being a boon companion to every one he meets, generally enables him to accomplish his object.

Over his competitor B., he was elected with much ease; and served for four successive years in the legislature, notwithstanding, he moved during the time more than one hundred and fifty miles, and was consequently dependent upon strangers for his second election. This is a forcible truth, of the great power of his talent for electioneering.

While in the legislature, there was a bill before it for the creation of a county. The author of it wished to run the boundary lines, so as to support his popularity; to this the Colonel was opposed, because his interests were affected by it. They were hammering at it for some time: whatever the author of the bill would effect by speaking, the Colonel would undo by logrolling; until the matter was drawing to a close, when he rose, and made the following speech:

"Mr. Speaker.—Do you know what that man's bill reminds me of? Well, I 'spose you don't, so I'll tell you. Well, Mr. Speaker, when I first came to this country, a blacksmith was a rare thing; but there happened to be one in my neighborhood, he had no striker, and whenever one of the neighbors wanted any work done, he had to go over and strike, till his work was finished. These were hard times, Mr. Speaker, but we had to do the best we could. It happened that one of my neighbors wanted an axe, so he took along with him a piece of iron, and went over to the blacksmith's to strike till his axe was done. The iron was heated, and my neighbor fell to work, and was striking there nearly all day; when the blacksmith concluded the iron wouldn't make an axe, but 'twould make a fine mattock;[72] so my neighbor wanting a mattock, concluded he would go over, and strike till his mattock was done; accordingly, he went over the next day, and worked faithfully, but towards night, the blacksmith concluded his iron wouldn't make a mattock, but 'twould make a fine ploughshare;[73] so my neighbor wanting a ploughshare, agreed he would go over the next day and strike till that was done; according he again went over, and fell hard to work, but towards night the blacksmith concluded his iron wouldn't make a plough-share, but 'twould make a fine *skow*;[74] so my neighbor, tired working, cried, a skow let it be—and the blacksmith taking up the red hot iron threw it into a trough of water near him, and as it fell in, it sung out *sknow*. And this, Mr. Speaker, will be the way with that man's bill for a county; he'll keep you all here doing nothing, and finally his bill will turn out a *skow*, now mind if it don't."

Whenever the Colonel was out of the legislature, he was either at work upon his little farm, or engaged in his favorite pursuit of hunting; and in this way, has the most of his life been spent. By hunting, he has supplied himself, and all his neighbors with meat; and there lives no man, who has undergone more hardships, done more acts of friendship, or who has been more exposed to all changes of weather, than David Crockett. He has lived almost entirely in the woods, and his life has been a continued scene of anecdote, to one fond of hair-breadth escapes, and hunting stories.

The following story will be read with intense interest, both, on account of the original ideas which it may present; and likewise, as it will serve to illustrate the character of Colonel Crockett in a new light. I shall give it as far as my recollection serves me, in the Colonel's own language.

"Well, as I have told you, it has been a custom with me ever since I moved to this country, to spend a part of every winter in bear hunting, unless I was engaged in public life. I generally take a tent, pack horses, and a friend 'long with me, and go down to the Shakes, where I camp out and hunt, till I get tired, or till I get as much meat as I want. I do this, because there is a great deal of game there; and besides I never see any body but the friend I carry, and I like to hunt in a wilderness, where no body can disturb me. I could tell you of a thousand frolics, I've had in these same Shakes; but perhaps the following one will amuse you:[75]

"Sometime in the winter of 1824 or '25, a friend called to see me, to take a bear hunt. I was in the humor, so we got our pack horses, fixed up our tent, and provisions, and set out for the Shakes. We arrived there safe, raised our tent, stored away our provisions, and commenced hunting: for several days we were quite successful; our game we brought to the tent, salted it, and packed it away. We had several hunts, and nothing occurred worth telling, save, that we killed our game.

"But, one evening as we were coming along, our pack horses loaded with bear meat, and our dogs trotting lazily after us, old Whirlwind held up his head and looked about; then rubbed his nose agin a bush, and opened. I knew from the way he sung out, 'twas an old *he* bear. The balance of the dogs buckled in, and off they went right up to a hollow. I gave up the horses to my friend, to carry 'em to the tent, which was now about half a mile distant, and set out after the dogs.

"The hollow up which the bear had gone, made a bend, and I knew he would follow it; so I run across to head him. The sun was now down; 'twas growing dark mighty fast, and 'twas cold; so, I buttoned my jacket close around me, and run on. I hadn't gone fur, before I heard the dogs tack, and they come tearing right down the hollow. Presently I heard the old bear rattling through the cane, and the dogs coming on like lightning after him. I dashed on; I felt like I had wings; my dogs made such a roaring cry; they rushed by me, and as they did I harked 'em on; they all broke out, and the woods echoed back, and back, to their voices. It seemed to me they fairly flew, for 'twasn't long before they overhauled him, and I could hear 'em fighting not fur before me. I run on, but just before I got there, the old bear made a break and got loose; but the dogs kept close up, and every once in a while they stopped him, and had a fight. I tried for my life to git up, but just before I'd git there, he'd break loose. I followed him this way for two or three miles, through briars, cane, etc. and he devilled me mightily. Once I thought I had him: I got up in about fifteen or twenty feet, 'twas so dark, I couldn't tell the bear from a dog, and I started to go to him; but I found out there was a creek between us. How deep it was I didn't know; but it was dark, and cold, and too late to turn back; so I held my rifle up and walked right in. Before I got across, the old bear got loose and shot for it, right through the cane; I was mighty tired, but I scrambled out and followed on, I knew I was obliged to keep in hearing of my dogs, or git lost.

"Well, I kept on, and once in a while, I could hear 'em fighting and baying, just before me; then I'd run up, but before I'd git there, the old bear would git loose. I sometimes thought 'bout giving up, and going back; but while I'd be thinking, they'd begin to fight agin, and I'd run on. I followed him this way, 'bout as near as I could guess, from four to five miles, when the old bear couldn't stand it any longer, and took a tree, and I tell you what, I was mighty glad of it.

"I went up, but at first it was so dark I could see nothing; however, after looking about, and gitting the tree between me and a star, I could see a very dark looking place, and I raised up old Betsy, and she lightened; down come the old bear, but he wasn't much hurt, for of all the fights you ever did see, that beat all. I had six dogs, and for nearly an hour they kept rolling and tumbling right at my feet. I couldn't see any thing but one old white dog I had; but every now and then the bear made 'em sing out right under me. I had my knife drawn, to stick him whenever he should seize me; but after a while, bear, dogs and all rolled down a precipice just before me, and I could hear them fighting like they were in a hole. I loaded Betsy, laid down, and felt about in the hole with her till I got her agin the bear and I fired; but I didn't kill him, for out of the hole he bounced; and he and the dogs fought harder than ever. I laid old Betsy down, and drew my knife; but the bear, and dogs just formed a lump, rolling about; and presently down they all went again into the hole.

"My dogs now began to sing out mighty often; they were getting tired; for it had been the hardest fight I ever saw. I found out how the bear was laying, and I looked for old Betsy to shoot him agin, but I had laid her down somewhere, and couldn't find her. I got hold of a stick and began to punch him; he didn't seem to mind it much, so I thought I would git down into the crack, and kill him with my knife.

"I considered some time 'bout this; it was ten or eleven o'clock, and a cold winter night. I was something like thirty miles from any settlement; there was no living soul near me, except my friend, who was in the tent, and I didn't know where that was—I knew my bear was in a crack made by the shakes, but how deep it was, and whether I could get out, if I got in, were things I could'nt tell. I was sitting down right over the bear, thinking, and every once in a while some of my dogs would sing out, as if they wanted help; so I got up, and let myself down in the crack behind the bear. Where I landed was about as deep as I am high; I felt mighty ticklish, and I wished I was out; I couldn't see a thing in the world, but I determined to go through with it. I drew my knife and kept feeling about with my hands and feet till I touched the bear; this I did very gently, then got upon my hands and knees, and inched my left hand up his body, with a knife in my right, till I got pretty fur up, and I plunged it into him; he sunk down and for a moment there was a great struggle; but by the time I scrambled out, every thing was getting quiet, and my dogs, one at a time, come out after me, and laid down at my feet. I knew every thing was safe.

"It began, now, to cloud up; 'twas mighty dark, and as I didn't know the direction of my tent, I determined to stay all night. I took out my flint and steel, and raised a little fire; but the wood was so cold and wet, I wouldn't burn much. I had sweated so much after the bear, that I began to get very thirsty, and felt like I would die, if I didn't git some water; so taking a light along, I went to look for the creek I had waded, and as good luck would have it, I found the creek, and got back to my bear. But from having been in a sweat all night, I was now very chilly; it was the middle of winter, and the ground was hard frozen for several inches, but this I had not noticed before; I again set to work to build me a fire, but all I could do, wouldn't make it burn. The excitement under which I had long been laboring had all died away, and I was so cold I felt very much like dying: but a notion struck me to git my bear up out of the crack; so down into it I went, and worked until I got into a sweat agin; and just as I would git him up so high, that if I could turn him over once more, he'd be out, he'd roll back. I kep working, and resting, and while I was at it, it began to hail very fine hail; but I kept on, and in about three hours I got him out.

"I then came up almost exhausted; my fire had gone out, and I laid down, and soon fell asleep; but 'twasn't long before I waked almost frozen; the wind sounded mighty cold as it passed along, and I called my dogs, and made 'em lie upon me to keep me warm; but it wouldn't do. I thought I ought to make some exertion to save my life, and I got up, but I dont know why, or wherefore; and began to grope about in the dark; the first thing I hit agin was a tree; it felt mighty slick and icy, as I hugged it, and a notion struck me to climb it; so up I started, and I climbed that tree for thirty feet before I came to any limb, and then slipped down. It was mighty warm work. How often I climbed it, I never knew; but I was going up and slipping down, for three or four hours, and when day first began to break, I was going up that tree. As soon as it was cleverly light, I saw before me a slim sweet-gum, so slick, that it looked like every *varment* in the woods had been sliding down it for a month. I started off and found my tent, where sat my companion, who had given me up for lost. I had been distant, about five miles; and after resting, I brought my friend to see the bear. I had run more perils than those described; had been all night on the brink of a dreadful chasm, where a slip of a few feet would have brought about instant death. It almost made my head giddy, to look at the dangers I had escaped. My friend swore he would not have gone in the crack that night, with a wounded bear, for every one in the woods. We had as much meat as we could carry, so we loaded our horses, and set out for home.["]

CHAPTER VII.

GENTLE reader, I know of no more agreeable way to commence this chapter, than by giving you another of Colonel Crockett's Dutch anecdotes, which he tells with great humor. There lived in one of the mountainous countries of western Virginia, many Dutchmen; and among them one named Henry Snyder; and there were likewise two brothers, called George, and Jake Fulwiler;

they were all rich, and each owned a mill. Henry Snyder was subject to slight fits of derangement, but they were not of such a nature as to render him disagreeable to any one; he merely conceived himself to be God Almighty, the Supreme Ruler of the universe; and while laboring under this infatuation, had himself a throne built, on which he sat to try the causes of all who offended him; and passed them off to Hell or Heaven, as his humor prompted him—he personating both the character of judge and culprit.

"It happened, one day, that some difficulty occurred between Henry Snyder and the two Fulwilers, on account of their mills; when to be avenged, Henry Snyder took along with him a book in which he recorded his judgments, and mounted his throne to try their causes. He was heard to pass the following judgments.

Having prepared himself, he called before him George Fulwiler.

"Shorge Fulwider, stand up. What hash you been doin in dis lower world?"

"Ah! Cot, Ich does not know."

"Well, Shorge Fulwider, hasn't you got a mill?"

"Yes, Cot, Ich hash."

"Well, Shorge Fulwider, din't you never take too much toll?"[76]

"Yes, Cot, Ich has—when der water wash low, und mein stones wash dull, Ich take leetle too much toll."

"Well, den, Shorge Fulwider, you must go to der left, mid der goats."[77]

"Well, Shake Fulwider, now you stand up. What hash *you* bin doin in dis lower world?"

"Ah! Cot, Ich does not know."

"Well, Shake Fulwider, hasn't you got a mill?"

"Yes, Cot, Ich hash."

"Well, Shake Fulwider, hasn't you never take too much toll?"

"Yes, Cot, Ich hash—when der water wash low, und mein stones wash dull, Ich take leetle too much toll."

"Well, den, Shake Fulwider, you must go to der left, mid der goats."

"Now Ich tries *mineself.* Henry Shnyder! Henry Shnyder! stand up. What hash *you* been doin in dis lower world?"

"Ah! Cot, Ich does not know."

"Well, Henry Shnyder, hasn't you got a mill?"

"Yes, Cot, Ich hash."

"Well, Henry Shnyder, didn't you never take too much toll?"

"Yes, Cot, Ich hash—when der water wash low, und mein stones wash dull, Ich hash take leetle too much toll."

"But, Henry Shnyder, vat did you *do* mid der toll?"

["]Ah! Cot, Ich gives it to der poor."

(Pausing.) "Well, Henry Shnyder, you must go to der right mid der sheep; but it ish a cot tam tight squeeze."

While the Colonel was a member of the legislature, some fellow started a report somewhat to his prejudice. After his return, at the first gathering he happened to meet with, he called the attention of the company, and mounted a stump, to explain; but his choler getting the better of his reason, he jumped down, swore he wouldn't explain, but he'll be damned if he couldn't whip the man who started the report. He could find no author, and his willingness to fight was taken as a fair proof of his innocence.

Colonel Crockett was already higher in the political world, than in early life he had ever expected to be; and had his inclination alone been consulted, his fame would have never reached Washington. He was so much wedded to hunting, that, I have no doubt he looked upon it as a sacrifice, to exchange that pursuit for any other.

The hunting stories which make a part of this work, are literally in his own style of narration; and of their truth I have not the least doubt. The reason why the names of his dogs are changed in almost every story, is, that a bear dog, if he fights regularly, is rarely good for any thing longer than one or two seasons.

Nothing delights the Colonel more than to be called upon by strangers to make a hunting party; and with the following one he was much pleased:

"I was setting by a good fire in my little cabin, on a cool November evening,—roasting potatoes I believe, and playing with my children,—when somebody halloed at the fence. I went out, and there were three strangers, who said they come to take an elk hunt. I was glad to see 'em, invited 'em in, and after supper we cleaned our guns. I took down old Betsy, rubbed her up, greased her, and laid her away to rest. She is a mighty rough old piece, but I love her, for she and I have seen hard times. She mighty seldom tells me a lie. If I hold her right, she always sends the ball where I tell her. After we were all fixed, I told 'em hunting stories till bed time.

"Next morning was clear and cold, and by times I sounded my horn, and my dogs come howling 'bout me, ready for a chase. Old Ratler was a little lame—a bear bit him in the shoulder; but Soundwell, Tiger, and the rest of 'em were all mighty anxious. We got a *bite* and saddled our horses. I went by to git a neighbor to drive for us, and off we started for the *Harricane*.[78] My dogs looked mighty wolfish; they kept jumping on one another, and growling. I knew they were run mad for a fight, for they hadn't had one in two or three days. We were in fine spirits, and going 'long through very open woods, when one of the strangers said, "I would give my horse now to see a bear." Said I "well give me your horse," and I pointed to an old bear about three or four hundred yards ahead of us, feeding on acorns. I had been looking at him for some time, but he was so fur off, I wasn't certain what it was. However, I hardly spoke before we all strained off, and the woods fairly echoed as we harked the dogs on. The old bear did'nt want to run; and he never broke till we got most upon him; but then he buckled for it, I tell you. When they overhauled him, he just *rared* up upon his hind legs, and he boxed the dogs 'bout at a mighty rate. He hugged old Tiger and another, till he dropped 'em nearly lifeless; but the others worried him, and after awhile they all come too,[79] and they give him hell. They are mighty apt, I tell you, to give a bear hell before they leave him. 'Twas a mighty pretty fight—'twould have done any one's soul good to see it, just to see how they all rolled about. It was as much as I could do to keep the strangers from shooting him; but I wouldn't let 'em fear they would kill some of my dogs. After we got tired seeing 'em fight, I went in among 'em, and the first time they got him down, I *socked* my knife into the old bear. We then hung him up, and went on to take our elk hunt. You never *seed* fellows so delighted as them strangers was. Damn if they didn't cut more capers, jumping about, than the old bear. 'Twas a mighty pretty fight, but I *b'lieve* I seed more fun looking at them than at the bear.

"By the time we got to the *Harricane*, we were all rested and ripe for a drive. My dogs were in a better humor, for the fight had just taken off the wiry edge. So I placed the strangers at the stands through which I thought the elk would pass, sent the driver way up ahead, and I went down below.

"Every thing was quiet, and I leaned old Betsy 'gin a tree, and laid down. I s'pose I had been lying there nearly an hour, when I heard old Tiger open. He opened once or twice, and old Ratler gave a long howl; the balance joined in, and I knew the elk were up. I jumped up and seized my rifle. I could hear nothing but one continued roar of all my dogs, coming right towards me. Though I was an old hunter, the music made my hair stand on end. Soon after they first started, I heard one gun go off; and my dogs stopped, but not long, for they took a little tack towards where I placed the strangers. One of them fired, and they dashed back, and circled round, way to my left. I run down 'bout a quarter of a mile, and I heard my dogs make a bend, like they were coming to me. While I was listening, I heard the bushes breaking still lower down, and started to run there. As I was going 'long, I seed two elk burst out of the *Harricane*, 'bout one hundred and thirty or forty yards below me. There was an old buck and a doe. I stopped,—waited till they got into a clean place, and as the old fellow made a leap I raised old Bet, pulled trigger, and she belched forth. The smoke blinded me so that I couldn't see what I did; but as it cleared away, I caught a glimpse of only one of 'em going through the bushes; so I thought I had the other. I went up, and there lay the old buck a kicking. I cut his throat, and by that time Tiger and two of my dogs come up. I thought it singular that all my dogs wasn't there, and I began to think they had killed another. After the dogs had bit him, and found out he was dead, old Tiger began to growl, and curled himself up between his legs. Every thing had to stand off then, for he wouldn't let the devil himself touch him.

"I started off to look for the strangers. My two dogs followed me. After gitting away a piece, I looked back, and once in awhile I could see old Tiger git up and shake the elk, to see if he was really dead, and then curl up between his legs agin. I found the strangers round a doe elk the driver had killed; and one of 'em said he was sure he had killed one lower down. I asked him if it had horns. He said he did'nt see any. I put the dogs on where he said he had shot, and they didn't go fur before they came to a halt. I went up, and there lay a fine buck elk; and though his horns were four or five feet long, the fellow who shot him was so scared, that damn me if he saw them. We had three elk and a bear, so we managed to git it home, then butchered our game, talked over our hunt, and had a glorious frolic."

While the Colonel was a member of the legislature, the tariff of '24[80] was passed by congress; and the member from his district supported it counter to the wishes of his constituents. An opposition was organized, and Colonel David Crockett was called upon by many of the people to become a candidate. There were already several in the field, when the Colonel, at the warm solicitation of his friends, entered the lists. Now there was a fair opportunity for the exhibition of that talent in which he excelled. Seventeen counties composed the district; and to be elected, his personal popularity had to overcome some talent, supported by wealth and family influence. Many speeches were made, many barbecues were eaten,—great exertions were used by all parties; and the election being over, the returns showed that in seventeen counties Colonel Crockett had been beaten *two votes*.[81]

His friends have ever believed that he was fairly elected; and few of those opposed to him have been sceptical enough to doubt it. It has been rumored that the election was conducted unfairly; and the following circumstance leaves a suspicion, amounting to too strong a probability. The law of elections required that the ballot boxes should be sealed up when the polls were closed, and remain so until the votes were counted by the judges. One of the sheriffs, who had been most violent in his opposition to the Colonel, instead of sealing up the ballot box, merely fastened it with a wire hasp and carried it home, retaining it in that situation till the votes were counted. Now, if his opposition did not induce him to take out a few Crockett votes, his carelessness left him under an imputation by no means creditable. Little doubt was entertained but that Colonel Crockett could have been returned by contesting the election; but he nobly said, "If it was not the wish of the people, clearly expressed, he would not serve them."

Being once more a private man, the Colonel returned to the bosom of his family; and as soon as the season would permit, occasionally sought his famous hunting ground, where he listened with rapture to the joyous cry of his dogs, or hung with delight on the far off echo of his old friend Betsy, as she distributed her death dealing power to the beasts of the forest.

In December of the year 18—, he set out with a friend for a trip to the *Shakes*. The close of the day found them putting up their little tent, and storing away their provisions. Their horses were hobbled and turned loose; their rude supper was prepared; and a short time found the Colonel, his friend, and dogs, stored away, and sleeping off the heavy night. There was something so wild in the description which the Colonel gave me of these *Shakes*, that I like to dwell upon incidents connected with them. Frequently would he be aroused from his sleep by the long howl of a gang of wolves, attracted to his tent by the odor of his provisions—so many in a gang as to intimidate the boldest; at other times, by the wild scream of the panther.

No one, he said, could tell the feeling which a situation of that sort brought about, to one separated as far as he had been from all assistance. Even his dogs seemed to partake of his feelings; for they would get up and come and lie close to him. The feeling was not fear, though he had cause to be afraid, from the many accidents which had happened. He remarked that he had not been a settler long in the Western District, when a gentleman had occasion to send his servant into the woods for a piece of timber. The servant remaining longer than was thought necessary, the master went to look for him. He was found; but dead, and most shockingly mangled, with five wolves lying around him, which had been killed with the sharp part of an axe. The ground bore the marks of there having been the most deadly and determined struggle, and that valor had yielded alone to numbers. A large gang had been attracted by the odor of his provisions. "Nothing is more common," said he, "than for wolves, when they meet with a single dog, to catch and eat him."

But to my tale. The next morning betimes, the Colonel and his friend were stirring; and having prepared their breakfast, they set out hunting.

"I was going 'long," said he, "down to a little *Harricane*, 'bout three miles from our tent, where I knew there must be a plenty of bear. 'Twas mighty cold, and my dogs were in fine order, and very busy hunting, when I seed where a piece of bark had been scratched off a tree. I said to my companion, there is a bear in the hollow of that tree. I examined the sign, and knew I was right.

I called my dogs to me; but to git at him was the thing. The tree was so large 'twould take all day to cut it down, and there was no chance to climb it. But upon looking about, I found that there was a tree near the one the bear was in; and if I could make it fall agin it, I could then climb up and git him out. I fell to work, and cut the tree down; but as the devil would have it, it lodged before it got there. So that scheme was knocked in the head.[82]

"I then told my companion to cut away upon the big tree, and I would go off some distance to see if I couldn't see him. He fell to work, and he hadn't been at it long before I seed the old bear poke his head out; but I couldn't shoot him, for if I did, I would hit him in the head and he would fall backwards,—so I had to wait for him to come out. I didn't say any thing; but it wan't a minute before he run out upon a limb and jumped down.

"I run as hard as I could, but before I got there he and the dogs were hard at it. I didn't see much of the fight before they all rolled down a steep hill, and the bear got loose and broke right in the direction of the Harricane. He was a mighty large one, and I was 'fraid my dogs would lose him, 'twas such a thick place. I started after him, and told my friend to come on. Well, of all the thick places, that ever you *did* see, that bear carried me through some of the thickest. The dogs would sometimes bring him to bay, and I would try for my life to git up to 'em, but when I would git most there he would git loose. He devilled me mightily, I tell you. I reckon I went a mile after that bear upon my hands and knees, just creeping through briars, and if I hadn't had deer-leather clothes on, they would have torn me in pieces.

"I got wet; and was mighty tired stooping so much. Sometimes I went through places so thick that I don't see how any thing could git through; and I don't *b'lieve* I could, if I hadn't heard the dogs fighting just before me. Sometimes I would look back, and I couldn't see how I got along. But once I got in a clear place; my dogs, tired of fighting, had brought the bear again to bay, and I had my head up, looking out to git a shoot, when the first thing I knew I was up to my breast in a sink hole of water. I was so damn mad, that I had a notion not to git out; but I began to think it wouldn't spite any body, and I scrambled out. My powder was all wet, except the load in my gun, and I did'nt know what to do. I had been sweating all the morning, and I was tired, and I looked like the devil with my wet leather clothes on; but I harked my dogs on, and once more I heard 'em fighting. I run on, and while I was going 'long, I heard something jump in the water. When I got there, I seed the bear going up the other bank of the Obion river—I hadn't time to shoot him before he was out of sight—he looked mighty tired. When I come to look at my dogs, I could hardly help from crying. Old Tiger and Brutus were sitting upon the edge of the water, whining because they couldn't git over; and I had a mighty good dog named Carlow,—he was standing in the water ready to swim; and I observed as the water passed by him, it was right red,—he was mighty badly cut. When I come to notice my other dogs, they were all right bloody, and it made me so mad that I harked 'em on, and determined to kill the bear.

"I hardly spoke to 'em before there was a general plunge, and each of my dogs just formed a streak going straight across. I watched 'em till they got out on the bank, when they all shook themselves, old Carlow opened, and off they all started. I sat down upon an old log. The water was right red where my dogs jumped in, and I loved 'em so much it made me mighty sorry. When I come to think how willingly they all jumped in when I told 'em, though they were badly cut and tired to death, I thought I ought to go and help 'em.

"It was now about twelve o'clock. My dogs had been running ever since sun rise, and we had all passed through a harricane, which of itself was a day's work. I could hear nothing of my companion; I whooped, but there was no answer; and I concluded that he had been unable to follow me, and had gone back to the tent. I looked up and down the river to see if there was a chance to cross it; but there was none—no canoe was within miles of me. While I was thinking of all these things, my dogs were trailing; but all at once I heard 'em fighting. I jumped up—I hardly knew what to do, when a notion struck me to roll in the log I had been sitting on, and cross over on that. 'Twas a part of an old tree, twelve or fifteen feet long, laying on a slant. I gave it a push, and into the water it went. I got an old limb, straddled the log, with my feet in the water, and pushed off. 'Twas mighty ticklish work: I had to lay the limb across, like a balance pole, to keep me from turning over, and then paddle with the hand that wasn't holding the rifle. The log didn't float good, and the water came up over my thighs. After a while I got over safe, fastened my old log to go back upon, and as I went up the bank I heard my dogs tree. I run to 'em as fast as I could; and sure enough, I seed the old bear up in a crotch. My dogs were all lying down under him, and I don't know which was the most tired, they or the bear.

"I knew I had him, so I just sat down and rested a little; and then to keep my dogs quiet, I got up and old Betsy thundered at him. I shot him right through the heart, and he fell without a struggle. I run up and stuck my knife into him several times up to the hilt, just because he devilled me so much; but I hardly pulled it out before I was sorry, for he had fought all day like a man, and would have got clear but for me.

"I noticed when the other dogs jumped on him to bite him, old Carlow didn't git up. I went to him, and seed a right smart puddle of blood under him. He was cut into the hollow, and I saw he was dying—nothing could save him. While I was feeling 'bout him, he licked my hand;—my eyes filled with tears;—I turned my head away, and to ease his sufferings, plunged my knife through his heart. He yelled out his death note, and the other dogs tried to jump upon him: such is the nature of a dog. This is all I hate in bear hunting. I didn't git over the death of my dog in some time; and I have a right to love him to this day, for no man ever had a better friend.

"After resting awhile, I fell to work and butchered my bear—I think he was the largest I ever saw. Then what to do, I didn't know. I was about, as near as I could tell, four miles from the tent, and there was a river between us. To leave my bear I couldn't do, after working so hard; but how to git him across, was the question. Finally I determined to carry him over on the same log I crossed on. I cut him up, threw away some of him, and brought at four turns as much as I could tote, and put it on the bank. The river was about three hundred yards from where I killed the bear; and 'twas hard work to git him there, I tell you. After I got it there, I put a piece on my log, straddled it, and brought it over; then went back, and kept doing this way till I brought it over. But 'twas a hell of a frolic, and I paid mighty dear for my meat. I packed it away in the crotch of a tree, to keep any thing from troubling it, and started for my tent. The sun was most down; and though it was a cold winter day, and I had been wet all the time, I wasn't cold much. I think that was the hardest day's work I ever had; and why some of my frolics haven't killed me, I don't know."

I asked the Colonel if he had crossed many rivers in that way. He said never before that time, but since then he had crossed them one hundred times; says he, "I just roll a chunk in, straddle it, and over I go."

"But to go on with my tale. I got to my tent an hour or two in the night, where I found my companion with a good fire: he seemed mighty glad to see me, for he did'nt like staying there by himself. I told him what sort of a day I had had of it, and he could hardly *b'lieve* me; so I told him I would take him next morning, and show him. I then dried myself, got warm, and went to sleep. Next morning we got our pack horses and went after my bear; 'twas all safe, and we brought it to our tent and salted it away. My dogs were so much worsted by the fight they had had the day before, and I was so sore from it, that we concluded not to hunt any more that day. My powder was all spoiled: my friend had'nt much; so next morning, instead of going hunting, we bundled up all our things and set out for home. 'Twas more than a day[']s journey; so the first night we camped about ten miles from my house. Having no powder at home, I told my friend if he would stay in the tent till I come back, I would go over the river to a little store, about twenty miles off, for a keg of powder which the merchant had promised to git for me. He agreed to do it; and the next morning

I left my dogs with him and went down to the river, where I knew there was a crossing place. I got down pretty early, and the log I expected to cross on was almost under water, and the river still a rising: but I thought as I was so far on my way, I would go over. The log did'nt reach all the way across, but where it stopped, a small tree grew up and leaned over the bank, so that when I quit the log I had been walking on, I had to climb the little tree to git to the bank. I fastened my rifle to my back, clim[b]ed up, and got over safe. I noticed all these things, because I knew I'd have to wade when I come back.

"Well, off I went to the store; I got there just about sun down, and met with a right jolly set: so instead of going back, I staid there and frolicked with them, and made shooting matches for two or three days. I then got my powder, and one morning before day, started off for my tent. The weather had turned much colder while I had been absent, and a smart snow had fallen, which made it mighty bad walking. I got to the river about two hours by sun, and as I expected, the river had risen and my log was covered. The water had risen considerably, but I did'nt know how much: I knew it would'nt do to stay there, for I should freeze; there was no log to float across on, and my only chance was to git back as I got over. I slung my keg of powder to my back and climbed down the little tree till I got to my log; this I found by feeling, and the water was about three feet over it. I kept feeling 'long, and got over safe; 'twas a mighty trying time; for right under the log was twenty feet deep, and if I had made one false step, 'twould all have been over with David Crockett.

"I had left old Betsy on the other side, so I had to go back for her, and pursue the same plan to git over; I got ready to start agin, in about an hour, and I then had to go through a wide swamp to strike the path leading to my tent. The water from the rise in the river was all over the swamp, and I had to wade all the time; and what made it worse, there was ice all over, which was'nt strong enough to bear my weight, but made it mighty hard to git along. Just as I had started off, I seed where something had broke the ice, and a notion struck me 'twas a bear, and I determined to follow it. I kept on about a mile, most of my time knee deep in water, when I struck the highland, and I found I was right in the path to my tent, and what I thought was a bear was some friends who had been down to the river to look for me. I took their tracks, and about dark I got to my tent; 'twas full of people, and they were mighty glad to see me. I had staid away so long, that my friends thought some accident had happened to me, and had gone to my house to git help to look for me. They told me that my family was in a great disturbance, believing I had been drowned; so to quiet 'em, we all bundled up, and went to my house that night.["]

CHAPTER VIII.

READER! let you and I hold a small confab.[83] My narrative has, before this, placed Colonel Crockett in situations, the truth of which, perhaps, you have doubted; but nevertheless, it is all true; and the work as far as it goes, has been, and will continue to be, an unvarnished picture of his life. So many incidents of an amusing nature have occurred to him, that it will be impossible for me to give more than a mere sample. Many of his queerest fantasies have no doubt been lost; but this chapter will place him in a situation, to say the least of it, novel in the extreme. You know I told you David was always a quirky boy; and now, to try your talent at guessing, I will tender you a copy of this work if you will divine where Colonel Crockett, in narrating a hunting story, will in truth place himself.

But before we commence his hunting story, let us merely for variety's sake, take another of his Dutch anecdotes.

"Well, I knew a young Dutchman once who was pretty well off, and who having, as he said, finished his *edecation*, was swelling[84] very largely. He had been riding about for some time, attending all the frolics in his reach, and came over to an uncle of his where I happened to be. His uncle said, "vell Shon vere you bin?" "Bin riding 'bout to see der vorld. Und uncle, vat you tink, I bin down to Yacop Ransowers, to von tam great big veddin, un dere vas a heaps of folks dere, un ve all trink, un eat, un after tinner, tey all said compliments; some said, 'much good may do you,' un some said, 'little vont sarve me;' so it come to my time, un I 'tots I must speak compliments too, un I jus rose up, un if I did'nt say, 'who keeps house, cot tam me?'["] The above story was told in the loud swelling language of the young Dutchman, who I have no doubt thought he had performed a wonderful feat when he spoke his *compliments too!*

Having disposed of the Dutch anecdote, we will now take the hunting story.

"Well, I had been at home some time—the weather was so cold I did'nt care much 'bout hunting, and Rees and a friend of his come over to my house one evening, and asked me if I did'nt want to go down to the Shakes and take a bear hunt. I told 'em I did'nt care much about it; but if they wanted to go I'd go with 'em: so next morning we fixed up, got our pack horses, and off we started for the Shakes. We pitched our tent right on the bank of one of those lakes made by the Shakes, and commenced hunting: we were tolerably successful: there was nothing strange about any of our hunts, only bear-hunting[f] is always the hardest work a man can be at. We killed our game and salted it away as usual, and on the third day 'twas so cold, and there was so much snow on the ground, that we all come to our tent earlier than usual; we made us a good fire and were lying 'round it, when Mr. Mars, who had been to Mill's Point,[85] rode up. He got down and told us that he was obliged to be at the land office very early next morning, and if we would set him across the lake there 'twould save him the trouble of riding 'round it, which was about twenty miles out of his way. There was an old flat[86] lying on shore; but we all told him we could'nt; 'twas too cold, and we were tired. But he kept begging us, saying he was obliged to be there; and after a while he pulled out a bottle of whiskey and passed it 'round. We soon emptied it, and it made me feel in a heap better humor; so when Mars fell to persuading us agin, I said I'd set him across, if one of the others would help me. Rees said he would, and Mars being in a great hurry, we went down to the lake, and getting his horse in, we pushed off. 'Twas a mighty rough establishment, oars and all. The oars were covered with ice, and the old flat had a good deal of snow in it, and she leaked mighty badly; but I thought she would carry us over; so after we had started off, Mars said if we carried him straight across he would have to swim a *slue*,[87] and there was so much mushy ice in it, he did'nt b'lieve he could git his horse across; but if we would land him up the lake, he could get on safe. To go straight across was about a mile, but to go w[h]ere Mars wanted us, was about three. However, we were all in a right good humor, and the sun was rather better than two hours high, so we agreed to land him where he wished.

"We pulled away, and just as we got about the middle of the lake, his horse made some motion in the boat, and set her to leaking worse than before. I told Mars she'd sink if he didn't bail her: so he took his hat, and went to work. We pulled as hard as we could, and Mars worked mighty hard; but the water run in as fast as he could get it out. By and by, though, we got to the bank, and just as Mars went to lead his horse out, the whole bottom went down. It had only been pinned on, and the weight of the horse broke it loose. Rees and I was a little wet, and when we got upon the bank we didn't know what to do. Mars looked half froze, with his wet hat—and his horse was shivering: he had to ride about fifteen miles, or a little upwards, before he could get to a house; and we were there, without a horse, separated by a lake from our tent, and had nothing to strike fire. Mars said he could do nothing for us, for he was all but froze, and must go on, as he had a long way to ride, and 'twas getting late. I told him 'twasn't worth while for him to stay, and off he started. We looked at him till he got out of sight, and we didn't know what to do. Well, there was Rees and I, shivering; and we must either get back to our tent, or freeze to death. I recollected there was, right opposite to where we started from, a canoe; but 'twas two miles to that place, and then to get to it we would have to cross the very *slue* which Mars had been afraid of swimming. This was the only chance. I told Rees 'twasn't worth while to consider—that there was no two ways about it—we must do it or die. So off we started. When we got to the *slue*, 'twas as Mars said, covered with mushy ice, and about thirty or forty yards across. We were mighty cold, and it made the chills run over me to look at it. I called to Rees, and told him, as he was tallest, he must go first. He didn't speak, but waded right in; he seemed to think 'twas death any how, and was resigned to his fate. I watched him as he went along. It kept getting deeper and deeper, till for nearly twenty yards he walked along with nothing out but his head. After he got out, I started in, and for nearly twenty yards I had to tiptoe, and throw my head back, and the ice just come along up to my ears—'twas this soft ice made of snow. I didn't speak—we were too near dead to joke each other. We went down to the lake, and there we found the canoe. 'Twas nearly full of snow and water; and I set to work to clean her out—and when I thought 'twould answer, I called to Rees to come on. He did'nt answer me, and I went to him and shook him—but he was fast asleep. I endeavored to rouse him up, but I couldn't make him understand any thing: so I dragged him along, and laid him in the canoe. I then straddled one end of it, put my legs as deep as I could in the water to keep them from freezing, and paddled over. Our friend we had left at the tent, had a fine fire. I could see it some time before I got ashore, and it looked mighty good. He had been preparing for us, as he knew we would be very cold when we got back. I hailed him as I run the canoe ashore, to come and take out Rees; for, says I, I believe he is dead. I got up, and thought I would jump out, and started to do so; but I came very near breaking my neck, for I couldn't step more than about six inches. I got out; I couldn't do any good by staying there, and I left my friend pulling poor Rees out, and started for the fire. I soon got to walking right good, and felt the fire before I got to it. But I was hardly at it before I began to burn all over. I kept turning round—my pains only grew worse. I was suffering the torments of hell, and I quit the fire. I turned towards the canoe. Our companion had poor Rees in his arms, his feet dragging the snow, coming towards the fire. I didn't say any thing to him, for I didn't know what to say; but while I was looking on, I recollected that there was a mighty big spring, not fur off; and a notion struck me to go and git into it. The sun was just down, and the sky looked red and cold, as I started off for the spring. When I got there, I put my legs in, and it felt so warm that I set right flat down in it—and I bent down, so as to leave nothing out but my mouth, and the upper part of my head. You don't know how good I did feel. I wasn't cold any where but my head. I some-times think now of that frolic; and I believe the happiest time I ever spent, was while I was in that spring. I felt like I was coming too; 'twas so warm, and every thing around me looked so cold. How long I remained there, I don't know; but I think an hour or two: 'twas quite dark when I got out. I went to my tent, and there I saw poor Rees wrapped up in some blankets, and laid before the fire, his friend watching over him. He was dull and stupid, and had not spoken. The fire had no other effect upon me than to make me feel comfortable. I took off my clothes, got dry, went to sleep, and never experienced any inconvenience. But all our attention could not get poor Rees entirely well. We stayed with him two or three days, and then carried him home; but he never walked afterwards. That frolic sickened me with hunting for one while."

CHAPTER IX.

To give my readers a better idea of the character of Colonel Crockett, I have here sketched for them my first interview with him.

Sometime in the month of ——, in the year ——, while travelling through the Western District, I heard Colonel Crockett, or the great bear hunter, so frequently mentioned,—and with his name were associated so many humorous anecdotes,— that I determined to visit him. Obtaining directions, I left the high road, and sought his residence. My route, for many miles, lay through a country uninteresting from its sameness; and I found myself, on the morning of the third day, within eight miles of Colonel Crockett's. Having refreshed myself and horse, I sat out to spend the remainder of the day with him—pursuing a small blazed trail, which bore no marks of being often travelled, and jogged on, wondering what sort of a reception I should meet with from a man, who, by quirky humors unequalled, had obtained for himself a never-dying reputation.

The character which had been given of the Colonel, both by his friends and foes, induced me to hope for a kind welcome; but doubting,—for I still believed him a bear in appearance,—I pursued my journey, until a small opening brought me in sight of a cabin, which, from description, I identified as the home of the celebrated hunter of the West.

It was in appearance rude and uninviting, situated in a small field of eight or ten acres, which had been cleared in the wild woods: no yard surrounded it, and it seemed to have been lately settled. In the passage of the house were seated two men in their shirt sleeves cleaning rifles. I strained my eyes as I rode up, to see if I could identify, in either of them, the great bear hunter: but before I could decide, my horse had stopped at the bars, and there walked out in plain, homespun attire, with a black fur cap on, a finely proportioned man, about six feet high, aged, from appearance, forty-five. His countenance was frank and manly, and a smile played over it as he approached me. He brought with him a rifle, and from his right shoulder hung a bag made of a raccoon skin, to which, by means of a sheath, was appended a huge butcher's knife. "This is Colonel Crockett's residence, I presume?" "Yes sir." "Have I the pleasure of seeing that gentleman before me?" "If it be a pleasure, you have Sir." "Well Colonel, I have rode very much out of my way to spend a day or two with you, and take a hunt." "Get down Sir; I am delighted to see you; I like to see strangers: and the only care I have is, that I cannot accommodate them as well as I would wish. I have no corn, you see I've but lately moved here; but I'll make my little boy take your horse over to my son-in-law's; he is a good fellow, and will take care of him." Walking in—"my Brother, let me make you acquainted with Mr. ———, of ———; my wife, Mr. ———; my daughters, Mr. ———. You see, we are mighty rough here. I am afraid you will think it hard times, but we have to do with the best we can. I started mighty poor, and have been *rooting 'long ever since*; but damn apologies, I hate 'em; what I live upon always, I think a friend can for a day or two. I have but little, but that little is as free as the water that runs—so make yourself at home. Here are newspapers, and some books."

His free mode of conversation made me feel quite easy; and a few moments gave me leisure to look around. His cabin within was clean and neat, and bore about it many marks of comfort. The many trophies of wild animals spread over his house and yard—his dogs, in appearance war-worn veterans, lying about sunning themselves,—all told truly, that I was at the home of the celebrated hunter.

His family were dressed by the work of their own hands; and there was a neatness and simplicity in their appearance very becoming. His wife was rather grave and quiet, but attentive, and kind to strangers; his daughters diffident and retiring, perhaps too much so, but uncommonly beautiful; and are fine specimens of the native worth of the female character—for, entirely uneducated, they are not only agreeable, but fascinating. There are no schools near them, and yet they converse well—and if they did not, one would be apt to think so, for they are extremely pretty, and tender to a stranger with so much kindness the comforts of their little cabin. The Colonel has no slaves; his daughters attend to the dairy and kitchen, while he performs the more laborious duties of his farm. He has but lately moved where he now resides, and consequently had to fix anew. He took me over his little field of corn, which he himself had cleared and grubbed, talked of the quantity he should make, his peas, pumpkins, etc. with the same pleasure that a Mississippi planter would have shewn me his cotton estate, or a James river Virginia planter have carried me over his wide inheritance.

The newspapers being before us, called up the subject of politics. I held in high estimation the present administration of our country.[88] To this he was opposed. His views, however, delighted me; and, were they more generally adopted, we should be none the loser. He was opposed to the administration, and yet conceded that many of its acts were wise and efficient, and would have received his cordial support. He admired Mr. Clay,[89] but had objections to him. He was opposed to the Tariff,[90] yet, I think, a supporter of the Bank.[91] He seemed to have the most horrible objection to binding himself to any man, or set of men. He said he would as live be a damned old 'coon dog, as obliged to do what any man, or set of men, would tell him was right. The present administration he would support as far as he would any other; and that was, as far as he believed its views to be correct. He would pledge himself to support no administration—when the will of his constituents was known to him, it was his law; when unknown, his judgment was his guide. I remarked to him, that his district was so thorough-going for Jackson,[92] I thought he would never be elected. He said, "he didn't care; he believed his being left out was of service to him, for it had given him time to go to work; he had cleared his corn-field, dug a well, built his cabins," etc.; and says he, "if they won't elect me with my opinions, I can't help it. *I had rather be politically damned than hypocritically immortalized.*" He spoke very highly of Benton,[93] and was delighted with P. P. Barbour[94] whom he would have preferred for President to Jackson or Clay; and of whom he remarked, "I'll be damned if Barbour ain't as quick as Dupont's treble."[95] He spoke with much pleasure of his former acquaintances at Washington, and assigned at my instance the reasons why he was beaten at the last election; but they were better summed up by an Irish gentleman, with whom I had the pleasure of conversing, while in the District. He said, "'twas a damn poor *bate* [beat] that, to be *baten* only three or four hundred votes in seventeen counties; and he would not have been *baten* at all, but that he carried on his back Jackson, and every damn lawyer, and printer, in the District."

His rifle next came upon the tapis,[96] and from him I learned that he was cleaning her up for a shooting match, to which I was invited. To gratify me, he, with his brother, went out and shot several times. One who is little accustomed to shooting, can form no idea of the skill of the backwoods marksmen. Even the fiction of Cooper, in the skill of his far-famed Hawkeye, I have seen surpassed.[97] And were the deeds of La Longue Carabine[98] and old Betsy brought into comparison, an impartial judge would have to decide in favor of the latter. Not only does the Colonel shoot well, who has indeed been a splendid shot, but the finest corps of riflemen in the world, might be selected from the north-western part of Tennessee.

Forty yards offhand, or sixty with rest, is the distance generally chosen for a shooting match. These are considered equivalent distances; that is, either may be selected—if no distance be specified, this is implied.

Off-hand shooting is always preferred by a good marksman, and is generally the closest. In shooting with rest, the rifle rebounds, and consequently throws its ball with much less accuracy. To prove this, take two rifle or gun-barrels, which, by placing them together, will touch only at each end, and you will find no difficulty in springing them together, by means of your two fingers. In speaking of the accuracy of the western riflemen, I can conceive of nothing that I could say, which would amount to fiction. I have known them, at the distance of one hundred yards, to shoot six balls out of eleven within less than half an inch of centre; and in all their shooting matches, no ball is termed a counter which is not found within an inch.[99] They use for patching,[100] cotton cloth, and wipe their rifles after every discharge. I think they would even shoot with more accuracy than they do, did they use percussion locks, which possess many advantages over the flint lock.[101]

The time having arrived, on we went to the shooting match. The place selected was a grove, near which stood a tipling house.[102] We found many persons already assembled, and they continued to flock in until several hundred were collected. They disposed of themselves in different groups about the grove, some lying down, others standing; and indulged pretty much in the same topic of conversation—that is, each man wanted his neighbor to put up something to be shot for. There was something very striking in their appearance. Almost every man was clad in the garb of a hunter,—with a rifle, a *'coon* skin bag, from which was suspended a large knife, and an alligator's tooth for a charger,[103]— than which nothing can be more beautiful. Many articles were brought to the gathering for sale; yet no person, though he might want them never so badly, thought of buying. They must all go through the process of being shot for, before any man would consent to own them. This was literally the case with every article. Whenever any thing very pretty was exhibited, you would hear many persons telling the vendor not to sell it, but to put it up—that is, make up chances, and have a shooting match.

There is no country in the world, which can beat the Western District in originality of names, setting aside the Hoosier, Kangaroo, and Nunnery.[104] I overheard two men bargaining for a horse: said one to the other, "I will give you two hundred dollars worth of dogs for him." Two hundred dollars worth of dogs! said I to myself—two hundred dollars worth of dogs!!—What can that mean? Upon asking for an explanation, I found out that bonds, or promissory notes, were termed dogs—and that they were said to be of a good or bad breed, according to the ability and punctuality of the obligor.[105]

But to my tale. The crowd, to brighten their ideas, or rather increase their propensity to shoot, which, by the by, needed no stimulus, occasionally took a little—and when it was summoned to the field where an ox or two was to be awarded to the victor, I could see many a man who was, "how came you so?" Each man who was to shoot, carried with him his target—this consisted of a small board which had been burned black, and rubbed smooth, on which a small piece of white paper had been pinned. The judges took possession of all the boards; and, from the centre spot on each, described four concentric circles, commencing with a radius of one-fourth of an inch, then half an inch, three-fourths of an inch, and one inch.

The judges having measured the distance at which they were to shoot, from a tree against which their targets were to be placed,—and having marked out on the ground a circle, to prevent their being intruded upon, under penalty of a *quart*,[106] all was ready. There was no regularity in shooting; each marksman called for his target when it suited him.[g] Taking his position, he cried out, put up my board—it was done; and the crowd flocked together on either side, from the target to the marksman, forming a lane of living people about four feet wide, with their heads inclining inwards, to see the effect of the shot. A man stood for a moment as if sculptured from marble, the muzzle of his gun pointing to the earth—then raising it gradually, it became horizontal, poised for an instant, and there burst forth a sheet of living flame—the ball was buried in the paper, and at the annunciation of it, a wild shout rent the air.

"Damn it, clear the track; and put up my board," was shouted from the lips of Crockett, and I discovered old Betsy poised aloft in the air. The lane was again formed, and Crockett lounged idly at his stand, with his gun upon his shoulder, which was carelessly thrown off, and discharged the moment it became horizontal. The same effect ensued—the ball was buried in the paper, and another wild shout rent the air. I have never witnessed more excitement; the scene was kept up for several hours by various marksmen—and the welkin did not ring with louder applause, when on Long Island the far-famed Eclipse passed Henry, one of Virginia's favorite sons, than did the backwoods of Tennessee, at each successful shot.[107]

I observed that many a marksman, after shooting two or three times, would hide his rifle in the woods, as he said, to allow it rest—and the idea at first seemed to me superstitious,—but there were two objects in doing so—it was hid to prevent any person from playing a trick upon it, and allowed to cool, that its barrel might not glimmer. A heated barrel always glimmers, and a good marksman never shoots when the rays of the sun may warp his vision; but, if practicable, seeks a shade.

Evening came on, and the crowd showed no disposition to disperse. A thousand shooting matches were in embryo—this man wanted a pair of shoes—another a hat—a third some cakes for his children—not one of which things would they dare to carry home, until it had gone through the regular process of being shot for. Whether this practice proceeds from a natural fondness for adventure, or from a spirit of economy, I know not—for I saw several men pay two or three prices for an article, before they were fortunate enough to get it. But methought, when one went home were, perhaps sat some

> ———————— "sulky sullen dame,
> Gathering her brows, like gathering storm,
> Nursing her wrath to keep it warm,"[108]

it would appease her but little to state, that their joint earnings had been spent for ginger cakes—but methought, it acted like a sedative, when it was announced, that they cost but a thimble of powder, with a small leaden ball.

The evening passed off amid a continual ringing of rifles, and night came on, and yet there was no disposition to disperse—it was damp and foggy, and consequently very dark; and, to my utter astonishment, candles were called for, to enable them to shoot. The distance was diminished: and, though their heads must have spun round like whirligigs, I think they rather improved in shooting. There was a candle held near each sight of the rifle, and one also on each side of the target; and in this manner did they continue through the night to dispose of the merchandise, which had been brought for sale during the day. I sat up very late; candles were continually called for, and new parties formed. Weary of the scene, I retired to the house to get a bed. There a new set of amusements presented themselves. In one room were to be seen three or four men sitting flat on the floor, throwing five corns;[109] and, at the same time, could be seen in other parts of the room, two grown boys, in the position that the Romans ate their meals, playing push-pin upon a hat; and, not far distant, a group of girls and boys, drawing straws.[110] Sleepy, and sick of every species of sporting, I sought another room—and there, to my inexpressible surprise, I beheld a little boy holding a lightwood-knot, while two others were playing at marbles in a chalk ring, marked out on the floor; and two more, leaning over a chair, were spinning round a *tetotum.*[111] By the light of the torch, I ascended a ladder leading into the loft, where, reposing myself, I was lulled asleep by a confusion of sounds, of which the English language cannot convey the least idea.

In the morning I arose with the first dawn of day, and mounted my horse. The noise had somewhat abated, though the candles were burning, and the rifles ringing—and they continued to do so while I was in hearing.

CHAPTER X.

THAT Colonel Crockett could avail himself, in electioneering, of the advantages which well applied satire ensures, the following anecdote will sufficiently prove:

In the canvass of the congressional election of 18—, Mr. *****[112] was the Colonel's opponent—a gentleman of the most pleasing and conciliating manners—who seldom addressed a person or a company without wearing upon his countenance a peculiarly good humored smile. The Colonel, to counteract the influence of this winning attribute, thus alluded to it, in a stump speech:

"Yes, gentlemen, he may get some votes by *grinning*, for he can *out-grin* me, and you know I ain't slow—and to prove to you that I am not, I will tell you an anecdote. I was concerned myself—[h]and I was fooled a little of the damn'dest. You all know I love hunting. Well, I discovered, a long time ago, that a 'coon couldn't stand my grin. I could bring one tumbling down from the highest tree. I never wasted powder and lead, when I wanted one of the creturs. Well, as I was walking out one night, a few hundred yards from my house, looking carelessly about me, I saw a 'coon planted upon one of the highest limbs of an old tree. The night was very *moony* and clear, and old Ratler was with me; but Ratler won't bark at a 'coon—he's a queer dog in that way. So, I thought I'd bring the lark down, in the usual way, *by a grin*. I set myself—and, after grinning at the 'coon a reasonable time, found that he didn't come down. I wondered what was the reason—and I took another steady grin at him. Still, he was *there*. It made me feel a little mad; so I felt round and got an old limb about five feet long—and, planting one end upon the ground, I placed my chin upon the other, and took *a rest*. I then grinned my best for about five minutes—but the damn'd 'coon hung on. So, finding I could not bring him down by grinning, I determined to have him—for I thought he must be a droll chap. I went over to the house, got my axe, returned to the tree, saw the 'coon still there, and began to cut away. Down it come, and I run forward; but damn the 'coon was there to be seen. I found that what I had taken for one, was a large knot upon a branch of the tree—and, upon looking at it closely, I saw that *I had grinned all the bark off, and left the knot perfectly smooth.*

"Now, fellow-citizens," continued the Colonel, "you must be convinced that, in the *grinning line*, I myself am not slow—yet, when I look upon my opponent's countenance, I must admit that he is my superior. You must all admit it. Therefore, be wide awake—look sharp—and do[i] not let him grin you out of your votes."

I have never met with a man, who had a happier [t]alent for turning every thing to his own advantage than Colonel Crockett. Never at a loss, he gives in his blunt way, to every sally of wit against him, the happiest answer that can be conceived—and I believe no person who has been the aggressor, ever left him, satisfied with his own success.

During his first canvass for Congress, while at a public gathering, Col. Crockett was, as he ever is, the centre of a crowd, which he was amusing with some comic story, when, to abash him, a friend of his opponent, with an impudent, yet smirking face, walked up, and pulling out a *'coon* skin, asked the Colonel to give him the change for it:—four hare skins are called a 'coon skin. Colonel Crockett, taking the skin, and feeling the fur, asked, "Where did you git this?"

"'Twas handed me while ago."

"Well, you take it back, and tell the fellow I say he cheated you—it's a counterfeit—the fur ain't worth a damn—the 'coon was sick—[j]you couldn't git any one of my dogs to tree *sich* a 'coon as that. Take it back."

The Colonel, though wild and wayward in his flights, seldom says anything without an interjection—and very often the keenest satire may be found lurking under the most ridiculous garb. But to place his character in a fair light, it is only necessary to advert to the circumstances under which he was elected. A hunter, poor, entirely without education, and without family influence, he was called up on by a large majority of the citizens in his district, to represent them—a district composed of seventeen counties, and containing at that time nearly 100,000 souls, without one single advantage, other than the mere gifts of nature. He had to contend with men of genius, fortune, and of refined education—and,[k] further, to withstand the fury of all the presses in his district,—[l]which sent forth sheet after sheet of violent abuse, of ludicrous caricatures, and of biting satire,—and yet, from beneath this accumulating weight, Colonel Crockett rose to distinction. Is this not a proof that nature has indeed been liberal to him? And, though we may laugh at his humors, yet we must all concede, that in the power of gaining men's hearts, with but one exception,[113] Colonel Crockett stands unrivalled. There are many persons who will attribute his success to a want of talent in his own district. But this is not the case. For, though the country has been but lately settled, there is in some portions of it the refinement of good society—and, throughout the district, you frequently meet with fine specimens of genius, and of education.

Colonel Crockett, as I before remarked, has been exposed to the wrath of the presses of his district; and paper bulletins have been used against him in every shape of which you can well conceive—in every style, from the chaste and sedate language of the bible, to the violent slang of modern party spirit. [I] think nothing could have been better calculated for effect, than a series of numbers, distributed in pamphlet form, entitled, "Book of Chronicles, west of Tennessee, and east of the Mississippi river,"—and which are really so severe, as well as amusing, that I must here insert a number.

"BOOK OF CHRONICLES,
West of Tennessee, and East of the Mississippi Rivers.[114]

"1. And it came to pass in those days when Andrew was chief ruler over the children of Columbia,[115] that there arose a mighty man in the river country, whose name was David; he belonged to the tribe of Tennessee, which lay upon the border of the Mississippi and over against Kentucky.

2. Now David was chief of the hosts of Forked deer, and Obion, and around about the Hatchee, and the Mississippi rivers; and behold his fame had spread abroad throughout all the land of Columbia, insomuch, that there were none to be found like unto him, for wisdom and valor; no, not one in all the land.

3. David was a man wise in council, smooth in speech, valiant in war, and of fair countenance and goodly stature; such was the terror of his exploits, that thousands of wild cats and panthers did quake and tremble at his name.

4. And it came to pass that David was chosen by the people in the river country, to go with the wise men of the tribe of Tennessee, to the grand Sanhedrim[116] held yearly in the twelfth month, and on the first Monday in the month, at the city of Washington, where the wise men from the east, from the west, from the north, and from the south, gathered themselves together to consult on the welfare of Columbia and her twenty-four tribes.

5. In those days there were many occupants spread abroad throughout the river country; these men loved David exceedingly, because he promised to give them lands flowing with milk and honey.

6. And it came to pass in the 54th year after the children of Columbia had escaped from British bondage,[117] and on the first month, when Andrew and the wise men and rulers of the people were assembled in the great Sanhedrim, that David arose in the midst of them saying, Men and brethren, wot ye not that there are many occupants in the river country on the west border of the tribe

of Tennessee, who are settled down upon lands belonging to Columbia; now I beseech you give unto these men each a portion for his inheritance, so that his soul may be glad, and he will bless thee and thy posterity.[118]

7. But the wise men from the south, the southeast, the west, and the middle country, arose with one accord and said, Lo! brethren, this cannot be done. The thing which our brother David asketh is unjust; the like never hath been done in the land of Columbia. If we give the lands away, it must be to the tribe of Tennessee, so that they may deal with the occupants as it may seem good in their sight. This has been the practice in old times, and with our fathers, and we will not depart therefrom. Furthermore, we cannot give this land away until the warrants are satisfied.

8. Behold, when David heard these sayings, he was exceeding wroth against the wise men and the rulers of the congregation, and against Andrew, and made a vow unto the Lord that he would be avenged of them. Then John, one of the wise men of the tribe of Tennessee, who lived at the rocky city,[119] arose in the midst, and said, If we give this land to the occupants instead of the tribe, all the occupants in the land of Columbia will beseech us for lands, and there will be none left to pay the debt which redeemed us from bondage; no, not an acre; and this saying pleased the wise men and the rulers, and they did accordingly.

9. Now there were in these days wicked men, sons of Belial,[120] to wit: the Claytonites, the Holmesites, the Burgessites, the Everettites, the Chiltonites, and the Bartonites,[121] who were of the tribes of Maine, Massachusetts, Rhode Island, Kentucky and Missouri, and who hated Andrew and his friends of old times, because the children of Columbia had chosen him to rule over them instead of Henry whose surname was Clay, who they desired for their chief ruler.[122]

10. And lo, when those men saw that David was sorely troubled in spirit, they communed one with another, and said, Is this not David from the river country in the west, who of old times was very valiant for Andrew to be ruler, and who perplexed our ranks in the Sanhedrim, and who was foremost in battle against our great chiefs Henry and John Q[123] when they were defeated by Andrew? Now Tristram, whose surname was Burgess,[124] answered and said, Men and brethren, as the Lord liveth it is he.

11. Then Daniel, whose surname was Webster,[125] and who was a prophet of the order of Balaam, said, Let us comfort David in his afflictions, his wrath is kindled against Andrew and his friends, and against the wise men of Tennessee; peradventure he will come over to us at the next election, to fight for Henry against Andrew, and Thomas whose surname is Chilton,[126] said, Thou speaketh wisely; let what thou sayest be done according to thy words.

12. Then Daniel drew nigh unto David and said unto him, Wherefore, O my brother, doth thou seem sad and sorrowful? Why is thy soul bowed down with

affliction? Hath the hand of the Lord smote heavily upon thee? Hath famine and pestilence destroyed thy land and all thy beloved occupants? Or has the wise men and rulers been unkind to thee? I pray thee tell me, and I will comfort thee.

13. And David lifted up his eyes and wept, and said, O Daniel! live forever. If the wise men and rulers had given my occupants the lands according to the manner I beseeched them, I could have been wise man and chief ruler in the river country for life. But if I join the wise men, and give it to the state of Tennessee, then they will share the honor with me, and the council of the state of Tennessee will give it to the occupants at twelve and one half cents per acre, and they will receive the honor instead of me; then the people of the river country will not have me for their wise man and chief ruler forever, and it grieveth me sore.[127]

14. And Daniel answered, and said unto David, Swear unto me that thee and all thy people in the river country will come over unto me and fight with me at the next election against Andrew and his people, in favor of Henry for chief ruler of Columbia; then I will help thee to get the lands for thine occupants; and David swore accordingly, and there is a league existing between them even unto this day.[128]

15. Now there was a man in the river country, about the centre way thereof, whose name was William.[129] He loved David as he loved his own soul; his soul and David's were knit as though they were but one; he was David's chief counsellor. When David wept, he wept; when David rejoiced, he rejoiced; if David bid him go he went; if David bid him come, he come.

16. So it came to pass when David returned from the great Sanhedrim, that William ran and fell upon his neck and wept for joy; then David said unto him, I have been discomfited in all my plans; I could not get my beloved occupants without dividing the honor with the wise men of my state,[m] and giving it to the whole tribe of the Tennessee; I wot not but the council would give it to them as cheap as I, but it would rob me of the honor, and then I cannot be wise man and chief ruler for life; I have therefore engaged to forsake Andrew, and join the ranks of Henry, for the chief ruler over the children of Columbia,—for the wise men of my tribe and the friends of Andrew hath forsaken me. Wilt thou, in whom my soul delighteth, go with me in these things?

17. And William answered, and said, Where thou goest I will go; where thou stayest, I will stay; what thou doest, I will do; and will have none other God but thee—when I forsake thee, let the Lord forsake me, do as thou wilt.[130]

18. And David said unto William, draw near unto me; I will counsel thee, for thou art my beloved disciple, in whom I am well pleased. Go thou through all the river country, and every neighborhood thereof; tell the people I will be elected by five thousand votes. As thou art a Baptist, they will put trust in thee.

19. If thou dost come to a people who knoweth thee not, if they are for me, say unto them, be strong and valiant on the day of the election:—if they are against me, say unto them thou art against me also,—but thou hast been all through the river country, and I will be elected by a mighty host: this will terrify them, and they will join me. If thou shalt come to an ignorant people, say unto them my adversary is guilty of corruption. If a Jackson man approach thee, say unto him, I have always been for Jackson.

20. If a Clay man encounter thee, then mayest thou tell him of the bargain with Daniel. If a Baptist greet thee, say unto him, I am religiously disposed, and think highly of the Baptists. If a Methodist shall enquire of thee, say unto him I always attend their camp-meetings. If a Cumberland Presbyterian shall call upon thee, say unto him I have joined his society.

21. But be thou circumspect in all things, and do not say unto the people that I have franked sack bags full of books into the river country against Andrew at their expense. Thou shalt not say unto the people that I have franked Hume's history of England,[131] or a sack of feathers; be careful to inform Roland, the High Priest,[132] of all these things, so that he may direct the congregation accordingly.

22. Remember now, my beloved disciple, that I am thy light and thy life; I have sent thee big coats, bibles, hymn books, and many articles from the great Sanhedrim, for thyself and family. I will send thee many other things if thou art faithful unto the end. Go forth, and the Lord prosper thee.

23. And William went unto all the river country, and did according to all that David commanded him; but the people were a stiff necked generation, and would not agree that David should bring Henry to be chief ruler over the children of Columbia, instead of Andrew; but with one accord said unto William, David hath beguiled us, we will desert him, and stick to Andrew, who hath brought us out of British bondage—and we will vote for William, whose surname is Fitzgerald[133]—and the people all said, AMEN!"

CHAPTER XI.

THE inhabitants of the Western District I love, and shall ever remember with pleasure, notwithstanding their propensity for fun and frolic, for they are kind, hospitable, and generous; and I should be unhappy, if I knew I had written a line calculated to wound the feelings of a single individual. My object has been, merely, to amuse myself,—to "lend a wing to weary time," and catch the "manners living as they rise." And, if this hasty production has the same effect upon others which it has had upon me, many a wandering exile may for a moment be relieved from the too sad thoughts of those now far away,—many a frightened poor soul may for a while cease to think of the dreaded *cholera*,—and many an afflicted patient bid farewell, for a time, to the *blues*. Indeed, I should believe any man a queer fellow, who cannot in this hotchpotch, find some page to his taste.

During my stay with Colonel Crockett, among other things, I asked him how he liked the various jests which had been published concerning him?[134]

"Oh, damn it," says he, "I don't care—those who publish them, don't intend to injure me."

"But," says I, "Colonel, what do you think of your last commission?"

"What commission?"

"The one which it is reported our worthy President has given you."

"Well, I don't know what that is."

"I perceive from the newspapers," said I, "that in order to quiet the fears of the world, you are authorized by the President to mount the Alleghany, and wring off the tail of the comet, when it makes its appearance."[135] He could not help smiling, but instantly replied,

"I'll be damn'd if I had a commission, if I didn't wring *his* tail off."

Although I have given in this work so large a space to hunting stories, I have failed to mention a species of hunting very much practised throughout the "far away west," and which is almost ever attended with invariable success. I allude to fire hunting, or the plan by which deer are killed of a night with a gun, very often with a rifle—and the darker the night, the better the prospect for success. I have known many a single hunter to kill five, six, and even seven of a night.

Fire hunting was unknown in this country until within some fifty or sixty years since, when it was introduced by Mr. Burnie, who lived among the Chickasaw Indians.[136] In Virginia, it was practised at a time anterior to this, but not with the same success. The facility with which Mr. Burnie killed deer of a night, infused into the superstitious Indians a belief that he was some superior personage, and that he effected it by means of physic, which is their *to kalon*,[137] or which solves all their mysteries. He delighted for some time in practising upon their fears—and literally astonished the natives. However, it was revealed—and is now generally practised, though prohibited by law.

To prepare for a fire hunt, it is necessary to get a common frying pan, the handle of which is lashed to a board, three or four inches in width, and five or six feet long, which is placed on the shoulder, and the arm thrown over it, to keep it in a horizontal position. The handle being lengthened, throws the pan several feet behind the hunter, in which there is a light wood fire kindled,— and he is then ready for a hunt. The light from the fire illuminates a circle, save where the shadow from the head falls, which diverging as it goes off, is in size considerable. Within this shadow, the huntsman sees and shoots his game, which manifests itself alone by its eyes, which are red and fiery, from the reflection of the light, and visible at some distance. The huntsman either walks or rides, shoots with the pan on his shoulder, and seeks the highland or swamp, or any place where he will probably meet with deer. To increase the shadow, or range of vision, it is only necessary to move the handle horizontally to the right or left, which causes the shadow to sweep the segment of a circle in any direction you please. The danger arising from this species of hunting is, that dogs, sheep, horses, and cows, are liable to be shot,—their eyes presenting an appearance similar to that of the deer. The most experienced hunter may be deceived by the eyes of a dog or sheep. Horses and cows, from the fact that their eyes are farther apart, may be distinguished—yet many of them have been sacrificed to a knowledge of this pursuit.

There is something very striking in viewing a walking light, meandering through the woods, while shooting upwards. It throws around a broad lurid glare, and lends to the woods, wherever a shadow falls, a gloom far greater than that of the night.

The sight is calculated to have much effect upon a human being: and I cannot reconcile it to myself to see even a deer fall, by so treacherous a plan—treacherous it seems to me, for having lain concealed all day in swamps to avoid man—having rid themselves of dogs, perhaps, by a long and weary chase, they move out under cover of night to pick their scanty subsistence, or to glean nutriment for their tender young. Little do they suppose, when all nature is wrapped in sleep, that there is an enemy in search of them, so captivating in appearance, as to lull asleep all fear, all suspicion of injury. They feed—their beautiful leopard-like young sport in gambols near them,—occasionally drawing the flowing teat: a flambeau[138] is seen approaching, shedding far and wide its broad lurid glare. This is the only object seen by them. As the hunter sweeps his circle, it flits about, reminding them only of a "marsh's meteor lamp,"[139] by the light of which so often they have cropped the tender herbage, while sporting o'er some grassy meadow. Nearer still it approaches,—and they gaze with rapture at the beautiful sight; a redder light bursts forth, and the dread crack of a rifle rings through the forest. The mother falls, and lies weltering in her blood. Her tender infants lick from her wound the crimson fluid as it exudes. They look about—they see nothing to alarm them. Tears fill their eyes,—which only make them a more prominent mark for the huntsman,—and, chained to the spot by the magic effects of the light, they there remain, until they are offered up as a sacrifice to maternal affection.

I have often heard the question mooted, who was the better marksman, the white or red man. My observation,—and I have had many opportunities of judging,—induces me to believe that there is no sort of comparison between them. The white man not only shoots with more precision, but traces with greater accuracy the various animals which are hunted, to their respective places of abode,—perceives things which an Indian can never see,—steers his course through the wildest forest, by signs invisible to other eyes, yet still correct,—and accomplishes, by means of his ingenuity, objects of which an Indian would have never dreamed.—[n]Among the celebrated hunters of the far-off west, Colonel David Crockett and John Bradshaw,[140] of the Western District, are most conspicuous. Between them, they have killed about fifteen hundred bears, exclusive of a proportionate quantity of other game; and I therefore think this question must be decided in favor of the whites, unless two red hunters can be found, whose deeds may in some measure compare to this.

But let us again take a peep at the Colonel,—for the election is coming on, and he must run for congress. Nor do not fancy, I beseech you, that since his last defeat, he has been altogether idle, or that his time has been spent exclusively in hunting—for, although he has made a very considerable impression on the wild beasts, he has likewise made some impression upon the men,—for which a Kentucky boatman can vouch, who had the pleasure of meeting with him, while in one of his quirky humors. This scene is better described in the Colonel's own language: "I had taken old Betsy," said he, "and straggled off to the banks of the Mississippi river—and meeting with no game, I didn't like it. I felt mighty wolfish 'bout the head and ears—and thought I would spile, if I wusn't kivured up in salt, for I hadn't had a fight in ten days—and I cum acrost a fellow floatin' down stream, settin' in the starn of his boat fast asleep. Said I, "hello stranger,—if you don't take keer your boat will run away with you"—and he waked up; and said he, "I don't value you." He looked up at me slantendicler, and I looked down 'pon him slantendicler—and he took out a chaw of tobaccur, and said he "I don't value you that." Said I, "cum ashore, I can whip you—I bin trying to git a fight all the mornin';" and the varmint flapped his wings and crowed like a chicken. I ris up, shook my mane, and neighed like a horse. He run his boat plump head foremost ashore. I stood still, and sot my triggurs,—that is, took off my shurt, and tied my gallusses[141] tight round my waist—and at it we went. He was a right smart koon, but hardly a bait for sich a fellur as me. I put it to him mighty droll. In ten minutes he yelled enough,—and swore I was a ripstaver. Said I, "ain't I the yallur-flower of the forest? And I am all brimstone but the head and ears, and that's aqui-fortis."[142] Said he, "Stranger, you are a beauty: and if I know'd your name I'd vote for you next election." Said I, "I'm that same David Crockett.

You know what I'm made of. I've got the closest shootin rifle, the best 'coon dog, the biggest ticlur, and the ruffest racking horse, in the district. I can kill more lickur, fool more varmints, and cool out more men, than any man you can find in all Kentuck." Said he, "Good mornin' stranger—I'm satisfied." Said I, "Good mornin' sir; I feel much better since our meetin';" but after I got away a piece, I said, "hello friend, don't forget that vote."

This scene, with some slight alteration, has been attributed, I understand, to an imaginary character Colonel Wildfire.[143] This I have not seen. But I am unwilling that the hard *earnings* of Colonel Crockett should be given to another.

I believe I have said nothing of the religious opinions of Colonel Crockett, and perhaps I should—as a chapter upon religion would be very appropriately situated, in a work of this nature—but am out of humor at present. And will only observe, that I once heard him, upon being invited, refuse to go to meeting; and the reason he assigned was, that he once heard the preacher state positively, that "he had seen a single stalk with thirty-three heads of cabbage on it."

But since the Colonel's defeat for congress, while we have been regaling ourselves with sundry topics he came very near making his exit. Believing that he did not grow rich fast enough, he loaded a boat with staves,[144] and sat out for New-Orleans. In floating down the father of waters, he one day fell asleep; and the crew, in rounding a point in the river, turned the boat bottom upwards. They swam to shore, and nothing was seen of the Colonel. But when all hope was gone, and they least expected it, the Colonel having examined the curiosities at the bottom, was seen *wading* out! Yes, gentle reader,—"walking the waters like a thing o' life"! You know it would have been extremely absurd, to have drowned himself in a stream which he had so often *waded*. Moreover, it would have tended to render fabulous the exploits of which he has so often boasted. He was reserved for a far higher destiny. He had to take another electioneering tour, and perform divers and various feats.

In this age of invention, when the power of steam is running the world mad,[145]—which is not only producing phenomena in mechanics, which future ages shall wonder at and admire, but which perhaps will yet account for the velocity of the comets, and even set the solar system in motion, and which, when applied to the mind, gives to the tongue a volubility unrivalled,—in this state of things, I say, with steam enough, it is not to be wondered at, that any man should make a stump speech.[146] I therefore will not claim for the Colonel the praise which would otherwise be his due, for having often spoken until his tongue was tired performing its offices,—for having often spoken until some veteran stump, which stood firm as the rock of ages, though the winter winds of a century had howled around it, was fatigued with his weight,—but I will claim for him the ingenuity of having discovered, that the best way to keep his arguments unanswered, when his opponent had commenced a reply, was to intimate to the crowd that down at a spring some three or four hundred yards hence, they would find a little steam [liquor], which soon left his adversary nothing to address, but the weary stump to which he had bid adieu.

But from a mind so fruitful in invention, as Colonel Crockett's has ever proved itself, something else should be expected, other than mere stump speaking. And, impressed with a belief that nature never made any thing save in a spirit of economy, as Captain Symmes very justly argues,[147] he resolved that his feet should aid him in the arduous enterprise in which he had engaged. And consequently, he has often shuffled them with the same advantage that he has moved his tongue.

No country presents a greater rage for "tripping on the light fantastic toe," than does the far away west. Here, "belles and matrons, maids and madams," all meet with a suitable partner in the other sex. You do not fancy, gentle reader, that they move with measured steps throughout a gay parterre,[148] or thread the mazy dance in some well-illumined hall? No. Nor do they listen to an Italian band, which warbles the soft airs of its native country. But, with music much more sweet—the *banjo*,—thrummed by some old trusty black, with a hall, whose roof is the star-spangled firmament, and whose floor is girded by the limits of the forest, with forms not screwed into fashion's mould, nor feet encumbered with light prunella's,[149] they trip the fairy dance. Governed by the republican maxim, that we are by nature free and equal, there is no necessity for introductions. And so great is the spirit of accommodation, that they all dance. Whether a lady solicits a gentleman, or a gentleman a lady, is a matter of indifference. Nor can this amusement get along altogether without steam—for there ever burns a furnace bright and ready, from which issues a supply sufficient to keep the *ball* in motion.

This is the famous bran dance of the west; and derives its name from the fact, that the ground is generally sprinkled with the husk of Indian meal. I cannot describe the costume, but do you conceive it,—though not so fine as Cinderella's, yet much more gaudy,—and believe the assembly with hearts as light as their heels, ready to go their *death* for a dance. To this place, during his electioneering tour, did the Colonel repair. And while the following lines fell from the lips of the faithful musician, accompanied by his *banjo*, not one in all the crowd moved with a better grace, or shuffled with more spirit.

Jay burd died wid de hoopin cof,
Snow burd died wid de kolic;
I met an old frog wid a fiddle on he bak,
Enquirin; de way to de frolic.
    Old fokes, young fokes, clare de kitchen,
    Old Firjinny neber tire.

Jay burd set 'pon de swingin' lim'
He look at me, I look at him;
I raise my gun, he seed me cock it,
An de way he flu was a sin to Crockit,
    Old fokes, young fokes, clare de kitchen,
    Old Firjinny neber tire.[150]

It is not to be presumed, that for a meeting of this sort the laws of nature are changed, and fair weather ever preserved. No. Far different is the issue. Invariably does it rain. But so far from putting an end to the frolic, with a fresh addition of steam, it ever adds wings to the heels; and while they regret the loss of the banjo, which the old black carefully hides, he bends forward, rolls up his sleeves, and claps in haste; at the same time singing some old Virginia jig, to which they all keep time with their feet—one of which I must here insert, for I love every thing connected with the land whose bare name, when mentioned as the birth place of a stranger, entitles him to hospitality and kindness.

    Ant Sara, ant Sara in de dary, doin' what?
    She sif de meal, she gim me de hus,
    She bake de bread, she gim me de crus,
    She bile de meat, she gim me de bone,
    She gim me a kik an' sen' me home,
Rube-re de se-de-bre, de punkin vine de juba,
Oh my old horse get ober dubble trubble.

    As I look away yonder, and de green corn growin',
    Pick goose, pick gander, brake bone, suck marrer
    Whoop, I'm gwine away.
Rube-re de se-de-bre, de punkin vine de juba,
Oh my old horse get ober dubble trubble.[151]

Aurora,[152] without regard to weather, never fails to behold the votaries of a bran dance; and gazes with delight on the mud, while creeping up between their tender toes. Unable to support its weight, it curls over, and gently rests upon them.

However, when the election came on, Colonel Crockett, so far from being again beaten by two votes, was returned by a majority of twenty-seven hundred. But he lost a vote, which he very much regretted. This was the vote of a Dutchman, who said, "Crockett was a clever fellow, and he liked him, but he couldn't vote for him; he tell too many cot tam hard tale from de dutch."

CHAPTER XII.

I have before observed, that there are few men who possess in the same degree with Colonel Crockett, the power of gaining men's hearts. And the following instance will serve to illustrate my remark.

Colonel Crockett, with a friend, having wandered off a distance from home, for the purpose of hunting, fell in with some dozen persons, utter strangers, engaged in a spree. Being kindred spirits, a union was soon formed—the bottle was passed round—and its frequent circulation brought about a free interchange of opinions. The election for congress was at hand; and the company fell to dissecting the character of each candidate. Being violently opposed to Colonel Crockett, they treated him with much severity. Crockett agreed with them in all their denunciations, and was among the loudest in abusing Crockett. But as the spirit began to operate, the company became more noisy, and Crockett's suppressed passion began to tire of confinement. While he was struggling to keep it down, one of the company waxing rather warm in his abuse, jumped up, and cried out, "I wish Crockett was here, I'd send him to congress, damn him—I'd lick him so he wouldn't know himself." This was more than flesh and blood could stand. The wish was hardly expressed, before, to the astonishment of all present, Crockett was up with his coat off, in a boxing attitude, telling them who he was, and inviting the fight. The company, though opposed to Crockett, had become much pleased with the two strangers, who had joined them; and they immediately interposed to prevent the fight. The novel situation in which they were placed, and the unexpected and ludicrous manner in which the collision had been brought about, rendered it an easy matter to restore harmony. And, to make it perpetual, Crockett invited the company to go with him to a neighboring store, and take a drink to better acquaintance; saying, that he improved upon acquaintance, and that the longer they knew him, the better they would like him. And so it turned out—for at the store they remained for some time, carousing, and listening to the Colonel's anecdotes; until, overpowered by his humor and kindness, they yielded with a good grace, and swore by the *Eternal*, that they "would live or die in defence of

Crockett." The store happened to be a precinct for holding elections; and it was observed by many, that of the twelve men at one time so violently opposed to him, he lost but a single vote.

In giving to the public this sketch of the backwoods, brief though it may be, I should think I had omitted an essential part of my duty, were I to fail to mention an itinerant class of gentry, now identified with every new country, whose adventures are as amusing as they are annoying to its inhabitants. I allude to the tribe yclept *Clock Pedlers*,[153] which term implies shrewdness, intelligence, and cunning. A pedler in disposing of a clock, feels the same anxiety that a General does on the eve of battle; and displays as much mind in bringing arguments to support his wishes, as Bonaparte did on the plains of Waterloo,[154] in the disposition of his forces. Their perseverance is so untiring, and it has been so often crowned with success, that a yankee clock now graces every cabin throughout the west. And the backwoodsmen, even the half-horse, half-alligator breed, when boasting of their exploits, always add, "I can stand any thing but a clock pedler."

Reader, did you ever know a full blooded yankee clock pedler? If not, imagine a tall, lank fellow, with a thin visage, and small, dark grey eyes, looking through you at every glance, and having the word *trade* written in his every action, and you will then have an idea of Mr. Slim. But to make it clearer, imagine this same individual, with a pedler's wagon, and what he would call a *good cretur*, riding where the roads are smooth, and always walking up hill; and, if you will then fill up his wagon with yankee clocks, throw in a package or two of horn combs,[155] and give him a box of counterfeit jewelry, he will be ready for a trip. Aye, not only ready for a trip, but rich. And every article he parts with, will carry with it a lasting impression of the "clock pedler."

Slim never travelled as if bound to any particular place, for he had business with every man he met and had an excuse for calling at every house. So that after passing through a neighborhood, he was perfectly familiar with the pecuniary concerns of every man in it.

The sun was getting low, when Slim, who was travelling the high road, with a perfect knowledge that there was a tavern about a mile ahead of him, left it to seek a cabin, which, with a modest but retiring aspect, showed itself in the woods at some short distance. The smoke, floating off from a dirt chimney, was mingling with the blue ether; and the children with loud, laughing voices, were playing in the yard. But no sooner did they see the clock pedler, than there was a race, each striving to be the first bearer of the news, that a gentleman with a carriage was coming.

Slim driving up, halted—and there walked out the proprietor of the cabin.

"Friend, can't you give a stranger in these parts some directions?"

"'Bout what, or where?"

"Wuh—my *horse* is tired, and I should like myself to git a pallet."

"If you had kept the road about a mile further, you would have found a tavern; but if you can rough it here, do so. My house is always open to a stranger."

Slim accepts the invitation, draws the wagon in the yard, and while rubbing his cretur down, chuckles to himself, "I've got that fellow."

They go to the house, take a little whiskey and water, eat supper, and draw around the fire.

Slim then makes a dead set to get rid of one of his clocks.

"Stranger, what's your name?"

"Baines."

"An' what's yours?"

"Slim."

"Mr. Baines, I haven't shown you my articles yet."

"What sort of articles?"

"I have a fine clock that I could spare, and some jewelry, and a few combs. They would suit your daughter there, if they ain't too fine—but as I got a great bargain in 'em, I can sell 'em cheap."

"Jewelry in these back-woods![o] 'Twould be as much out of place on my gal here, as my leather hunting shirt would[p] be on you. And as for a clock, I have a good one, you see it there."

Slim finds a thousand faults with it, knows the maker—never did see one of that make worth a damn—and winds up with, "Now let me sell you a clock worth having."

"No. I have one that answers my purpose."

"Not so bad a beginning," says Slim to himself. Slim then brings out his horn, or as he calls them, his *tortoise shell* combs, and his counterfeit jewelry, all of which he warrants to be *genuine*—overwhelms the young lady with compliments upon her present appearance, and enlarges upon the many additional charms his articles would give her—wishes to sell a comb to her mother, who thinks one for her daughter will be sufficient. "Your daughter, madam?"[q] Slim would never have suspected her of being old enough to have a daughter grown. The mother and daughter now begin to see new beauties in the pedler's wares. They select such articles as they would like to have, and joining with the pedler, they pour forth on old Baines one continued volley of sound argument, setting forth the advantages to be derived from the purchase. The old man seeing the storm that is about to burst, collects within himself all his resources, and for a long time parries, with the skill of an expert swordsman, the various deadly thrusts which are made against him. But his opponents return to the charge, in no wise discomfitted. They redouble their energies. With the pedler in front, they pour into the old man volley after volley. No breathing time is allowed. He wavers—falters. Flesh and blood can't stand every thing. And, like a wall before some well directed battery, grows weak, for a moment totters,—then falls, leaving a clear breach,—through this the pedler enters. And having disposed of two *tortoise shell combs*, and a little *double refined jewelry*, the women retire from the field of action, and the pedler, taking advantage of the prostrate condition of his adversary, again reiterates the defects in his clock, and concludes with, "Now let me sell you one cheap."

"No, I'll be damned if you do," says Baines.

(Reader, the only apology for this oath is, would you not have sworn under the same circumstances?)

Slim disappears, but soon returns, bearing in his arms a yankee wooden clock. Baines looks thunder struck.

"Let me put it up."

"No, it's no use."

"I know that. I don't want you to buy it. I only want to put it up."

Still asking permission, yet having it denied, Slim is seen bustling about the room; until, at the end of the dialogue, his wooden clock having encroached upon the dominions of an old family time-piece, is seen suspended with all the beauty, yet bold effrontery, of a yankee notion—while the old family time-piece,[r] with a retiring, yet conscious dignity, is heard to cry out, "Oh tempora! Oh mores!"[156] And concludes her ejaculations by thundering anathemas against this modern irruption of the Goths.[157]

Slim having accomplished so much, draws around the fire, and soothes the old man by discussing the quality of his farm. Baines begins to go into the minutiæ of his farming operations, and the clock strikes nine.

"Now just notice the tone of my clock. Don't you see the difference?"

"A man may buy land here, at a dollar an acre."

"I like always to see in a house a good time-piece; it tells us how the day passes."

"Wife, hadn't we better kill that beef in the morning?"

"Did you notice that clock of mine had a looking glass in it?"

Baines proposes to go to bed. Slim always likes to retire early; and, going to his apartment, cries out, "Well now, old man, buy that clock. You can have it upon your own terms. Think about it and give me an answer in the morning."

"What do I want with the clock?"

"Oh, you can have it upon your own terms. Besides, a man of your appearance ought to have a good clock. I wouldn't have that d—n thing of yours. Did you notice the difference when they were striking?"

Baines going to his room, says, "No, I'll be damned if I buy it."

Soon the house becomes quiet. Slim collects his scattered forces, and makes preparation for a renewal of the attack in the morning. The daughter dreams of tortoise shell combs and jewelry. The mother, from Slim's compliment, believes herself both young and beautiful. And the old man never turns over but the corners of a clock prick him in the side.

Morning comes, and with its first light Slim rises, feeds his cretur, and meeting with Mr. Baines, makes many enquiries after his health, etc.; professes to be in a hurry, and concludes with, "Well, as I must now leave, what say you about the clock?"

"Why, that I don't want it."

Slim bolts into the chamber, where the ladies are scarcely dressed, after whom he makes many enquiries—then jumps into a chair, and sets both clocks to striking, ridicules the sound of the old man's, and commences the well-formed attack of the last night, which he keeps up for nearly an hour, only interrupted by the repeated striking of the clocks.

They then take a fog-cutter,[158] eat breakfast, and Slim returns to the charge. The old man is utterly confounded. Slim sees his advantage, follows him over his farm, every part of which he admires, and which only supports his argument, that a man so well fixed ought to have a good clock. They return to the house, take a little more whiskey and water, and Slim is struck with the improved appearance of the room. His clock sets it off.

Slim, clapping Baines by the shoulder, "Well, now, old gentleman, let me sell you the clock."

"But what shall I do with mine?"

"Oh, I'll buy that. What do you ask for it?"

"It ought to be worth ten dollars."

"Mine cost me forty dollars—but give me thirty to book, and it's a trade."

"Well, I b'lieve—No, I'll be damned if I want it."

"My dear fellow, my clock is fastened up now. Besides, you have made me waste all day here—you ought to take it."

Baines does not exactly see how that is—ˢhesitates—and Slim proceeds to take down the old clock. It is all over now, the money is paid, and Slim is soon ready to leave—but, before going out, he remarks, "It would be as well to leave the old clock here, as I shall be back in a day or two." Slim then mounts his wagon and drives off. And methinks, I can see the rueful countenance of Baines, while gazing at the wagon until it disappears. His thoughts I leave to the imagination of my reader.

About three years after the happening of this event, in passing along, I chanced to call upon Mr. Baines. After being seated a few moments, said I, "Hello, stranger, how came you with a yankee clock in these wild woods?"

"Ah! G-d damn the clock," sighed he, and narrated the above story, showing at the same time his old clock, which, as yet, has never been called for.

Colonel Crockett being elected, we have to transfer him from the wilds of a forest, where his only aim was to compass the ingenuity of wild beasts, or master them in deadly struggle, to a scene which required him at once to forget all former recollections, and enter upon the performance of new duties. We should not therefore wonder, if the character which had been thus idly thrown aside, should in some inadvertent moment leap forth, and for an instant claim the ascendancy. Nor should it be a matter of detraction, if it had asserted its rights, and claimed for itself entire supremacy. For, though opinions may change with wind, the features of a man's character are too deeply stamped, to be altered at will.

So much rubbish has been thrown over the character which I have attempted to trace, that I fear it appears like an object seen through a dark fog, rather indistinctly, —its outlines are not clearly perceptible. I must therefore be pardoned, while, for an instant, I set it forth in a clearer light.

To analyze the mind of Colonel Crockett, and assign the motives which have prompted him to do those particular acts which have given him so much notoriety, must fall to the lot of some philosopher. For myself, I do not feel disposed to dip as deeply in metaphysics as would be requisite to give this matter a fair elucidation. But I take a great pleasure in bearing testimony to the high natural endowments of this gentleman; for I have never seen a character, strip it of all adventitious circumstances, which I could take more pleasure in beholding. Precluded by necessity, from all intercourse with books,—shut out by circumstances, until late years, from that species of society which alone could have benefitted him,—he is really

"Rara avis, et simillima nigroque cygno;"[159]

and yet, at the same time, a fine specimen of human nature.

Many men without the advantages of education, have been great; but it was reserved for the gentleman whose character I have attempted to sketch, bereft of fortune, of education, and of the advantages of society, to be taken wild from the woods, and transferred to the floor of a legislative hall. And yet in Colonel Crockett, in this character, notwithstanding all his eccentricity, we find many of those traits which, of themselves, ennoble and add lustre to our race. What spring of action, other than generosity the most pure, could have often induced him to breast the storms of winter, and force his way through heaps of drifted snow, to supply the wants of some poor famished family, dependent upon the precarious subsistence of hunting, as all families must be, who first make war with the forest. Was there another motive, for having often rescued from the hands of an officer, by his own means, the bed of a widowed woman, with helpless children? Was there another motive, for having often, with his hard earnings, purchased a blanket for a suffering soldier? What spring of action, other than a high and noble daring of soul, could have often prompted him, at the thoughtful hour of midnight, when imbosomed deep in a forest, to peril his life for the sake of a dog—for the sake of that faithful animal which could make no requital? Here there was no approving voice of the world, to urge him on—no loud acclamation of a crowd, to stimulate to action.

Many a spirit will dare to do a deed, in the face of the world, which rather than do when alone, unseen, and apart from assistance, would crouch and fawn like a guilty thing. But, methinks, it is only in a moment of this sort, that the high and lofty attributes of our nature exhibit themselves as the true gift of that being after whom we were fashioned. There are many persons who will look upon these traits of character as mere acts of folly—[t] but to them nature has indeed been poor. They never felt the more generous impulses of our nature. We need not therefore wonder, when this character has been assailed, that presses have been closed to his vindication, and that torrents of abuse, which few in this world are able to withstand, have often burst upon him in all their fury. Notwithstanding this, I do not mean to be understood as saying, that Colonel Crockett is entirely fit for the station which he has often filled, through the kindness of his constituents; for the necessary qualifications of a representative are various and many, and we rarely find them combined in the same individual; yet, so far as the most perfect frankness of manner, an independence of which few can boast, and an honesty of purpose which no one doubts, are considered requisites, Colonel Crockett is qualified in an eminent degree.[u] When one suddenly changes the faith which for a long time he has professed, and is benefitted by the change, we may attribute to him some improper motive; but if by changing, he sacrifices every thing, we must believe it the effect of principle, and there is nothing left at which even envy can cavil.[160] This was the case with him; but in conversing on the subject he laughs and says, "I have never changed. I think now as I did when I started, but

Jackson has turned round." "*I had rather be politically damned than hypocritically immortalized*," is a sentiment which would have honored a far more erudite society than that of the backwoods; and those gentlemen who have supported its author, have the pleasure of knowing that their votes were conferred on one whose intentions at least were honest.[161] To test the worth of a man, strip him of the accidental advantages which fortune may have given him; and, pursuing that plan, how few would be found superior to the subject of this biography. To a person who, like myself, could never behold the magic which gave to a man a character merely because he was rich, or because he was descended from some proud family, it is pleasant to contemplate one rising superior to fortune, and possessing at the same time the ennobling virtues of our race.

CHAPTER XIII.

COLONEL Crockett was no doubt highly gratified by the result of the election. His triumph was a forcible proof of the power of native intellect struggling against opposing circumstances; and, anticipating much pleasure in the boundless field for enterprise which lay before him, in the winter of 1827 he emerged from the wild woods, and occupied a seat in congress. Unacquainted with forms, and a stranger to etiquette, his appearance gave rise to much amusement. But few persons ventured more than once to entertain themselves at his expense. Though rude in speech, his repartee never failed of its object. The notoriety which he had obtained from several speeches made before he reached Washington, rendered him conspicuous as an original,[162] and induced almost every person to seek his society.

But in order to keep up the thread of my narrative, it will be necessary to accompany him on his journey from his residence to Washington City.[163] "When I left home," said he, "I was happy, *devilish*, and full of fun. I bade adieu to my friends, dogs, and rifle, and took the stage, where I met with much variety of character, and amused myself when my humor prompted. Being fresh from the backwoods,ᵛ my stories amused my companions, and I passed my time pleasantly. When I arrived at Raleigh, the weather was cold and rainy, and we were all dull and tired; and upon going in the tavern, where I was an entire stranger, I did not feel more comfortable, for the room was crowded, and the crowd did not give way that I might come to the fire. I felt so damn mean from being jolted in the stage, that I thought I had rather fight than not; and I was *rooting* my way 'long to the fire, not in a good humor, when some fellow staggered up towards me, and cried out, "Hurrah for Adams."[164] Said I, "Stranger, you had better hurrah for hell, damn you, and praise your own country."ʷ

Said he, "And who are you?"

"I'm that same David Crockett, fresh from the backwoods, half horse, half alligator, little touched with the snapping turtle—can wade the Mississippi, leap the Ohio, ride upon a streak of lightning, and slip without a scratch down a honey locust—can whip my weight in wild cats,—and if any gentleman pleases, for a ten dollar bill, he may throw in a panther,—hug a bear too close for comfort—ˣ and whip any man opposed to Jackson."[165]

"While I was telling what I could do," said the Colonel, "the fellow's eyes kept getting larger and larger, until I thought they would pop out. I never saw fellows look as they all did. They cleared the fire for me; and when I got a little warm, I looked about, but my Adams man was gone." I asked Col. Crockett, if he had ever used the above expressions before? He said, "Never; that he felt *devilish*, and they all popped into his head at the time; and that he should never have thought of them again, if they hadn't gone the rounds of all the papers."[166]

"At Raleigh," continues the Colonel, "I became pretty well acquainted, and left there for Petersburg, Va., where happening to get hold of a newspaper, the first thing I saw was a piece headed "Hero of the West," giving an account of my visit to Raleigh. I discovered that it was a source of much amusement; and, not wishing to be known, I determined to obey one of our backwoods sayings, "Lay low, and keep dark stranger, and *prehaps*[167] you'll see some fun." And so I did; for I never let any body know who I was, until I got to Washington."

An anecdote is related as having happened to the Colonel, some where on his route, which partakes strongly of originality. While at dinner, at some public house, where the waiters were very officious in their services, and extremely polite to the Colonel, handing to him every thing on the table, and, among other things, they pressed him to take some chicken; he declined, begging them "if they cared a damn for him, to take it away—for that he had been fed upon chickens until he was nearly feathered."

He arrived in Washington, and had been there but a short time, when he received a note inviting him to dine with the President. Unaccustomed to formality, he did not exactly comprehend its meaning, and required of a friend an explanation, which was cheerfully given; and who also being invited, tendered his services to go along with the Colonel, and introduce him. This was done accordingly, and propriety of action marked his behavior. I was much struck with his simplicity of manner, in narrating to me this event. "I was wild from the backwoods," said he, "and I didn't know nothing 'bout eating dinner with the big folks of our country, and how should I, having been a hunter all my life? I had ate most of my dinners upon a log in the woods, and sometimes no dinner at all. I knew whether I ate dinner with the President or not, was a matter of no consequence, for my constituents were not to be benefitted by it. I did not go to

court the President, for I was opposed to him in principle, and had no favors to
ask at his hands. I was afraid, however, I should be awkward, as I was so entirely
a stranger to fashion; and in going along, I resolved to observe the conduct of
my friend, Mr. Verplanck,[168] and to do as he did; and I know," said he, "that I
did behave myself right well."

The Colonel's originality of character, induced some person to write a humorous, yet false account, of this dinner scene, which could never have been believed
by any person who knew him, but which the Colonel thought proper to deny, as
it was used to his prejudice by his enemies.[169]

The account alluded to is here inserted, and with it the certificates which
go to disprove it. The Colonel is supposed to have returned from Washington,
after his first winter, and to be at a house-raising[170] among his constituents,
where, to their numerous enquiries relative to his visit to Washington, he gives
the following account.

"The first thing I did," said Davy, "after I got to Washington, was to go to
the President's. I stepped into the President's house—thinks I, who's afeard?
If I didn't I wish I may be shot. Says I, "Mr. Adams, I'm Mr. Crockett, from
Tennessee." "So," says he, "how d'ye do Mr. Crockett?"; and he shook me by
the hand, although he know'd I went the whole hog for Jackson. If he didn't
I wish I may be shot. Not only that, but he sent me a printed ticket to dine
with him. I've got it in my pocket yet. If I havn't I wish I may be shot." (Here
the printed ticket was exhibited for the admiration of the whole company.) "I
went to dinner, and I walked all round the long table, looking for something
that I liked. At last I took my seat just beside a fat goose, and I helped myself
to as much of it as I wanted. But I hadn't took three bites, when I looked way
up the table at a man they called *Tash*, (attache.) He was talking French to
a woman on t'other side of the table. He dodged his head, and she dodged
her's, and then they got to drinking wine across the table. If they didn't I wish
I may be shot. But when I looked back again, my plate was gone, goose and
all. So I jist cast my eyes down to t'other end of the table, and sure enough I
seed a white man walking off with my plate. I says, "hello, mister, bring back
my plate." He fetched it back in a hurry, as you may think; and when he set
it down before me, how do you think it was? Licked as clean as my hand. If
it wasn't I wish I may be shot. Says he, "What will you have sir?" And says
I, "You may well say that, after stealing my goose." And he begun to laugh.
If he didn't I wish I may be shot. "Then" says I, "mister, laugh if you please;
but I don't half like sich tricks upon travellers. If I do I wish I may be shot."
I then filled my plate with bacon and greens; and whenever I looked up or
down the table, I held to my plate with my left hand. If I didn't I wish I may

be shot. When we were all done eating, they cleared every thing off the table, and took away the table cloth. And what do you think? There was another cloth under it. If there wasn't I wish I may be shot. Then I saw a man coming 'long carrying a great glass thing with a glass handle below, something like a candlestick. It was stuck full of little glass cups, with something in them that looked good to eat. Says I, "Mister, bring that thing here." Thinks I, let's taste them first. They were mighty sweet and good—so I took six of 'em. If I didn't I wish I may be shot."[171]

Correspondence between Mr. Crockett of Tennessee, Mr. Clark of Kentucky, and Mr. Verplanck[172] of New-York, all three members of the House of Representatives.

House of Representatives,
January 3d, 1829.

Dear Sir—Forbearance ceases to be a virtue, when it is construed into an acquiescence in falsehoods, or a tame submission to unprovoked insults.

I have seen published and republished in various papers of the United States, a slander, no doubt characteristic of its author, purporting to be an account of my first visit to the President of the nation. I have thus long passed the publication alluded to with silent contempt. But supposing that its republication is intended, as in its origin it evidently was, to do me an injury, I can submit to it no longer, without calling upon gentlemen who were present to do me justice. I presume, sir, that you have a distinct recollection of what passed at the dinner alluded to; and you will do me the favor to say distinctly, whether the enclosed publication is not false. I would not make this appeal, if it were not that like other men I have enemies, who would take much pleasure in magnifying the plain rusticity of my manners into the most unparalleled grossness and indelicacy. I have never enjoyed the advantages which many have abused; but I am proud to hope, that your answer will show that I have never so far prostituted the humble advantages I do enjoy, as to act the part attributed to me. An early answer is requested.

I am sir, most respectfully,
Your obedient servant,
DAVID CROCKETT.

Hon. James Clark, of Ky.

A similar request to the above, was communicated to the Hon. Mr. Verplanck, of New-York.

WASHINGTON CITY, Jan. 4, 1829.

Dear Colonel—In your letter of yesterday, you requested me to say, if the ludicrous newspaper account of your behavior when dining with the President, which you enclosed to me, is true?

I was at the same dinner, and know that the statement is destitute of every thing like truth. I sat opposite to you at the table, and held occasional conversation with you, and observed nothing in your behavior but what was marked with the strictest propriety.

I have the honor to be, with great respect,

Your obedient servant,
JAMES CLARK.

Col. D. CROCKETT.

WASHINGTON, Jan. 4, 1829.

Dear Sir—I have already several times anticipated your request, in regard to the newspaper account of your behavior at the President's table, as [I] have repeatedly contradicted it in various companies where I heard it spoken of. I dined there in company with you at the time alluded to, and had, I recollect, a good deal of conversation with you. Your behavior there was, I thought, perfectly becoming and proper; and I do not recollect or believe that you said or did any thing resembling the newspaper account.

I am yours,
GULIAN C. VERPLANCK.

Col. CROCKETT.

That Colonel Crockett should have had to produce certificates of his behavior, is certainly a novel circumstance, but tend much to prove how various were the attacks, and how wanton the abuse, which was heaped upon him. So much use was made by his enemies in his own district, of the above publication, that justice to himself induced him unwillingly to appear before the public, in order to vindicate himself from so ridiculous a charge. His rusticity of manner, blended with great good humor, frequently gave rise to much fun. He was ever the humorous hero of his own story, and defended himself from the sallies of his acquaintances with so much pertinacity, that no time, no place, not even the pomp of wealth, nor the pride of name, could awe him into silence, when jocosely assailed. The following circumstance is a forcible proof of this remark. "After the dinner was over," said the Colonel, "I, with the remainder of the company, retired to the famous 'East Room.' I had drank a glass or two of wine, and felt in a right good humor, and was walking about gazing at the furniture, and at the splendid company with which it was filled. I noticed that many persons observed me; and just at that time, a young gentleman stepped up to me and said, "I presume sir, you are from the backwoods?"

"Yes sir," said I.

A friend whispering to me at the time, said it was the President's son—ʸand as I had never been introduced to him, I know'd he wanted to have some fun at my expense, because, after I spoke the first word, you might have heard a pin drop. All was silence. So I thought I would keep it up. Mr. A. then asked me, "What were the amusements in the backwoods?"

"Oh, said I, "fun [is] alive there. Our people are all divided into classes, and each class has a particular sort of fun, so a man is never at a loss, because he knows which class he belongs to!"ᶻ

"How is that" said Mr. A.

"We have four classes," said I, "in the backwoods. The first class have a table with some green truck on it, and it's got pockets; and they knock a ball about on it to git it in the pockets," (billiard table,) "and they see a mighty heap of fun. They is called the quality of our country, but to that class I don't belong."

"Then there is the second class," said I. "They take their rifles, and go out about sun-rise, and put up a board with a black spot on it about a hundred yards off, and they shoot from morning till night for any thing you please. They see a mighty heap of fun too; and I tell you what, I am mighty hard to beat as a second rate hand in the class."

"The third class," said I, "is composed of our little boys. They go out about light with their bows and arrows, and put up a leaf against a tree, and shoot from morning till night, for persimmons, or whortleberries,[173] or some such thing; and they see a mighty heap of fun too."

"But the fourth class," said I, "oh, bless me! they have fun. This is composed of the women, and all who choose to join them. When they want a frolic, they just go in the woods and scrape away the leaves, and sprinkle the ground with corn bran,[174] and build some large lightwood fires round about, raise a banjo, and begin to dance. May be, you think they don't go their death upon a jig, but they do, for I have frequently gone there the next morning and raked up my two hands (placing them together,) full of toe nails."

"By the time," says the Colonel, "I had finished giving an account of our amusements, the whole house was convulsed with laughter, and I slipped off, and went to my lodgings."

I asked him, what prompted him to tell the above story?

He said, that "most persons believed every thing which was said about the backwoods, and he thought he would tell a good story while he was at it. Besides," said he, "the object in questioning me at such a place, was to confuse me, and laugh at my simplicity, and I thought I would humor the thing."

The above scene gave rise to much amusement, and considering the company in whose presence it occurred, it is certainly without a parallel. And nothing could give a more forcible proof of the most perfect independence of character—perfectly at home in the presence of a president, foreign ministers, senators, congress men, and the polished ladies of Washington City.

CHAPTER XIV.

As a member of congress, Colonel Crockett was ever at his post, faithful and assiduous in his attention to the welfare of his constituents; and his great personal popularity rendered him a valuable representative to his district. He who consumes most time, and makes most noise, is rarely a serviceable member. But he attends to the interests of his constituents, who, without wasting time in idle declamation, is ever at his post, voting upon all subjects which in any manner affect the people of his district. A political life of this nature would merely form a tissue of dry details, uninteresting and unnecessary, save as a work of reference.

Although possessed of many requisites for a representative, it was not his political life which has given him so much notoriety, but his talent for humor and originality. As a boon companion, no one stood higher than Colonel Crockett; and his conduct has been often characterized by acts of generosity, which reflect much credit upon him as a man, and lustre upon the state of society in which he originated. Few persons, with the same means, have ever performed more acts of kindness, and still fewer with so perfect a disregard to all future recompense. Were it proper, these remarks might be illustrated by private anecdotes, which would place the character of Colonel Crockett in a very fair light. It has become customary in the common publications of the day, to make every backwoodsman rant and rave in uncouth sayings, and in new coined words, difficult of pronunciation. This being done, the character is finished, and the hero turned loose as a genuine son of the wild woods. Nothing can argue a greater ignorance of the true character of a backwoodsman,[aa] than a sketch of this nature.[175] I have before remarked, that so far from this being true, they express themselves in the simplest language possible. The most extravagant ideas they clothe in simple language, and they delight us by quaintness of expression and originality of conception. If there be any one distinguishing feature in their character, it is a generosity and nobleness of soul, seldom met with in a more polished society. Did I want a friend who would stick by me through all the trials of adversity in life, give me the backwoodsman, a stranger to form and fashion, who uncorrupted by intercourse with the world, has held communion only with his own heart, and worshipped God only in the beauty of nature. Though their rusticity may often give rise to amusement, yet there is a high and lofty bearing in their deportment. They have been so long companions with danger, that they become strangers to fear. They have nothing to conceal, and are consequently frank in their manners. It would be difficult to hire an inhabitant of a polished city to do, what a backwoodsman first did from necessity, and habit afterwards renders familiar. To sleep in the wild woods apart from assistance, with no music save the hungry howling of the beasts of the forest, and to cross rivers whose depth is unknown, at all seasons of the year, form but small items in the life of a backwoodsman. To me it seems, that a determined purpose of mind is a part of their character. Often I have been struck with their fearlessness, upon seeing them in the most inclement season ride their horses in a stream, careless of its depth or hidden dangers, and force their way across.

In sketching the life of Colonel Crockett, we find so much levity, good sense, good humor, and such a propensity for fun, that his character is often seen in different lights. Yet, I think, any person may recognize the original from the picture drawn. The following circumstance shows a singular conception of ideas.

During the Colonel's first winter in Washington, a caravan of wild animals was brought to the city and exhibited. Large crowds attended the exhibition; and prompted by common curiosity, one evening Colonel Crockett attended.

"I had just got in," said he, "the house was very much crowded, and the first thing I noticed was two wild cats in a cage. Some acquaintance asked me "if they were like the wild cats in the backwoods?"—and I was looking at them, when one turned over and died. The keeper ran up, and threw some water on it. Said I, "Stranger, you are wasting time. My looks kills them things—and you had a damn sight better hire me to go out here, or I will kill every damn varmint you've got." While I and he was talking, the lion began to roar. Said I, "Turn him out, turn him out, damn him, I can whip him for a ten dollar bill, and the zebra may kick occasionally during the fight." This created some fun, and I then went to another part of the room, where a monkey was riding a pony. I was looking on, and some member said to me, "Crockett, don't that monkey favor General Jackson?" "No," said I, "but I'll tell you who it does favor.

It looks like one of your boarders, Mr. —— of Ohio."[176] There was a loud burst of laughter at my saying so, and upon turning round, I saw Mr. ——, of Ohio, in about three feet of me. I was in a right awkward fix; but I bowed to the company, and told 'em, "I had either slandered the monkey, or Mr. ——, of Ohio, and if they would tell me which, I would beg his pardon." The thing passed off; and next morning as I was walking the pavement before my door, a member come up to me and said, "Crockett, Mr. ——, of Ohio, is going to challenge you." Said I, "Well tell him I am a fighting fowl. I 'spose if I am challenged, I have the right to choose my weapons?" "Oh yes," said he. "Then tell him," said I, "that I will fight him with bows and arrows."[bb]

There was another circumstance occurred while Colonel Crockett was in Washington, which goes far to show how perfectly a stranger to every thing like fashion he is. A young gentleman of worth and respectability had been paying his addresses to a daughter of Colonel Crockett's; and having obtained her consent, wrote to her father in Washington, requesting his permission that they might be married. The Colonel approving of the match, wrote in answer to his letter the following laconic reply:

"WASHINGTON, ——.
Dear Sir—I received your letter. Go ahead.
DAVID CROCKETT."[177]

I have never known a character more free from restraint under all circumstances, or more truly independent, than Col. Crockett. After the adjournment of congress, the Colonel returned home; and he who but a short time before had been mixing with the fashion of our own and foreign countries, and representing a district composed of seventeen counties, in the congress of one of the first nations upon earth, might then be found with a hoe or plough, laboring for the subsistence of his family. What a beautiful commentary is his election upon our republican institutions! Not only a proof that the power of our institutions is derived directly from the people, but what an example of the easy access of the humblest individual, to the highest offices within the gift of our government, that he, whom the satellites of a regal government would despise for his poverty—that he whose daily labor in the field was required to provide for the necessities of life for a family—that he, entirely uneducated, should, because the people willed it, be called upon to represent persons of wealth, of family influence, and of education: not a greater mark of their power, than that he whom our senate had denigrated, should be chosen by the people to preside over the same body.

In attending to the duties of his farm, and in hunting when the season permitted, Colonel Crockett spent his time between the meetings of congress. Having gathered in his corn, and provided for the wants of his family, the time drew near for him to return to Washington. For a change of scenery, he determined to take the steam-boat[cc] as far as Wheeling.[178] And accompanied by several friends, he went down to Mills' Point for that purpose. There they had to wait some time for a boat. There was likewise a young gentleman present, who was waiting to go down the river. A boat appeared, descending the river. The young gentleman raised a signal and hallooed, but all in vain. The boat swept gracefully by, heedless of his cries. Colonel Crockett having witnessed the scene, and seeing the situation of the young man, turned to him—"Stranger, do you know what I would have done with that boat if I had been in your place?"

"No. What could you have done?"

"Well, I'll tell you what I'd have done. I would have just walked right on board of her, taken her by the *bill*,[179] and have dipped her under. Damn 'em, they are all afraid of me upon these waters, but they don't know you. You see when I speak to them if they don't obey me."

It was but a short time before a boat was seen struggling up against the current. The Colonel raised his flag, and upon nearing the point where he stood, the boat curved beautifully round, and in a few moments was lying at the shore waiting for her passenger. The Colonel seeing the young man said, "Stranger, didn't I tell you so. You see they are afraid of me." Colonel Crockett had become so notorious, that the boats were all anxious to get him as a passenger. He was an inexhaustible fountain of fun to every company in which he happened to be thrown.

During their passage up the river, a small company had assembled around the Colonel at the bow of the boat; and while there the machinery got out of order, and the boat began to go along with the current.

"Heave anchor," cries the captain.

"Hold," cries Crockett. "Pay me for the wood you would burn, and I will get out and tow her up; and for double price, damn her, I will take her over the falls."

He then went on to Washington, where he remained until congress adjourned.

Colonel Crockett's term of service having expired, he again announced himself as a candidate for congress. The character which he had acquired for eccentricity, organized a powerful opposition against him, and no one ever entered the field against greater odds. He was caricatured in the shape of almost every living wild animal, and his innocent ebullitions of humor were gravely arraigned against him. Every species of vituperation was showered on him, but without effect. He was too deeply seated in the affections of his constituents. Living among them as poor as the poorest, in a hut the work of his own hands, his interest was perfectly identified with their's. He was their companion under all circumstances. He hunted with them, or if his assistance was wanted he was ready to cut logs, and help a friend to put up his cabin, help him to dig a well, and *fix out and out*,[180] and then he was ready to divide his meat and bread with him. No friend ever asked a favor which could be granted, that was denied. To confer a favor always gave him a pleasure; and it was this innate love of conferring benefits, which served to render him so popular. Nothing could be more perfectly original, and at the same time more humorous, than his mode of getting rid of the various charges which were preferred against him. And indeed his manner shows, that he was possessed of more good humor than falls to the lot of most of us.

As a husband, no one can be more kind and indulgent than the Colonel. As a father, he is not only affectionate, but even a companion for his children. Yet notwithstanding these circumstances, the malevolence of some person originated a report that he was unkind to his wife, that she had most of the labor to do, and that he would not even give her shoes. The report was entirely false, and gave the Colonel no concern. Indeed, the vilest slander, when entirely destitute of truth, gives us much less concern than one of a much milder nature, founded though remotely on fact. At some public gathering the report was told to the Colonel, who, with the utmost good humor, said it was a lie—that his wife neither wanted for shoes, nor did she have much work to do, for that he always gave her his old boot legs to make shoes of, and cut up wood enough when he went to Washington to last her till he got back. Pursuing a plan of this sort, so entirely new, nothing disconcerts him. And that circumstance indeed which occurs in his presence must be a singular one, which he does not turn to his advantage. Believing that honest poverty is no crime, he is not ashamed of his circumstances, and frequently alludes to them in some amusing manner.

In the section of country in which Colonel Crockett lives, there are very few slaves. Almost every man has to labor for the subsistence of his family. Many of his constituents are poor, yet they live comfortably, and are happy and cheerful; and there is a greater interchange of neighborly acts among the citizens of his district, than I have seen any where in the west. To an agriculturist who wishes to get rich, the Western District holds out few advantages, on account of the failure which has marked the cotton crop for several years past.[181] It is too far north for cotton, but is an excellent grain and corn country. And to one who has a family dependent upon his own exertions, and who would be content to live comfortably, no country presents more advantages than does the north-western part of the district of Tennessee. The soil is light, very productive, and easy of cultivation, and you there meet with good water, which is rarely to be found in the more settled parts of the district. The country is very much intersected with rivers, which flow into the Mississippi, and which, when they are cleared out and their navigation improved, will render lands in that section of the country very valuable.[182]

Colonel Crockett was acquainted with the situation of his constituents. They had settled upon public lands lying waste and uncultivated—they had improved them—they had rendered them more valuable by making roads and building bridges, and rendering that section of the country accessible to the more settled parts of the west—they had breasted all the dangers and difficulties attendant upon settling a new country—they had labored under so many disadvantages, that the Colonel thought their claims upon the justice and clemency of the general government were of a high order. And to place those lands within the reach of every citizen of his district, that he might provide a home for himself and family, was with him an overruling passion. His attention was directed closely to this subject while in congress, and it was so managed by him, that if in his zeal for the welfare of his constituents he had not asked too much, he might have conferred upon them a sensible benefit, and have given them their lands at a much less price than perhaps any future representative will be able to do. If in the matter however he erred, his error must be attributed to his wishes for the welfare of his constituents, and to a firm belief on his part that his views were correct, and that at some future day he would bring his favorite scheme to bear.[183]

The above subject generally formed a part of his discourse in his public harangues, or his *war talks*, as electioneering speeches are called in the west. He also frequently discusses and gives his views upon questions affecting the general interests of our country. He has ever been a strong friend to internal improvements; and as will be seen, it was this subject afterwards which induced him to withdraw his support from General Jackson. As a speaker, Colonel Crockett is irregular and immethodical in the arrangement of his discourse. He seizes upon whatever comes first, which he expresses in bold and strong terms. His language, though rude and unpolished, is forcible; and his discourse is pleasing from the humor and singular comparisons which pervade it, and from the numerous anecdotes with which he illustrates his subjects. His electioneering tour was arduous and laborious, yet he surmounted all difficulties; and the result of the electioneering showed that he was returned to congress by a majority of thirty five hundred votes. Thus, so far from losing ground, he had actually gained upon the affections of his constituents.

The election being over, the Colonel returned home to cultivate his little field of corn; and when leisure permitted, again sought the company of his dogs and rifle. He has been so long wedded to hunting, that it now seems a part of his business. An old hunter never forgets the sound of the horn, but even when too old to join in the chase, its cheering voice gives animation to his weather-beaten frame, and carries him back to youthful scenes, where, in the rapture of the moment, he forgets that he is no longer young. None but a hunter can tell how the heart swells at the joyous sound of the horn, or how it dances with delight at the approach of an animating chase, or how elastic the step and how buoyant the feelings when one rises with the first dawn of light, and sallies forth to hunt the deer, or rouse from his lair the more hated beasts of the forest. Bears, panthers, wild cats, and wolves, create much excitement for the hunter. The first are hunted principally as a matter of profit; the latter because they are very destructive to hogs and sheep, and also because they have frequently been known to attack individuals when alone and apart from assistance. An attack from wild animals east of the Mississippi river, is now somewhat a rare circumstance; but you can scarcely meet with an old hunter who is not able to tell you of some desperate struggle, or hair breadth 'scape.

I believe there is no animal so willing to attack the human species as our common panther. When irritated by hunger it is reckless of consequences, and makes its attacks under all circumstances. While travelling through the late Choctaw purchase,[184] I stopped with a Mr. Turnbull, an old settler, who amused me with many anecdotes connected with the wildness of the country; and among others, with an account of the fight he had had with a panther, marks of which he now carries, and will carry to his grave.

He had built a cabin at some distance in the woods, and had but lately taken possession of it, when sitting by a good fire on a damp, rainy evening, he was endeavoring to quiet his child, which was crying, and for that purpose placed it upon his shoulder, and walked his apartment. The door was open, and he turned to it to examine the weather, when a panther, attracted perhaps by the cries of the child, sprung upon him, fastening its fore claws in his head, and its hind claws in his thighs. Mr. Turnbull, who is full six feet high, large and muscular, dropped his child, and being without arms seized the panther by the throat with one hand, and with the other hugged it closer to him, and then fell on the floor so as to keep the panther at bottom. At first he said he could feel its claws working their way into his flesh, but the strong grasp which he had on its throat soon caused it to loosen its hold, and he then, retaining his grasp, dragged it to the fire, which was burning brightly, and threw it in. The panther upon being so roughly treated, endeavored to escape out of the chimney.

Whenever it would attempt to spring out, he would pull it back by the tail. He pursued this plan until it was disabled from the fire, and then seizing his axe knocked it in the head. His wife was present and a witness of the scene, but so much alarmed as to be unable to render any assistance. Exclusive of this, he was once, when riding with a friend, pursued some distance by a panther. They prepared for battle, and it followed them for some distance seeking an opportunity, though it did not make an attack. Their general mode of attack is to couch themselves upon a tree, and spring off upon whatever comes near them. I heard a hunter say that he had once seen as many as five panthers in view, on the trees adjoining a large salt lick, where they were waiting to spring upon deer.

The following anecdote was narrated to me as having actually occurred. There lived in the west three brothers, John, Dick, and Bill, famed for their propensity for quarrel and love of fighting. They invariably attended every public place, and elicited a fight if there was a possible chance. And what was very remarkable, the oldest brother present would always claim the privilege of fighting, though a younger one might have brought about the quarrel. So steadfastly was this privilege adhered to, that Bill, the younger, never could have a fight, but would often cry and say "that his brothers wouldn't let him have a fight, though he b'lieved he was a better man than any of 'em." He was so anxious to try his prowess, and begged so hard for a chance, that it was agreed among them that the next fight which could be raised, should belong exclusively to Bill. Not long after this determination, John and Bill went out upon a hunting excursion. They had wandered about for some time in the woods, when stopping to rest, they discovered a panther couched upon a limb, and in the act of springing upon them. Before John, who had his rifle, could shoot it [,] it had lit upon Bill, who drew from its sheath his hunting knife, and with his hands and feet commenced a desperate fight. The panther would no sooner light upon him, than its hold was cut loose, which rendered it frantic, and for a long time they fought with all the spirit of desperation. During this scene, John, the oldest brother, stood by, leaning carelessly on his rifle, apparently an unconcerned spectator of the fight. The fight was still prolonged. Bill's clothes were stripped from him, and he with the panther literally besmeared with blood. Fortunately Bill's knife found its way to the panther's heart, and freed him from his antagonist. This was no sooner done, than naked, his body streaming with blood from the nails of the panther, he ran up to his brother John to take vengeance for his not having assisted him; who only laughed, and told him of the promise which he had exacted, that the first fight which could be raised should belong exclusively to him; saying at the same time, "it had been a beautiful fight—that Bill had given good evidence of manhood, and had acquitted himself with great credit." The compliment was pleasing to Bill. He went to a branch, washed the blood from his body, borrowed some of his brother's clothes, and ever afterwards thanked him for being permitted to win for himself so much reputation. Bill was at once exalted above his brothers, and ever afterwards retained his reputation. For he who had whipped a panther a fair fight, could never get a chance of losing his hard earned fame by fighting with a man.

Wild cats also have frequently been known to attack persons. The following story was told to me by a gentleman cognizant of the circumstances. A person who had removed from the east to our western forests, had selected a site for his residence, and was engaged in putting up the necessary houses for a settlement. His negroes at night were encamped at his door, and it happened that while they were preparing their supper, a wild cat sprung upon an old negro woman, one of the group, and though her cries speedily brought assistance, they were scarcely able to preserve her life. It was several times beaten off, but strange to tell, returned, and each time sought her from the crowd as its victim. Wolves abound in large numbers throughout the west, but the settlements have become so thick, that they rarely now venture to attack individuals. It is somewhat remarkable, that though you may hear innumerable wolves at night, you rarely ever see them during the day. I have often heard old hunters remark this; and I suppose it is owing to the circumstance that their sense of smelling is very acute, which enables them to elude their enemies. Farther, as a proof of their sagacity, they generally travel constantly in windy weather, and always against the wind, by which means they are able to detect an enemy before it approaches them, trusting to their heels should they be pursued. It is idle to hunt them with dogs, for they never tire, but have been known to catch and eat a dog out of the very pack which was pursuing them. A panther, though more ferocious, will flee from a dog, and is easily treed. These are some of the circumstances which, blended with the wild appearance of the country, create so much interest to the traveller, and readily render a trip to the unsettled portions of the west, a delightful recreation to one tired of a city life. But exclusive of the game above enumerated, you find occasionally a few elk, and every species of game common to our country. Partridges, pheasants, woodcocks, and turkeys, abound in large numbers—for a genuine son of the backwoods rarely condescends to molest them. Nor must I forget the many species of ducks which infest our western waters in great numbers, and easily fall a prey to the hunter. The prairies in some parts of the west, and the barrens in other parts, form the best hunting grounds; and they are so extensive and open, that nothing could afford a fairer field to the sportsman. Having been raised in one of the oldest states in the union, where my ambition never rose higher than to stop the woodcock in his circling flight, or bring the partridge tumbling to the ground, my spirits danced with delight when as a hunter I first trod our western forests, where instead of meeting with some lone bird lamenting the loss of its mate, to whom the deadly shot of the sportsman would give relief, I roused the bounding deer from its covert, or drove before me, in wide extended fields, clouds of birds, from morning until night. My fondness for shooting small game, such as turkeys, partridges, and woodcocks, gave the old hunters much amusement; and they laughed at me with the same pleasure that an old weather-beaten tar does at a landsman just seeking the ocean for his home. The habits of the wild pigeon[185] have long been a subject of much curiosity. The great numbers in which they appear, the singular propensity that they have to roost together, have for some time been a source of speculation. They frequently fly as much as eighty miles to feed, and return to their roost the same evening. This was proved by shooting them at their roost of a morning when their craws were empty, and then shooting them again in the evening when they returned. Their craws were then found filled with rice, and it was computed that the nearest rice field could not be within a less distance than eighty miles. I have often seen pigeon roosts in the older states, but they scarcely give an idea of one in the west. I have seen a cloud of those birds cover the horizon in every direction, and consume an hour in passing. And near a roost, from an hour before sunset until nine or ten o'clock at night, there is one continued roar, resembling that of a distant water-fall. A roost frequently comprises one hundred acres of land, and strange, though literally true, as can be attested by thousands, the timber, even though it be of the largest growth, is so split and broken by the immense numbers which roost upon it, as to be rendered entirely useless. There are few persons hardy enough to venture in a roost at night. The constant breaking of the trees renders it extremely dangerous; and besides, there is no necessity for shooting the birds, as the mere breaking of the limbs kills many more than are taken away. A pigeon roost in the west resembles very much a section of country over which has passed a violent hurricane. Wolves, foxes, etc. are constant attendants upon a pigeon roost.

It is as a hunter that I like most to dwell upon the character of Colonel Crockett, for in that capacity he is really great. I do not know that I ever enjoyed more pleasure than I did during my first hunt with Colonel Crockett. The character he had obtained, the great quantities of game he had killed, and the sagacity of his dogs, all of which had often in my presence been the theme of conversation, created a restless anxiety on my part at once with him to mingle in the chase, and be a witness of his far-famed skill. So, having determined on the following morning to take an elk hunt, we cleaned our guns, prepared for the chase, and with pleasant conversation whiled away the early part of the evening. I then retired to bed, feasting on anticipation, and even anxious to annihilate time. At last the heavy night passed away and morning came, and with it came hope, and happiness, and buoyancy of spirit. I arose and went out; the Colonel was already up, and seizing an old horn which swung from the logs of the cabin, he sounded it until the woods seemed alive, while echo answered to its joyous notes. Then the dogs which were scattered about the yard rose from their couches, yawned, stretched themselves, and lent their deep toned voices to its cheering sound.

The morning was not more beautiful than usual. The sun bounded up into the heavens, and tinged with its golden beams the tops of the forest; but this it had often done before, and yet I thought nature never looked so cheerful, so lovely. Happy myself, I saw every thing only through the medium of my own feelings. I did not think that the music which had so many charms for me, was but the death note of preparation for the execution of some noble elk, or panting stag. While my heart thrilled with pleasure at the scene before me, I did not recollect that every blast which floated off, carried with it to quaking hearts the idea of a long and weary chase, a certain yet protracted death. However, my feelings ran but a short time in this strain. The arrival of several of the neighbors with their dogs who had been invited to join us, their rifle-guns[dd] and accoutrements, their wild and picturesque dresses, and the tumultuous barking of the dogs, infused into us only animation, and a desire for the chase. So having obtained our breakfasts, we were soon on foot, moving merrily forward to a small hurricane, which had been agreed upon for a drive.[186] The time consumed in arriving there we whiled away by the narration of anecdotes and sage prophecies, with regard to our probable success.

Having also settled among ourselves the way that the elk, if roused, would run, I selected for myself a stand, with a certain expectation of a shot. Colonel Crockett selected a small opening within sight of me, and the remainder of the hunters stationed themselves at different points of the hurricane. We were then ready. The sound of the horn, and the cheering hark of the driver, told us that he had already entered the hurricane. For some time all was quiet, and nothing broke in upon the stillness of the scene, save the "*look about*," "*hark about dogs*," from the lips of the driver. Time never seemed to me to move so heavily; and weary, I seated myself, where in fancy I listened to the cry of the dogs, and killed many a noble elk, as he bounded by me. But this delusion lasted not long before I was waked up by the music of a living chase. At first the dogs opened in long yells, at irregular intervals, and slowly they appeared to move through the tangled thicket,—then burst forth one long, loud roar, as they dashed off, and they swept through the woods like the blast of a tornado. "He's up, he's up," with a loud whoop, was shouted from the lips of the driver, and the woods re-echoed with the roar of the dogs. Trembling with anxiety I jumped up and cocked my gun, expecting every moment to see the elk. I turned towards Colonel Crockett. He was lounging idly against an old beech tree, his rifle leaning against it, and he apparently an unconcerned spectator of the scene.

For some moments it was difficult to tell which way the dogs were running,—then their notes became fainter, and my heart grew sick while I thought they were leaving me. They stretched on until they were almost lost to the ear. They circled, they tacked, they were at fault. I heard them coming, and my heart grew glad as their music increased. Another moment,—with wide stretched eyes I looked in every direction,—and all was still, though the dogs were circling near me. Colonel Crockett, calm and unmoved, now held his rifle—the bushes crack, his leaps are heard—'tis the elk that's coming. The Colonel shrunk behind a tree, and raised his rifle. The game is in view—not an elk, but a lovely stag is bounding by us. Colonel Crockett bleated—the stag was deceived, it stopped, and with panting sides and lofty head, looked wildly round. I raised my rifle; the Colonel's rung through the forest, and with it the cry of *"here, here, here dogs,"* he running in a direction counter to that in which the deer was standing. In an instant the deer bounded away like lightning, and "a panther, a panther!" was shouted from the lips of Colonel Crockett. I ran up to him, and learned that while he was in the act of shooting the deer, a panther, roused from his lair by the cry of the dogs, had passed by, at which he thought he had discharged his rifle with effect. The horn was soon sounded, the dogs after much trouble were called off from the deer, the huntsmen were assembled, the cause was explained, and we then proceeded to examine the spot where Colonel Crockett said he had shot. But a few moments sufficed to convince us that the panther was wounded; the deer was gladly forgotten, and with joyous shouts we placed the dogs upon the panther's trail, and followed on. Nothing could be more animating than their eager cry. Long and weary was the chase, which was sure to lead us wherever most difficulties opposed our progress. The joyous shouts of the huntsmen so animated the dogs, that they gave the panther but little rest. For a long time he eluded their pursuit; but they caught him upon the brink of a little branch, and never did I hear such a fight. The wild screams of the panther, and the loud yelling of the wounded dogs resounded through the forest. I scrambled on through briars, bushes, etc. and arrived just in time to see the panther with one desperate effort tear himself from the dogs and slip off. With unabated vigor they followed on, and for some time held a running fight, when the panther, to relieve himself, took a tree. The peculiar notes of the dogs told of this joyous event, and fierce was the struggle who should reach there soonest. Who was the fortunate person I have now forgotten, though I well recollect that I was not. A short time, however, brought us together, and merry were we at the panther's expense. He was couched in the crotch of a tree, looking composedly down upon the dogs, his eyes gleaming with rage. Fearing he may jump down and give us more trouble, we all formed a line, and at a given signal, fired our balls into the panther's body. He fell without a struggle, and instantly every dog was upon him, worrying him as if he was alive. I have often known old hunters, when their dogs were loth to take hold, shoot their guns in the air, and it always produces the desired effect—they immediately seize. The panther measured, from tip to tip, a little more than nine feet. The day was well nigh spent, and dragging him along as a trophy of our victory, we returned to the house, where, over a bottle of whiskey and some good water, we remained and listened with attention until each hunter gave, in his own way, his ideas of the day's hunt.

CHAPTER XV.

THE chief circumstance which characterized Colonel Crockett's second term in congress, is the change which he is supposed to have undergone in his sentiments toward the present executive.[187] In alluding to this subject, he stated that he had ever been a friend to internal improvements—that he believed they were consistent with the spirit of the constitution—ee that the situation of the west particularly required them—and that it was good policy in the present flourishing state of our financial department, to carry on a scheme of gradual improvement. He alluded particularly to the situation of the west, the poverty of its inhabitants, and its sparse population—to their having to contend with the difficulties incident to a new country, clearing lands, opening roads, and building bridges, and to their inability under these circumstances, of carrying on any general state improvement. He also adverted to the bounteous gifts of nature, a soil rich and productive, intersected with innumerable rivers, and stated the numerous advantages which would flow from these sources, should they by the assistance of the general government, be rendered safe and navigable. He adverted to public roads, and the facilities which they would afford to the inhabitants of the west; likewise to the good which would result from their cementing together the various western interests. He alluded to the large quantity of lands owned by the general government in the western states—to the immense revenue derived from that source, and thence inferred, as a matter of right, the propriety of spending a large portion of that revenue in the internal improvement of the same section of country.

In supporting General Jackson, he had always done so under a firm belief that he was a friend to internal improvements, and when he vetoed the Maysville Road Bill,[188] he thought he swerved from the political faith he had formerly professed; and I felt bound, said he, in duty to myself, to differ with him in opinion. He said he never had, and never would, swear allegiance to any man—that to General Jackson he was not more opposed than to any other person—that he could not bind himself to do whatever General Jackson thought right, but would support his views when he thought them correct, when he was instructed to do so, or when he knew that it was the wish of his constituents; but under other circumstances, his judgment must ever be his guide.

Colonel Crockett's conduct on this occasion was certainly the effect of principle, and his bitterest enemies cannot with any shadow of justice impeach it. Standing high in the affections of his constituents, popular above any other man in his district, he might have retained his seat in congress as long as he wished it, without a chance of being beaten—and to do this, he had only to follow in the wake of public opinion. But being a friend to internal improvements, believing that the situation of his country required them, he could not lend his support to an administration going directly counter to his own views. By blindly following it, he would certainly retain his seat in congress. By opposing he might lose it. But that freedom and independence which have hitherto stamped his character, induced him to obey the dictates of his own judgment, and trust for re-election to the justice of his constituents. Surely, he could not have given a better example of correct principle and honest intention. By pursuing the dictates of his own judgment there was every thing to lose, and nothing to gain—and yet he obeyed them. The Jackson party[189] was then, as it now it, dominant throughout the United States. The Clay party[190] did not expect to succeed in their election. And if it did, what was the reward held out to Colonel Crockett for his support? There was none. His want of early education would have disqualified him for any office which he would have had. And yet, so fashionable is the slang of party spirit, that he is said by the Jackson editors to have been *bought up*. Previous to his withdrawing his support from General Jackson, he was the first in the house of congress to denounce the political course of Martin Van Buren,[191] then Secretary of State, which he did in strong and harsh terms, some of which have lasted until the present time, and have been adopted by opposition editors for their poignancy, and, as they think, aptitude, without being aware that they are indebted for them to a hunter of the west.

It would be difficult for any writer to give such an account of the west, its manners, customs, etc. as would be admitted on all hands to be correct. The beauty of its scenery and the fertility of its soil, require much commendation; but then there are so many difficulties and inconveniences attendant upon the settling of a new country, that a person is apt to be influenced by the circumstances under which he is situated. So far is this true, that even in the west you meet with many persons who differ in opinion with regard to the advantages which it presents. In the west, you meet with every shade of character of which you can possibly conceive, from the pious and devout Christian, to him who disregards his God, and sets at defiance all the laws of man. You also meet with representatives from every civilized country in the world—and having all gone there for the purpose of bettering their fortunes, they are generally shrewd, intelligent, and enterprising, much more so than the mass of people in an older country—for it requires some energy of character in a man, to sever the ties of affection which bind him to his native place, and seek a home in a strange land. Thrown together under circumstances of this nature, unacquainted with each other's former character, they are in general less confiding than they are in a country where society is more settled. Yet there is more civility than you would expect to meet with, and much apparent frankness of manner. The citizens, as yet, have paid no attention to the luxuries, and very little to the comforts of life; but nature has here been so bountiful in her gifts, that the time is not far distant when the Mississippi valley will, in point of wealth, be the first agricultural country in the world, filled with a population brave, enterprising, and industrious.

Although the west is settled by representatives from every country, it is very largely indebted for its inhabitants to Virginia, Georgia, and the two Carolinas. One, to witness the immense emigration from those states to the west, would assign it at once as the cause of their increasing so slow in population.[ff] Emigrants from these states, as well as from Kentucky, form by far the larger proportion of the population of the west. Whether this disposition to move is peculiar to that people, or whether it arises from the existence of some temporary cause, I know not. The south would perhaps attribute it to the injurious effects of the tariff system,[192] saying, to bear its burdens we must have rich lands. The north would assign as its cause the evils of slavery. But if this latter is true, it is somewhat remarkable that southerners in moving should, with but few exceptions, always settle in a slave state, and this though they may own no slaves of themselves. I should suppose it was owing to the fact, that in the south, there are but few manufactories, and consequently the great mass of the people are raised upon plantations in the cultivation of the soil; and when entering upon life for themselves, they generally pursue the same avocation. The western soil being productive, and had at a less price than lands of equal value in their native states, holds out inducements to emigrate. This disposition to move must be owing in a great measure to the habits of the people, from the circumstance that it is a very rare occurrence to see in the west a northern man who is a planter or farmer. Northern emigrants who come here—and they form but a small proportion of the population—generally settle in the towns or little villages, where their tact for trade enables them to get along with more advantage to themselves than they could derive from agriculture. Possessed of this particular talent, they live easily, and generally accumulate fortunes. The Yankees, as all men north of the Potomac are here termed, are generally well educated, and have become as celebrated in the west for shrewdness and cunning, as they are in the south. Their shrewdness has given rise to many anecdotes, and, among others, I hear from Colonel Crockett the following.

"Two foreigners, who were fresh from our mother country, in travelling through the west on horseback, happened to pass an evening at a house situated on the banks of the Mississippi river, when they met with a Yankee pedler, who had just disposed of his stock of goods, and was ready to go to any part of the world where interest might call him. By shrewd guesses, he soon found out every thing in relation to the circumstances, residence, and business of his companions, and then kindly gave a history of himself. He no sooner announced himself as a Yankee, than the foreigners, who had often heard of the shrewdness of their character, were all anxiety that he should play them a Yankee trick. This he modestly declined. They insisted; and offered to give him five dollars for a good Yankee trick. The money was taken, with a promise either to refund it, or play a good trick—and morning was selected as the time for the exhibition of the Yankee's skill. Pleased with each other, they all retired to bed in the same apartment; and when morning came, the Yankee rose with the first light, gently dressed himself in the clothes of one of the foreigners, took a pair of saddlebags to which he had no title, and quietly leaving the house, was observed to go on board of a flat boat bound for New Orleans. The foreigners soon after woke, and upon getting up to dress, beheld the sad reality of a Yankee trick. Having much money in their saddlebags, they found out which way the Yankee had gone; and obtaining a small skiff, set out after him. The skiff was light; and, moving rapidly, an hour or two brought it along side of the flat boat, where sat the Yankee perfectly composed, in quiet possession of their clothes and saddlebags. With much apparent pleasure he arose, enquired after their healths, and asked how they were pleased with the trick. The idea that they then had of the Yankee, I leave to the imagination of my reader. However, he soon delivered their saddlebags, which had not been opened, and exchanged clothes. The foreigners having deposited their saddlebags in the skiff, very much dissatisfied, were about to leave, when the Yankee insisted upon their taking a parting glass together; and, while drinking, he stepped back, jumped in the skiff, and pushed off. Amid the execrations of the crew he plied his paddle, and the skiff darted away from the flat boat. Going up stream, pursuit with the flat boat was idle, and he was observed to land on the Arkansas shore, where, I have no doubt, before this he has doubled the money thus obtained."

The frontier settlers in the west are either from Kentucky or the southern states, and living as they do, almost excluded from society, they have established for themselves a character and language peculiar to them as a people. Wedded to hunting, and careless of society, they manage always to live on the extreme frontier of a settlement, by selling out the clearing which they have made, and plunging again into the forest, whenever the tide of population approaches too near to them. Many accumulate a competency from this habit of moving, which often becomes so confirmed as to render them unhappy should they be constrained to remain in one place more than a year or two.

Those persons who navigate our western waters in flat boats, have many peculiarities in their habits and language. The great exposure to which they are subject, the great labor they frequently perform, and their propensity for fun and frolic, have rendered them remarkable as a class. The introduction of steam boats so extensively on our western waters, has served to destroy, in a great measure, the use of flat boats, and has driven to other occupations many of the persons thus engaged; but a fine sketch of this class of persons, as they have existed, may be found in the character of Mike Fink,[193] by a gentleman of Cincinnati.

Colonel Crockett having served out his second term in Congress, was again a candidate for re-election, and though every exertion was used by him, he failed of success. The country was flooded with handbills, pamphlets, etc. against him; and it was about this time that a series of numbers, entitled 'The Book of Chronicles,'[194] made their appearance. Many of his constituents had served under General Jackson throughout the last war. Their homes, their wives, and children, had been defended by him from the attacks of the Indians. These circumstances were called up by his opponents, and reiterated daily to his constituents. It was a powerful lever, and one that turned the fate of the election. But the contest was warm and doubtful, and it required all the exertions of the opposing party to gain it, under those circumstances—a strong proof of the personal popularity of Colonel Crockett.

Under the last census his district has been materially changed. Several counties have been thrown out, and among them some that were most violent in their opposition to him. He is still a candidate for the ensuing election, with flattering hopes of success.

BILLY BUCK.[195]

EARLY[gg] in the month of November 1831, while travelling through the west, I became acquainted with Mr. A——, of ——, to whom I owe many obligations for his great attention. He was a native of Virginia, bred in her most polished society, and had, in early life, from disappointment in a love affair, left his paternal mansion and taken up his abode in the "far-off west." He brought with him taste, and science, and fortune, and formed him a little paradise in the depths of the forest. His cabin, though rude without, was finished within, save that no lovely woman presided as its mistress. It was rather too neat for a bachelor; and its great order and arrangement might have infused into a stranger some little ceremony; but, if so, it vanished at the appearance of its owner, whose countenance beamed with good humor, affability, and frankness. Enjoying his pipe, with slippers on, he met me at the door, and gave me a cordial reception.

Having roughed it for some time on frontier fare, I was delighted to find myself in so good quarters, and partook liberally of his hospitality. After a sumptuous supper, we drew around a good fire, lit our pipes, and enjoyed the sweets of conversation. I found him intelligent, communicative, and a dear lover of hunting. He delighted in talking of his dogs, narrated many anecdotes of them, dwelt upon their pedigree, all in a manner so new, that to me it was extremely interesting. They borrowed fame from a long line of proud ancestry, on whose escutcheon[196] there was no blot; and from the many hard races they had run, had already carved for themselves honorable distinction. I was pleased to hear, that next morning had been fixed upon for a drive; and but little pressing was requisite to enlist my feelings in an amusement of which I had heard so much, and of which I longed to taste the sweets. So, after a promise on my part to join in the hunt, I retired to bed, anticipating boundless pleasure on the morrow. I courted sleep, to pass away the heavy night; but, restless, I tossed to and fro, and ever and anon started at the sight of a deer, or was aroused by the full cry of a pack of dogs, coming straight towards me. At length, weary nature sought repose; and the long winding of the horn, as it floated off until it died away, like the notes of a bugle heard far o'er the waters, announced the coming of morn.

Buoyant and light of spirits, I arose, dressed, and went out. There I found the company already gathering, and enjoying, by way of anti-fog, that greatest of all human inventions, a mint julap.[197] All nature was, as yet, hoar and crisp with frost. The golden horizon of the east told that the sun was just rising. The cheering sound of the horn, the loud answers of the dogs, as they rallied round us, anxious for the chase, and the bustle of preparation, all formed a scene more easily conceived than described. Damon and Pythias, two loving brothers, whom a Virginia mother bore—Union and Nullifier, two southern dogs of glorious metal—Tariff, whose warm covering denotes him of northern origin—Atlantic, who had been rocked asleep by the heaving of the briny billows—Miss Lavinia, from old Kentuck, than whom a lovelier pup was never whelped—Rolla, who had been cradled in the "far-off west," and cried out "this is my own, my native land,"—with several younger dogs,—formed the finest pack my eyes ever beheld. Their joyous barking had roused up Billy Buck, his master's pet [deer]; and, to add more interest to the scene, as was sometimes usual, while we were getting ready, they were harked on after him. "Hark forward!" was the cry, and all, save old Rolla, jumped off in eager haste, and flew like lightning, o'er a lovely plain. Their voices echoed through the far deep woods, and even the feathered tribe hovered o'er them, as though they were partakers of the sport.

My spirits bounded with joy, as Billy Buck, spurning the earth with lovely leaps, seemed to exult in the majesty of his strength. It was a scene of thrilling interest. But being all prepared, the horn's longest notes were heard floating off, the cheering cry of the dogs was hushed, and in a moment more they were all trotting lazily homewards, dissatisfied at being called off from the chase. However, the cheering hard of the huntsman soon infused fresh animation into the dogs, and my spirits fluttered with delight as we sought our horses, amid their joyous cry. I found, in place of my own horse, a gallant charger had been prepared for me, who moved restlessly, animated by the passing scene, when, to mount him, I seized his flowing mane. The dogs hushed up, and on we went to the drive, still cheered by the narration of some glorious hunt.

Having arrived there, each hunter was placed at his stand, while the driver, by a circuitous path, entered the drive at its head. For a time all was quiet, and no noise broke in upon the stillness of morning save

"The woodpecker tapping the hollow beech tree,"[198]

or the more cheerful voices of warbling songsters, as they answered each other in the far deep woods. Lounging idly at my stand, I was watching the exhalation from the frost, which vanished at the approach of the "God of day," when the short note of the horn, told me that the driver was ready. "Look about boys! hark about!" was his cheerful cry, as the dogs busied themselves in the depths of the forest. *Toot*, sounded the horn, to tell the standers where the driver was, and then all was still. And then there floated on the breeze, mellowed by distance, the long howl of a hound. Listening with suspended breath, I stood; another faint howl broke upon the ear, and nought was heard of the hunting party. A deep stillness reigned for some time, and then the huntsman's gathering resounded through the forest, in mournful accents. It announced that the drive was over, and called us together. Rather dispirited we met; a different drive was agreed on, and lazily we sought our stands. There followed a scene somewhat similar to the one described. And the huntsman's gathering again echoed through the wild woods. We again met, a council of war was held, and by a small majority it was decided that we should return to the house, wet our whistles, get dinner, and drive again in the evening.

Slowly we walked our horses homewards. Numerous excuses were made for our not finding a plenty of deer, about which I did not care a straw; for I was disheartened—having come out filled with anticipation of boundless pleasure. When within about half a mile of the house, Tariff, raising his head, snuffed the breeze, and gave a long deep howl, whose echo had not died away ere it was caught up by Union, and Nullifier, Damon, Pythias, Atlantic, and Miss Lavinia chimed in; and at the joyous hark of the huntsmen, they all bounded forward. Old Rolla brought up the rear, yet followed on as if he doubted. I was told to remain where I was, with an expectation that the deer would run out by the same way he entered. Each huntsman hurried to his stand, and the woods re-echoed with the finest music ears ever heard. My horse was hid; and with gun ready cocked, and fluttering spirits, I stood behind a tree, looking deep into the woods; and starting at the crack of a limb, or the fall of a leaf. The whole forest seemed alive, and there was a moment of wild and intense interest; when the music, so far from approaching me, died away in faint echoes, and all was still. Wearied with the high excitement under which I had been laboring, I uncocked my gun, sat down, and began to breathe more freely. There was no noise—none—all nature seemed asleep. How changed the scene! A moment past, and all was life, and animation: now a death-like silence reigns. I was wondering what could have become of the dogs, when a confused, though distant noise broke upon my ears. Hush! I hear it—loud—still louder—and the whole woods again echo to the living music of the dogs. They come toward me. With ready gun, but nervous hand, I stand prepared. With one continued roar the woods resound. I hear it running—I catch a glimpse—my gun is raised—pointed—and as it leaps into a clear place, I discover old Rolla coming to me. A moment more—the deer has tacked, and stretching away to the left, he and the dogs are buried in the forest.

Dispirited, I again sat down. Old Rolla was seated upon his hind legs. I harked him on: he merely got up, turned round, and again seated himself. Hark! the dogs tack. I hear them running away to the right. All nature was hushed, as if to hear the lively and joyous sound. Another moment—they come towards me—I jump up—once more seize my gun, and listen with breathless expectation. He must break out now. Near, still nearer, they come; and—no—they are at fault; the deer has dodged. Circling round, with noses to the ground, they dash back upon their former path. They double; they bother, and full towards me comes the joyous pack. I hear the bushes cracking: yes, I hear his leaps: my heart beats violently—I tremble from head to foot. A deer is seen about forty yards off, coming to me. I raise my gun—take aim—the deadly trigger is pulled, and it snaps. In my confusion, the priming[199] is shaken out; and ere I can replace it, lovely Billy Buck stands before me for protection. With panting sides and open mouth, he rubs his soft velvet horns against me; and looking in my face, a stream of tears flowing from his fine black eyes, he begs assistance. Convulsive shudderings seize his frame at the approaching yell of the dogs. He smells old Rolla, who understands the language; for he rubs up against him, licks off the perspiration as it exudes from his trembling limbs, and plants himself between him and the coming dogs. A thousand reflections pass like lightning through my mind. What shall I do? The dogs I know not; they will not heed me. Kill them, to save Billy Buck. But, hark—they are in sight—Nullifier leads the van: Billy Buck gets behind me, and rubs me with his head; they rush forward; then, one wild moment of distracting interest. Old Rolla seizes Nullifier, and throws him on the ground; is here, now there, opposing the torrent like some mighty hero, in a deadly conflict. I cry out; my voice is lost amid their deafening yells. I kick them, cuff them, beat them with my gun; but they heed neither me nor noble Rolla. They sweep past, and I hear the dying bleat of Billy Buck. I turn round, raise my gun, cock it, point it—they are all upon him—'tis too late. My gun falls harmless from my hands, and I walk off in a different direction. Old Rolla follows; yet often looking back, till we are lost to the scene.

I may, from the decay of mind, forget my father; I may forget my mother; I may forget her who first taught my youthful heart to love; but never, while there exists the least glimmering of memory, can I forget the dying bleat of Billy Buck.

THE END.

Explanatory Notes

1. The epigram is from Horace's *Satires* (Book I, Satire I, Line 24): "What is to prevent one from telling truth as he laughs?" The quote underscores the author's humorous intent for the volume.

2. The reference is to the 1832–1833 cholera outbreak, which affected not only cities in the United States but also Europe, North Africa, and India. See Charles E. Rosenberg, *The Cholera Years: The United States in 1832, 1849, and 1866* (1962; repr., Chicago: Univ. of Chicago Press, 1987), 13–39.

3. An "apology" or apologia is a "written defense or justification of the opinions or conduct of a writer, speaker, etc." (*Oxford English Dictionary* [2018] online). It is the ancestor of the preface. It is a standard opening for a work, often designed to fend off possible criticism. The author attacks this convention, but uses it satirically as well.

4. The description, in the opinion of the author, is a then-stereotypical view of Native Americans in much popular literature.

5. Rodomantades are vainglorious boasts, or extravagantly boastful, arrogant, or bombastic speeches or pieces of writing. From the Middle French *rodomontade* (*Oxford English Dictionary* [2018] online). Ambrose Bushfield is a frontier character from James Kirke Paulding's *Westward Ho!, A Tale* (New York: J. & J. Harper, 1832). Paulding's character of Bushfield is an extension of his earlier work in *Letters from the South* (New York: James Eastburn & Co., 1817). See his sketch "The Fight" and, more significantly, his play *The Lion of the West* (1830), and his character, Nimrod Wildfire, based upon Crockett. See also Joseph Arpad, "The Fight Story: Quotation and Originality in Native American Humor," *Journal of the Folklore Institute* 10 (1973): 141–72; and for a broader context, see Elliott J. Gorn, "'Gouge and Bite, Pull Hair and Scratch': The Social Significance of Fighting in the Backcountry," *American Historical Review* 90 (1985): 18–43. For a brief biography of Crockett, see the online *Tennessee Encyclopedia of History and Culture*, https://tennesseeencyclopedia.net/.

6. Such manufactured words were used in literary depictions of frontiersmen, particularly those focused on humor. These wild coinages and exaggerated phrases continued to flourish, especially in the tall tales presented in the Crockett Almanacs, 1835–1856. Thus, all inhabitants of the wilderness, white and red, suffer from stereotypical portrayals, according to the author. Another commonplace of these humorous works is the assertion that they are "strictly true."

7. The "blue devils" are those who are depressed, i.e., those who are blue or have the blues.

8. This refers to the maize or corn dance. The dance is both a thanksgiving ceremony and a celebration of many tribes.

9. One then-current theory was that the ancestor races of the present Native Americans were not only more advanced but much larger in size. It followed the theories of the Comte de Buffon on the degeneration of the New World as compared to the Old, both in the human and natural environments. The ancient race referred to here is sometimes called the "race of the mound-builders."

10. The author of a manuscript who notes that animals whose saliva could destroy trees could not be determined. It smacks of being a tall tale. Interestingly, in *The Literary Panorama and National Register* (London, 1819, p. 281), there is a definition of "lignivorous" as "eating the trunks of trees."

11. Cannæ, Pharsalia, Austerlitz, and Waterloo were all major military defeats of, respectively, the Roman Republic, Pompey the Great, Russia, and Napoleon.

12. The Indian Removal Act became law on May 28, 1830, when signed by President Andrew Jackson. On December 6, 1830, he noted in his Second Annual Message to Congress that, "It gives me pleasure to announce to Congress that the benevolent policy of the Government, steadily pursued for nearly thirty years, in relation to the removal of the Indians beyond the white settlements is approaching to a happy consummation." Crockett opposed the bill, which eventually led to the "Trail of Tears," the removal of the Cherokees to the Indian territories in 1838 and 1839, a forced march on which approximately four thousand people died. For more information, see http://www.loc.gov/rr/program/bib/ourdocs/Indian.html and http://www.cherokee.org/AboutTheNation/History/TrailofTears/ABriefHistoryoftheTrailofTears.aspx. For a brief overview of Indian removal, see Andrew K. Frank, "Native American Removal" in *A Companion to the Era of Andrew Jackson*, ed. Sean P. Adams (Chichester, West Sussex, UK: Wiley-Blackwell, 2013), 391–411. For a brief biography of Jackson, see the online *The Tennessee Encyclopedia of History and Culture*.

13. While the exact locations of these excavations could not be determined, Southern Ohio abounds in native archaeological sites. See, for example, the Hopewell culture at https://www.nps.gov/hocu/learn/historyculture/places.htm.

14. Enrico Causici, *Conflict of Daniel Boone and the Indians*, 1826–1827, sandstone. It is located in the rotunda of the US Capitol, above the south door. For a view of the sculpture, see https://www.aoc.gov/relief-sculpture.

15. Samuel Lorenzo Knapp's sketch of Boone in *Lectures on American Literature: With Remarks on Some Passages of American History* (New York: E. Bliss, 1829), 262.

16. The name of the "gentleman," if he exists, could not be determined.

17. The New Madrid Earthquakes (December 16, 1811; January 23 and February 7, 1812) were a series of earthquakes that occurred near the borders of present-day Arkansas,

Missouri, and Tennessee. A reconstruction of their magnitude on the Richter scale produced approximate values of 7.5, 7.3, and 7.5, respectively. Aftershocks continued into 1813. These earthquakes were among the largest east of the Rocky Mountains in more than five hundred years. See https://earthquake.usgs.gov/earthquakes/events/1811-1812newmadrid/summary.php. The earthquake in 1812 created Reelfoot Lake in West Tennessee, near Crockett's home in Rutherford. Crockett refers to the surrounding region as "the shakes" at the beginning of chapter V. See also *A Narrative of the Life of David Crockett of the State of Tennessee*, ed. James A. Shackford and Stanley J. Folmsbee (1834; facs. ed., Knoxville: Univ. of Tennessee Press, 1973) for a fuller and autobiographical version of his life.

18. Greene County lies in northeastern Tennessee, roughly seventy miles northeast of Knoxville. The county shares its eastern border with North Carolina. At the time of Crockett's birth, Tennessee was not yet a state, and Greene County was under the jurisdiction of North Carolina.

19. These tales became a staple of and the seedbed for ever more outlandish yarns in the Crockett Almanacs (1835–1856). The mention of such tales in this 1833 publication underscores their previous circulation.

20. Andrew Jackson, major general during the Battle of New Orleans and then president of the United States. Crockett, formerly an ardent supporter of Jackson, had by this time turned his opponent over the issues of Indian removal, squatters' rights, and the establishment of a National Bank.

21. Sullivan County is located in northeast Tennessee and shares its northern border with Virginia. The Crockett Tavern, however, is in Hamblen County, due west of Greene County.

22. The Dutchman referenced is Jacob Siler.

23. The superior beauty of curved lines as compared to straight ones is a major component of English painter William Hogarth's aesthetic theory as argued in *The Analysis of Beauty* (London: Printed by John Reeves for the Author, 1753).

24. Crockett was briefly engaged to Margaret Elder, but, as the narrative indicates, she eventually married another man instead. The "plays" were games at which marriagable youths could meet with propriety.

25. "Best bib and tucker" refers to their finest clothes.

26. Apollonius of Tyana, a Pythagorean philosopher, who in Philostratus' *Life of Apollonius* (c. 170–245 AD) is described as wearing only modest garments made from linen rather than more costly animal fur.

27. "Roached" means cut so short that it stands up. A term initially used to refer to animal hair, particularly horses' manes. Later nineteenth-century usage in the American South employed the term for "a hairstyle in which the hair is brushed so as to stand up or sweep back from the face" (*Oxford English Dictionary* [2018] online).

28. A "jump-jacket" is a long, loose outer coat for men, often reaching down to the thighs and with buttons down the front.

29. "Kiver taters" is a dialect rendering of "cover potatoes" (a dance step).

30. "Yallerest flower" means the best at what it is / the best at what is being done (here, dancing). *Crockett's Yaller Flower Almanac for '36* (New York: Robert H. Elton, [1835]) echoes this usage with its front page, noting that it is "The Ringtail Roarer! Ripsnorter!" and "Circumflustercated Grinner's Guide." Pictures of its covers and those of twenty other almanacs are currently available at the Dorothy Sloan Books website, catalog for Auction 21, "Davy Crockett Almanacs," http://www.dsloan.com/Auctions /A21/crockett_almanac-pictures.html.

31. Jim Crow is a name that first appeared in the 1828 song by Thomas Dartmouth "Daddy" Rice ("Jump Jim Crow"). In blackface, Rice performed the minstrel role of the stereotypical black man "Jim Crow." The name quickly came to be used more generally as a derogatory racial term for any black male. The song has many variant verses. See also the reissuing of C. Vann Woodward's *The Strange Career of Jim Crow* (1955; repr., New York: Oxford Univ. Press, 2002).

32. "After-claps" is a delicate way of referring to a hangover.

33. The source of this quote is Sir Walter Scott's "Truth of a Woman" from *The Betrothed* (Edinburgh: Arthur Constable and Co., 1825), one of his Waverly novels. For a full e-text, see https://www.poemhunter.com/poem/the-truth-of-woman/. See also Alexander Pope, "Of the Characters of Women," Epistle II (1735), *Moral Essays*, available online at http://www.bartleby.com/203/144.html.

34. This line is from Lord Byron's *Childe Harold's Pilgrimage* (1812), Canto 2, verse XXXIV, l. 3.

35. "Reaping and flax-pulling" are harvesting.

36. Here the author refers to the social custom of using an intermediary party to introduce strangers, particularly strangers who are of the opposite sex. Crockett, in this less formal rural setting, is able to introduce himself to the young ladies without such an intermediary.

37. The farmer hosting the gathering presides.

38. These are lines 14–16 of Robert Burns's song "For A' Man's A Man For A' That" (1795). For full text, see Burns Country website, http://www.robertburns.org/works/496 .shtml.

39. Conundrum: a game involving word-play and punning, potentially a game in which a riddle is answered with a pun. Railroad stockings refers to a particular style of stocking worn in the nineteenth century that are striped and easy to knit. For a description and instructions, see the *Sacramento Daily Record Union*, October 1, 1881, p. 6, center column at https://chroniclingamerica.loc.gov/lccn/sn82014381/1881-10-01 /ed-1/seq-6/.

40. "Sell the Thimble" is likely a variation on "Hunt the Thimble" or "Hide the Thimble," a nineteenth-century game in which one person looks for a thimble that

other players have hidden or are passing around to one another. In some versions, players make increasingly louder and louder noise as the seeker gets closer to the thimble. "Grind the Bottle" is a game similar to musical chairs.

41. The earliest mention of this kissing game/play party song is in the present volume. See Constance Rourke, *American Humor: A Study of the National Character* (New York: Harcourt, 1931), 53–54; and Phil Jamison, *Hoedowns, Reels, and Frolics: Roots and Branches of Southern Appalachian Dance* (Urbana: Univ. of Illinois Press, 2015), 108.

42. Crockett's betrothed and eventual wife is Mary (Polly) Finley. See note 44.

43. A filley (or filly, as it is spelled next) is a young female horse less than four or five years old, but is also a slang term (as in its next usage) for a young girl.

44. David married Mary (Polly) Finley on August 14, 1806, in Jefferson County, Tennessee. For another version of the story, see Crockett, *Narrative*, 61–67.

45. The Elk River is a tributary of the Tennessee River. It flows through the southern portion of Middle Tennessee and meets the Tennessee River in northern Alabama. The move likely took place in late September or early October 1811, and Crockett settled in Lincoln County.

46. This refers to the War of 1812 or the Creek War (1813–1814).

47. Tallisahatchee and Talladago were two battles fought during the Creek War (1813). The Battles of Pensacola (1814) and New Orleans (1815) were also fought during the War of 1812. Andrew Jackson led forces in all four of these battles.

48. Andrew Jackson (1767–1845) was major general of the Tennessee militia and later seventh president of the United States. Crockett served under Jackson during the Creek War and the War of 1812. The "separation" referred to here, which occurred during Jackson's presidency, is at least threefold. David Crockett, as a congressman from Tennessee, opposed Jackson's Indian Removal Act (see note 12), vocally repudiated Jackson's attacks upon the National Bank, and supported squatters' rights. Jackson's removal of federal funds on September 10, 1833, occurred after the publication of the present volume and only increased Crockett's anti-Jackson stance.

49. Crockett married a widow, Elizabeth Patton, in 1816. Their blended family had five children. His first wife, Polly, however, was alive after David's return from the war and died in the summer of 1815. See the *Narrative*, 125.

50. "Laurens County" is Lawrence County, Tennessee, a county located in the southern portion of Middle Tennessee and that shares a border with Alabama.

51. Crockett served as a justice of the peace from 1817 to 1819. He was also elected as town commissioner of Lawrenceburg during this time. Crockett later served in the Tennessee state legislature from 1821 to 1824.

52. James Coffield Mitchell (1786–1843), a Tennessee state legislator who went on to serve in Congress from 1825 to 1829. During his time in the state legislature (1813–1815,

1819–1823), he represented Hamilton, McMinn, and Rhea counties. See the *Biographical Directory of the United States Congress* for more information.

53. The "gentleman from the cane" remark insinuates that frontiersman Crockett is an uncivilized person from the wilderness.

54. A "freshet" is a flood. This one bankrupted him.

55. Perhaps here the word "interested" implies that the world takes an active interest against a person, as well as introducing a financial pun.

56. "Coruscations of his genius" is a common phrase in the early nineteenth century. Coruscation refers to "a vibratory of quivering flash of light, or a display of such flashes; in early use always of atmospheric phenomena" (*Oxford English Dictionary* [2018], online). In this passage, "flashes" is the likely meaning.

57. The author here equates the frontier areas with the wilderness, a place with few or no settlements.

58. Gibson County is located in West Tennessee. An 1818 treaty with the Chickasaw nation ceded their land in Tennessee to the United States. It was opened to settlement by proclamation on January 7, 1819.

59. For the earthquake of 1812, please see note 17.

60. Ibid.

61. The Obion River is located in the northern corner of West Tennessee. It passes north of Rutherford and continues down until it meets the Mississippi River.

62. The "two considerable lakes" may be the two parts of Reelfort Lake or Reelfoot Lake and the adjacent bodies of water of Buzzard Slough and Upper Blue Basin.

63. The undergrowth referred to is a canebreak.

64. A "quiz" is a prank or practical joke.

65. The candidate referred to as "B." is Dr. William E. Butler, then town commissioner of Jackson, Tennessee, who Crockett ran against for reelection to the Tennessee state legislature, albeit in a new district, in 1823. For a variant version of this campaign, see *Narrative*, 66–70.

66. The phrase "knocking along" means "making do."

67. Chewing tobacco was formed into twists for sale.

68. For a longer and much anthologized version of "A Useful Coonskin," please see the first chapter of *Col. Crockett's Exploits and Adventures in Texas* (Philadelphia: T. K. and P. G. Collins, 1836), 13–22; or Claude M. Simpson and Allan Nevins, eds., *The American Reader* (Boston: Heath, 1941), 562–64.

69. In the notes to Crockett's *Narrative of the Life of David Crockett of the State of Tennessee* (1834; repr., Knoxville: Univ. of Tennessee Press, 1973), the editor explains that Crockett used this image of Dr. Butler's rug as a campaign issue, saying that the rugs on his floors were of better material than the wives of voters could wear on their backs (166n2). See note 126. And see Lofaro, ed. *Boone, Black Hawk, and Crockett in 1833*, lxviii–lxix, for part of the genesis of the story.

70. Dutch jokes and anecdotes were a popular form of amusement in Crockett's day, often related in a mock-Dutch accent.

71. A "pole cat" is a skunk.

72. A mattock is a "tool similar to a pick but with a point or chisel edge at one end of the head and an adze-like blade at the other, used for breaking up hard ground, grubbing up trees, etc." (*Oxford English Dictionary* [2018], online).

73. A ploughshare is "the large pointed blade of a plough, which, following the coulter, cuts a slice of earth horizontally and passes it on to the mouldboard" (*Oxford English Dictionary* [2018], online).

74. Skow are "strips of wood for wattle-work [staking tree branches to make fences, walls, or roofs], barrel-staves, fixing thatch, etc." (*Oxford English Dictionary* [2018], online). Crockett's neighbor settles for an iron skow.

75. Crockett also later tells a variant version of this tale. See his *Narrative*, 185–91.

76. Traditionally the miller would charge a "toll" on grains milled on his machinery. Often this toll would simply consist of a certain portion of a farmer's ground meal or flour.

77. This is a reference to the Gospel of Matthew 25:31–33: "When the Son of Man shall come in his glory, and all the holy angels with him, then shall he sit upon the throne of his glory: And before him shall be gathered all nations: and he shall separate them one from another, as a shepherd divideth his sheep from the goats. And he shall set the sheep on his right hand, but the goats on the left."

78. A "harricane" is a canebreak, possibly in the Shakes near Reelfoot Lake.

79. To "come too" is to awake.

80. This refers to the Sectional Tariff of 1824, which imposed higher import taxes on British goods, particularly agricultural goods. The tariff was mainly supported and passed through Congress by northern and faced opposition by southern congressmen.

81. Crockett did unsuccessfully run for a congressional seat in the US House of Representatives in the 1825 election, losing to the incumbent, Adam Rankin Alexander (1781–1848). See the *Biographical Directory of the United States Congress* for more information about Alexander. Alexander got 42 percent of the vote, Crockett 38.1 percent, James Ferrill 13.4 percent, and Thomas H. Pearsons 6.6 percent. Crockett did not lose by "*two votes.*"

82. The phrase "knocked in the head" means that the plan failed.

83. A "confab" is a private conference.

84. His "swelling" means that he was overly proud.

85. This location is possibly Mill's Point, Kentucky, though there are also nineteenth-century references to a Mill's Point between Camden, Tennessee, and Waverly, Tennessee.

86. The "old flat" is a flatboat, which was "a large roughly-made boat formerly much used for floating goods, etc. down the Mississippi and other western rivers" (*Oxford English Dictionary* [2018], online).

87. A "slue" is a variant spelling of "slew" and is "a marshy or reedy pool, pond, small lake, backwater, or inlet" (*Oxford English Dictionary* [2018], online). The context makes clear that it is some additional body of water.

88. The administration is that of President Andrew Jackson.

89. Henry Clay (1777–1852) was a US statesman who served as representative and senator from Kentucky in Congress, Speaker of the House, and secretary of state. See the *Biographical Directory of the United States Congress* and the *American National Biography* for more information.

90. Presumably this is the Tariff of 1824. See note 80.

91. What is referred to as "The Bank" is the Second National Bank of the United States run by Nicholas Biddle. See *American National Biography* for more information. In 1832, President Jackson blocked passage of a bill that would reauthorize the bank's charter and then removed all government funds from it. The bank was eventually liquidated in 1841.

92. Crockett began his political career as a supporter of President Andrew Jackson, but later opposed him on several key issues: Crockett was for squatter's rights, and, as earlier noted, against Indian removal, and for the Second National Bank.

93. Thomas Hart Benton (1782–1858) was a US senator from Missouri who served from 1821–1851. He then served in the US House of Representatives for one term from 1853–1854. See the *Biographical Directory of the United States Congress* and the *American National Biography* for more information.

94. P. P. (Philip Pendleton) Barbour (1783–1841) was a US congressman from Virginia and later a justice of the Supreme Court. He also served as Speaker of the House from 1821–1823. In 1833, he was serving as a judge for the Federal District Court for Eastern Virginia. See the *Biographical Directory of the United States Congress*, the *Biographical Directory of Federal Judges*, and the *American National Biography* for more information.

95. The Dupont here refers to the Dupont gunpowder manufacturing family. See *American National Biography* for more information. The "treble" here might refer to quickness, something akin to the much-later patented treble wedge gun, which speeded the loading of cartridges.

96. The phrase "upon the tapis" is a translation of the French idiom *sur le tapis*, which literally means "on the tablecloth" but signifies "under discussion or consideration." (*Oxford English Dictionary* [2018], online).

97. Here the author refers to James Fenimore Cooper's Leatherstocking Tales, published between 1823 and 1841: *The Pioneers, The Last of the Mohicans, The Prairie, The Pathfinder,* and *The Deerslayer.* Only the first three books were available to the author by 1833. Hawkeye is one of the many aliases of the character Natty Bumppo, who appears in all of the novels. Natty Bumppo ranks among the most famous and iconic representations of the frontiersman in American literature and was known for his marksmanship.

98. "La Longue Carabine" is another name of Natty Bumppo, one supposedly given him by natives.

99. Target shooting was a popular pastime on the American frontier, with settlements often holding weekend or holiday matches. Here "offhand shooting" is described as opposed to shooting from a bench or using something to rest the gun upon to steady the shooter's aim. For a literary depiction, see "The Shooting Match" from Augustus Longstreet's *Georgia Scenes* (Augusta: Printed at the S[tates]. R[ights]. Sentinel Office, 1835), 215–35.

100. "Patching" refers to "the wadding of a bullet." (*Oxford English Dictionary* [2018], online).

101. A flintlock firing mechanism uses a small piece of flint that, when struck against a steel "frizzen," sparks. The spark drops into the firing pan to ignite the gunpowder. The successor to the flintlock was the percussion lock, which used a percussion cap of brass or copper in place of the steel "frizzen."

102. A "tippling house" is a tavern.

103. A charger is "a device for loading the magazine of a rifle." (*Oxford English Dictionary* [2018], online). It dispenses a small amount of black powder for priming the gun.

104. "Hoosier" is a slang term for someone from Indiana; "Kangaroo" and "Nunnery" may be other nicknames, or the writer may simply be stating words that seem strikingly original to him.

105. An "obligor" is a creditor.

106. The phrase "under penalty of a quart" means that the fine consists of a quart of liquor.

107. This passage parodies Shakespearean diction and meter. "Welkin," a term signifying the heavens, is often used in Elizabethan drama. The author here also refers to a famous match race between the horses "American Eclipse," bred on Long Island, NY, and "Sir Henry" from Virginia. The race drew over six thousand spectators to the Union Course on Long Island, among whom was Andrew Jackson, then governor of Florida. "American Eclipse" won two of the three four-mile heats and was pronounced the winner of the $10,000 purse.

108. This again is a passage from Robert Burns's poem "Tam O'Shanter" (1791).

109. Five corns is a game in which players use five large, hollowed-out corn grains. All five corns are held in the hand, then released in such a way so that (hopefully) all five hearts land with the hollowed-out side facing upward.

110. This refers to the Ancient Roman practice of eating, not while sitting, but while reclining on couches. "Push-pin" is a game in which two players each put a pin on the top of a hat. They each take turns lightly tapping the hat until one of the pins falls off. "Drawing straws" involves a player trying not to draw the shortest straw out of a bundle of straws.

III. A "teetotum" is a toy that resembles a top.

II2. William Fitzgerald, a Jackson supporter.

II3. The "one exception" may refer to Christ.

II4. This pamphlet was distributed during Crockett's congressional campaign against William Fitzgerald in 1831. The pamphlet is written in a biblical style, with an obvious allusion to the First and Second Books of Chronicles in the Old Testament. First and Second Chronicles recounts, along with many genealogical lists, the history of the Jewish people (mainly after the establishment of the monarchy). Second Chronicles focuses primarily on the fall of the kingdom of Judah and the exile of the Jews into Babylon. It is also worth considering how the language of this pamphlet resonates both with biblical diction and language that was often also used in describing Native Americans (e.g., tribes, both of Israel and of America). See notes 129 and 133 for more information about Fitzgerald.

II5. The reference is to the then-current time, when Andrew Jackson was president of the United States (i.e., "Columbia"). The states are the "tribes."

II6. "Sanhedrim" is an alternate spelling of the Sanhedrin, an ancient Jewish high court which dealt with religious issues. In the New Testament, it is the Sanhedrin who charge Christ with blasphemy and send him to Pontius Pilate.

II7. The "54th year ... bondage" is 1830.

II8. The context of this debate is over a bill for squatters' rights that Crockett sponsored. The "warrants" referred to are "land warrants" that were issued from various state land offices that allowed a person to claim possession of a certain amount of public land. The warrants were transferable and title was not established until the land was surveyed and registered. For registration, the land had to be free of all prior claims.

II9. The reference is to John Blair (1790–1863). He was from Upper East Tennessee (Jonesborough) and was a congressman from 1823–1835. He was also a member of the Tennessee state legislature from 1815–1821 and from 1849–1850. See the *Biographical Directory of the United States Congress* for more information.

I20. "Belial" is literally the Hebrew word for "worthless" (*beli + ya'al* / without + value). "Sons of Belial" became a phrase with the connotation "sons of worthlessness." Later Jewish and Christian traditions spoke of a demon with the name Belial.

I21. The formulation of the various political factions is a mock version of the tribes of Canaan listed repeatedly in the Pentateuch: the Hittites, the Amorites, the Canaanites, the Perizzites, the Hivites, and the Jebusites.

I22. The Claytonites were the supporters of Henry Clay of Kentucky, named later in the paragraph, who was defeated for president in the four-candidate field in the election of 1824. He was a senator from Kentucky from 1831–1852. All those named were, in general, opposed to Jackson. John Holmes (1773–1843) was a representative from Massachusetts from 1817–1820 and a senator from Maine from 1820–1832. Tristam Burges (one "s"; 1770–1853) was a representative from Rhode Island from 1825–1834. His first name is subsequently misspelled in the next paragraph as "Tristram." Edward

Everett (1794–1865) was a representative from Massachusetts from 1825–1834 and senator from 1853–1854. Thomas Chilton (1798–1854) was a representative from Kentucky from 1827–1830 and 1833–1834. David Barton (1783–1837) was a senator from Missouri from 1821–1830. See the *Biographical Directory of the United States Congress* for more information about Holmes, Burges, Everett, Chilton, and Barton. See also the *American National Biography* about Holmes and Everett.

123. Henry Clay had unsuccessfully run for president against Andrew Jackson twice. The first time both men lost to John Q. Adams in 1824. The second time Jackson won the presidency. Clay would go on to lose the presidential race of 1844 as well. This passage refers to the Election of 1824, in which Jackson won the popular vote but lost the election in the House of Representatives to John Q. Adams. Henry Clay ran in this election but only carried three states. The Election of 1832, in which Jackson defeated Henry Clay, might also be meant here, though John Q. Adams did not run. See note 164 for more information about Adams.

124. See note 122 for Burges.

125. Daniel Webster (1782–1852) was a representative from New Hampshire from 1813–1816 and a representative and senator from Massachusetts from 1823–1840 and 1845–1850. He was a major leader in the anti-Jackson faction. He is here linked to Balaam, considered by some a false prophet in the Old Testament. See the *American National Biography* for more information.

126. See notes 69 and 122. Chilton also later helped Crockett prepare his autobiography, the *Narrative*.

127. Crockett was never able to pass his land bill. The 12 ½ cents per acre was the compromise that he agreed to with James K. Polk, then head of the Tennessee delegation, but the deal fell through. Interestingly, David's son, John Wesley Crockett, was able to revive the bill, and it became law in February 1841 in somewhat modified form. The price per acre remained the same.

128. "A league" is a group bound together in a common cause.

129. The "William" referred to is probably William T. Fitzgerald (see note 133). It is unlikely that he tried to promote Crockett's candidacy for reelection, since he was Crockett's opponent. "William" might be, however, an unidentified supporter of Crockett.

130. On the whole, this passage imitates the language of Ruth's speech to her mother-in-law Naomi in the Book of Ruth: "For whither thou goest, I will go; and where thou lodgest, I will lodge; thy people shall be my people, and thy God my God. Where thou diest, will I die, and there will I be buried: the Lord do so to me, and more also, if ought but death part thee and me" (Ruth 1:16–17).

131. David Hume's *History of England* was published between 1754 and 1761. The reference is to its weight (six volumes) versus that of feathers. The statement indicates that Crockett has abused his franking privilege (free postage) as a congressman to attack Jackson.

132. The identity of "Roland, the High Priest," is unknown.

133. William T. Fitzgerald (1799–1864) was a representative from Tennessee who defeated Crockett in the ensuing election and served in Congress from 1831–1833. He was a supporter of Andrew Jackson. See the *Biographical Directory of the United States Congress* for more information. Jackson was, of course, delighted with the election. Earlier in 1831, in an April 23 letter to Samuel Jackson Hayes, the president used Crockett as the standard for deceit and base behavior. After the congressman's defeat, Jackson also wrote that with "Chilton beaten, & Crockett left at home, the character of Tennessee, & Kentucky, will be relieved from the foul stain of being represented by such men . . . " (Jackson to Hardy Murfree Cryer, August 18, 1831). Quotations taken from *The Papers of Andrew Jackson, 1831*, ed. Daniel Feller, et al. (Knoxville: Univ. of Tennessee Press, 2013), 9:206, 507, respectively. Like Crockett, Thomas Chilton was reelected in 1833 and was Crockett's primary helper in crafting the *Narrative*. For more on Chilton, see the *Biographical Directory of the United States Congress*.

134. Many tales circulated about Crockett in the newspapers of his day. See the introduction, "Stereotype and Synthesis as National Compromise: The Evolution of the Early Frontier Hero" in Lofaro, ed. *Boone, Black Hawk, and Crockett in 1833*.

135. See xlviii, n12, for early newspaper mentions/versions of this story. The tale is elaborated posthumously in *Davy Crockett's Alamanack of Wild Sports in the West* (Nashville: Published by the Heirs of Col. Crockett, 1837 [1836]), 2.

136. There were several Burnies living in Virginia at this period, but no clues exist as to which was among the Chickasaw. Chickasaw records today do list "Burnie" as a last name among currently-living members of the tribe, and the Chickasaw did join with US forces in fighting the Creek Indian War in 1813.

137. The phrase "*to kalon*" is Greek for "the beautiful." Here it likely refers to Burnie as a representation of what the Chickasaw held to be their ideal.

138. A "flambeau" is a torch.

139. "Marsh's meteor lamp" is a will o' the wisp (i.e., the light of the torch "flits about") and refers to the fact that marsh gas can ignite in combination with oxygen to smolder for a considerable time. The phrase is taken from Lord Byron's poem "The Prisoner of Chillon" (1816): "And through the crevice and the cleft / Of the thick wall is fallen and left; / Creeping o'er the floor so damp, / Like a marsh's meteor lamp" (lines 32–35).

140. John Bradshaw was an early settler in northwestern Tennessee and a close friend of Crockett who supported his political ambitions. Along with Crockett, Bradshaw, as the text states, was a noted bear-hunter.

141. "Gallusses" are suspenders.

142. This story also contains the manufactured language and dialect renderings typical of the tall tale humor of the period. A "ripstaver" is a "ring-tailed roarer," a powerful

wild person; "yallur-flower" means the boaster is the "prettiest"; "aqui fortis" is aqua forte, or drinking alcohol; and a "ticlur" (tickler) is a large hunting knife.

143. Colonel Nimrod Wildfire is a character in James Kirke Paulding's play *The Lion of the West* (1830). Wildfire's speech and mannerisms are intentionally based on and attributed to Crockett. For an example, Wildfire makes this declaration makes in Paulding's play: "My name is Nimrod Wildfire—half horse, half alligator, and a touch of the airthquake—that's got the prettiest sister, fastest horse, and ugliest dog in the District, and can out-run, outjump, throw down, drag out and whip any man in all Kaintuck."

A version of Crockett's boastful speech does, in fact, occur in Paulding's play in the second scene of Act II. See James Kirke Paulding, *The Lion of the West and Bucktails*, ed. Frank Gado (Lanham, MD: Rowan & Littlefield, 1994), 127–28. This version of the play was somewhat revised and retitled *The Kentuckian; Or, A Trip to New York*. Paulding's even earlier relation of a fight between a batteauxman and a wagoner is a likely source for the story. See James Kirke Paulding, *Letters from the South* (NY: James Eastburn & Co., 1817), Letter XXIX, II, 89–92. See also note 5.

144. "Staves" are wood for making barrels, i.e., barrel staves. The quotation "walking the waters like a thing o' life" is a standard biblical commentary on Proverbs 15:15. It is apropos in that it is often used in regard to the possibility of a shipwreck. See, for example, *The Biblical Encyclopedia*, ed. James Comper Gray and George Moulton Adams (Cleveland: F. M. Barton, 1903), 2:837. Also quoted in the story "The Vow," *Southern Literary Messenger* 9 (April 1843): 209, in reference to a ship navigating rough seas well.

145. Steam power was increasingly used for railroads, steamboats, etc.

146. Candidates at the time traveled from location to location to speak. They often stood upon a tree stump while giving their speeches in order to be seen by their constituents.

147. Captain John Cleves Symmes Jr. (1780–1829) was famous for his "Hollow Earth" theory, in which he claimed that there existed holes at the earth's poles through which man could travel to reach the center of the earth. It was also popularly called the "Holes at the Poles" theory.

148. "Gay parterre": A parterre is "the part of the ground floor of a theatre in front of the orchestra; the stalls" (*Oxford English Dictionary* [2018], online).

149. A "prunella" is a "strong silk or worsted fabric . . . used for the uppers of shoes" and can sometimes be used, as it is here, to signify "a shoe with uppers made of such material" (*Oxford English Dictionary* [2018], online).

150. Several versions of this traditional tune are on YouTube; given that it was a dialect song and now considered offensive, all these versions are instrumental. See https://www.youtube.com/results?search_query=Jay+burd+died.

151. Again, a version of this traditional tune is on YouTube; given that it was a dialect

song and now offensive, this version is instrumental. See https://www.youtube.com /watch?v=sMffW4_2bwY

152. "Aurora" here refers to the dawn.

153. The word "yclept" is from Middle English and means "called" or "named." The traditional comic figure of the shrewd Yankee peddler, especially of clocks, likely soon reached its high point in Nova Scotian Thomas Chandler Halliburton's (1796–1865) *The Clockmaker; or the Sayings and Doings of Sam Slick of Slickville*, first appearing as sketches in a Halifax newspaper in 1835, and then collected and published in book form there the next year, under the title listed above. Slick's colloquial, vernacular Yankee voice, in peddling clocks and giving his views on gullible "human natur," took full comic advantage of those marked by pride and greed, and displayed his beguiling forms of trickery to great advantage. His popularity reached beyond Canada and the United States to England and Germany. "Slim's" salesmanship closely parallels the methods of Sam Slick.

154. Napoleon Bonaparte (1769–1821) was defeated by Arthur Wellesley, 1st Duke of Wellington (1769–1852) at the Battle of Waterloo on June 18, 1815.

155. "Horn combs" were inexpensive combs made from animal horns. Finer, more expensive, ones were made from tortoise shells.

156. "Oh tempora! Oh mores!" is Latin for "Oh the times! Oh the customs!" and was used by Cicero both in his Second Oration Against Verres and his famous First Oration Against Catiline.

157. The Goths were "a Germanic tribe, who in the third, fourth, and fifth centuries, invaded both the Eastern and Western empires, and founded kingdoms in Italy, France, and Spain" (*Oxford English Dictionary* [2018], online). Here the reference to the new clock by the old underscores its tastelessness.

158. A "fog-cutter" is a drink of liquor to clear the throat.

159. "Rara avis, et simillima nigroque cygno" is from Juvenal's *Satires* (Cambridge Univ. Press, 1966), 32. The full line runs: "rara avis in terris nigroque simillima cygno" ["A rare bird in the lands, and very like a black swan"]. The shortened quotation would be translated, "A rare bird and very like a black swan."

160. To "cavil" is "to raise captious and frivolous objections; to object, dispute, or find fault unfairly or without good reason" (*Oxford English Dictionary* [2018], online).

161. Crockett's break with Jackson actually occurred later than his first term in Congress. See note 92.

162. An "original" is a unique, or one-of-a-kind person.

163. "Washington City" is Washington, DC.

164. "Adams" is John Quincy Adams (1767–1848), who ran presidential campaigns against Jackson both in 1824 and 1828. He was elected to the presidency in 1824 (see note 123), but lost his reelection campaign in 1828. See the *American National Biography* for more information.

165. This section is reminiscent of warrior posturing, similar to what we would see in ancient heroic texts like *Beowulf*. See also "flyting," an Old Norse tradition of stylized insults exchanged between two opposing parties. Here, Crockett is quite clear about his support for Jackson in his first term as congressman.

166. Such instances of bragging as here represented did make the rounds in newspapers of the period. See also note 142.

167. The use of "prehaps" is intentional and meant to represent backwoods speech.

168. Gulian Verplanck (1786–1870) was congressman from New York during the Jacksonian Era and also a literary figure who belonged to the "Knickerbocker Group." See the *Biographical Directory of the United States Congress* and the *American National Biography* for more information. Washington Irving was the group's most famous member.

169. Most of the false accounts are quoted in the following section.

170. A house-raising is "the construction of a house, esp. the setting up of the wooden framework, as a communal activity; the gathering of neighbors to do this" (*Oxford English Dictionary* [2018], online).

171. The backwoodsman, particularly a backwoodsman of the Old Southwest, blundering in a "civilized" setting is a common trope of the period. See William Alexander Caruthers, *The Kentuckian in New York. Or the Adventures of Three Southerns. By a Virginian* (New York: Harper and Brothers, 1834). Note that this plot device of a rural innocent coming to the city is an ancient one. For a solid study of the Greek and Roman antecedents of this device, see Jennifer L. Ferris-Hill's introduction to her *Roman Satire and the Old Comic Tradition* (New York: Cambridge Univ. Press, 2015).

172. Crockett's letter and those of Clark and Verplanck were printed in *The National Gazette and Literary Register* (Philadelphia, PA) on January 5, 1829, and in other newspapers. James Clark (1779–1839) was a congressional representative from Kentucky. He later became the governor of Kentucky in 1836. See the *Biographical Directory of the United States Congress* and the National Governors Association database for more information.

173. Whortleberries are "the blue-black fruit of the dwarf shrub *Vaccinium myrtillus*." It is the southwestern dialect form of the word huckleberry (*Oxford English Dictionary* [2018], online).

174. While "bran" is "the husk of wheat, barley, oats, or other grain, separated after grinding; in technical use, the coarsest portion of the ground husk" (*Oxford English Dictionary* [2018], online); it is used here to help make the ground (and earlier in this work, a cabin floor) easier to dance upon.

175. This is a reference to the humorous tales of the Old Southwest and other newspaper anecdotes about the frontier and the Old Southwest. Early examples of works in this tradition include Mason L. Weems's *Awful History of Young Dred Drake* (1818) and H. C. Jones's *Cousin Sally Dillard* (1830), as well as episodes in James Kirke Paulding's previously noted *Letters from the South* (1817).

176. There are fourteen congressmen from Ohio in 1828, and it is unclear who is the target of Crockett's wit.

177. Crockett's short letter of reply is also printed in the *New-Bedford (MA) Mercury* (April 26, 1833) and is likely extracted from *Sketches*. The phrase "go ahead" connoted both speed and certainty and was widely associated with Crockett. His motto, on covers of several Crockett Almanacs, was "Be always sure you're right, then Go Ahead!"

178. This is Wheeling, West Virginia, on the Ohio River.

179. Here, "bill" refers to the portion of a boat's anchor that points upward when secured on board. It may also refer to a "yard," the spar on a mast from which sails are set.

180. To "*fix out and out*" is a colloquial expression for setting the table fully for a meal.

181. The reference here is to the nationwide economic downturn in the late 1820s and early 1830s. The cotton market, which had experienced a massive spike in production with the rise of new industrial technologies, hit its low point in the early 1830s. The value of cotton began steadily rising, however, by the 1832–1833 harvest.

182. The recent completion of the Erie Canal (1825) stirred many proposals for canalization of America's waterways, and internal improvements such as this were a key belief of the Whig Party, which later courted Crockett as a potential presidential candidate.

183. Crockett did not achieve his goal, but his son, John Wesley Crockett, congressman from the same Tennessee district as his father (1837–1841), did. See note 127.

184. The author likely means the state of Mississippi. The Choctaw were the first tribe forced west of the Mississippi River under the Indian Removal Act (1830).

185. "The wild pigeon" referred to is likely the passenger pigeon. See James Fenimore Cooper, *The Pioneers: Or the Sources of the Susquehanna; A Descriptive Tale* (1823; repr., Albany: State Univ. of New York Press, 1980), 242–50, for portrayals of the migration of passenger pigeons. Hunting rendered these wild birds extinct by about 1900.

186. A hunting drive is a method of hunting in which a hunter (with the assistance of dogs or other hunters) flushes game out of dense cover, often toward a desired area to shoot the game. On "hurricane" or "harricanes" (canebreaks) please refer to note 78.

187. The "present executive" is Andrew Jackson; he was inaugurated on March 4, 1829.

188. In May 1830, Andrew Jackson blocked a congressional bill that would have authorized the government to invest in the Maysville, Washington, Paris, and Lexington Turnpike Road Company, a private venture. The company intended to build a road between Lexington, Kentucky, and Maysville, Kentucky, that was to be called the National or the Cumberland Road and would have been one of the first to be "macadamized." See also Craig I. Friend, *Along the Maysville Road: The Early American Republic in the Trans-Appalachian West* (Knoxville: Univ. of Tennessee Press, 2005).

189. The "Jackson Party" are the supporters of Andrew Jackson (i.e., Jacksonian Democrats).

190. The "Clay Party" are the supporters of Henry Clay (i.e., Whigs).

191. Martin Van Buren (1782–1862) was secretary of state under Andrew Jackson, his vice president in the second term, and succeeded Jackson as president. Crockett's antipathy to Van Buren's views led the Whigs to publish what might well be termed the first anti-presidential campaign biography, *The Life of Martin Van Buren, Heir-Apparent to the Government* . . . (Philadelphia: Robert Wright, 1835) under Crockett's name. The actual author is believed to be Augustin Smith Clayton (1783–1839), a congressman from Georgia (1831–1835). See the *American National Biography* for more information about Van Buren. See the *Biographical Directory of the United States Congress* and the *American National Biography* for more information about Clayton.

192. The "tariff system" is the Tariff of 1828, also called by southerners the "Tariff of Abominations." It protected northern industries, but drove up the price of imported goods upon which much southern trade with England depended. Members of the House of Representatives from the South voted 64 to 4 against the bill, which eventually passed 105 to 94.

193. For a sound short review of the life and legend of Mike Fink, see Michael Allen, *Western Regimen, 1763–1861: Ohio and Mississippi Boatmen and the Myth of the Alligator Horse* (Baton Rouge: Louisiana State Univ. Press, 1994), 8–14ff. The publication referred to is likely Morgan Neville's "The Last of the Boatmen," which appeared in *The Western Souvenir, A Christmas and New Year's Gift for 1829*, ed. James Hall (Cincinnati, N. & G. Guilford, 1828), 107–22.

194. A reference to an earlier pamphlet that attacked Crockett politically, one version of which is reprinted in this volume (63–66). Crockett was not without his defenders. The *National Intelligencer* newspaper (Washington, DC) published a spirited denial of many of the charges, as well as a solid affirmation of Davy's character and his record as a congressman in its issue of June 23, 1831.

195. The sketch "Billy Buck" has no known relationship to Crockett, and no reason has been uncovered for its inclusion in the volume by the editor. The sketch constitutes a separate seventeenth gathering for the pages of the book, so it was not needed as "filler" to eliminate a series of blank pages bound at the rear. Since the volume as a whole represents a collection of sketches strung together by the narrator, the editor may have simply wished to include another anecdote, albeit a quite sad and sentimental one. It was dropped when *Life* was republish as *Sketches and Eccentricities*. To complete Crockett's life, see "A Selective Crockett Chronology," xix–xx.

196. An escutcheon is "the shield or shield-shaped surface on which a coat of arms is depicted; also, in a wider sense, the shield, with the armorial bearings" (*Oxford English Dictionary* [2018], online).

197. An "anti-fog," as noted earlier as a "fog-cutter" in note 158, is a drink of liquor to help awaken the early riser. A "mint julap" is an alternate spelling of mint julep, a cocktail made up of bourbon, sugar, water, and garnished with mint leaf.

198. The quotation is from a ballad by Irish poet Thomas Moore. "Every leaf was at rest, and I heard not a sound / But the woodpecker tapping the hollow beech tree," is the refrain of the popular and often reprinted poem that is variously titled "Song," "Ballad Stanzas," "The Woodpecker," etc. See "The Woodpecker" in *The British Minstrel: A Choice Collection of Modern Songs* (London: Thomas Allman, 1848), 101.

199. Priming, here, signifies "gunpowder placed in the pan of a firearm to ignite a charge after itself being ignited by friction, a spark, etc." (*Oxford English Dictionary* [2018], online).

Textual Notes

This section documents any changes or significant variations from the original text, including points of grammar and variations in spelling. Each entry below begins with the designated letter for the note. In the right-hand column, the text to the left of the bracket is the word, letter, or symbol under discussion. The material to the right of the bracket depicts the two possible spellings or grammatical variations separated by an (>) symbol.

a. ther] ther > their. (In some printings of the first edition, "their" is misprinted as "tr." No order of publication of the several variants can conclusively be determined.

b. Crockett's name is inconsistently printed throughout as, alternatively, "Col. Crocket" and "Colonel Crockett." These variants are allowed to stand in this edition.

c. for ever – Line break with two words, no hyphen it is often printed as two words in the text.

d. Usually the first word in a chapter is in small caps, and "The" is here corrected. See note gg.

e. "Betsy" – Crockett's rifle's name is also at times spelled "Betsey."

f. "bear-hunting" – is here hyphenated at a line break, but the word was never spelled with a hyphen prior to this.

g. Period added.

h. Original text has two shorter dashes separating "myself" and "and."

i. Originally there is no space between "and" and "do."

j. Although this dash is solid, the preceding three instances in this story are smaller double dashes.

k. The comma is suspended in the middle of the line, rather than the bottom. This is either a mistake or the printer was running out of type for commas and used an apostrophe instead.

l. Original text has two shorter dashes.

m. The comma is suspended in the middle of the line, rather than the bottom. This is either a mistake or the printer was running out of type for commas and used an apostrophe instead.

n. Original text has two shorter dashes.

o. "back-woods" – Spelled earlier as one word.

p. "would" – The *u* in "would" is either printed upside down as an *n* or an *n* was mistakenly chosen by the typesetter.

q. The question mark replaces the exclamation point in the original text. Also, the printer here used a single quotation mark and an apostrophe to simulate the proper double quotation marks.

r. The hyphen is at the bottom of the line.

s. Original text has two shorter dashes.

t. Original text has two shorter dashes.

u. The period is set in the middle of the line.

v. "backwoods" is an end-line hyphenated word. The intended word could be meant to be spelled with or without the hyphen.

w. The use of quotations marks in this entire section is erratic by modern standards. Though Crockett is telling the story, and the double quotation marks open the story at the beginning of the paragraph, the dialogue narrated within the story also uses double quotation marks instead of the proper single quotation mark for internal dialogue. This continues through the end of the Raleigh story.

x. Original text has two shorter dashes.

y. Original text has two shorter dashes.

z. The sentence ends with a quotation mark, but it should likely be preceded by an exclamation mark.

aa. "backwoodsman" is an end-line hyphenated word and could be spelled with or without the hyphen after "back." The hyphen is also at the bottom, rather than in the middle of the space.

bb. In the original text, there is no set of closing quotation marks.

cc. "steam-boat" is also spelled "steam boat" and "steamboat" in the text.

dd. "rifle-guns" is an end-line hyphen break in the original, but the word is clearly meant to be hyphenated.

ee. Original text has two shorter dashes.

ff. The period is set in the middle of the line.

gg. "Early" is not originally in block capitals, though the first word in every other chapter but one (Chapter V) has been. See note d.

Index